SIR WALTER RALEGH
The first English Imperialist

# THE MARITIME
### AND
# COLONIAL EXPANSION
# OF ENGLAND

## UNDER THE STUARTS
### (1603–1714)

BY

## A. D. INNES

SOMETIME SCHOLAR OF ORIEL COLLEGE, OXFORD

AUTHOR OF

*England under the Tudors, A Short History of the British in India,*
*England's Industrial Development, etc.*

LONDON
SAMPSON LOW, MARSTON & CO., LTD.

MADE AND PRINTED IN GREAT BRITAIN BY PURNELL AND SONS
PAULTON (SOMERSET) AND LONDON

43444

# PREFACE

THE Prelude to the Expansion of England was her Oceanic development under the Tudors. The story itself begins with the birth of the great Commercial Company that became the parent of her Oriental Empire and the almost simultaneous birth of her first successful Colonial settlement in the West—at the moment when the crowns of England and Scotland were united by the accession of the King of Scots to the English throne, as the legitimate heir of the House of Tudor. At that time, she was not yet the premier maritime or commercial power, and was not yet in possession of a yard of land outside the British Isles.

In this country, all of us inevitably think of the Stuart Period as the century of Constitutional conflicts culminating in the Revolution which established Constitutional Monarchy. Our Histories, with rare exceptions, tell us little of the Greater Britain growing up beyond the seas almost untouched by the constitutional struggles at home—and still less of the stolid struggle of a handful of Englishmen to establish by the methods of peaceful trading a lucrative commerce with the gorgeous East when the mighty Mogul empire was at the height of its power and splendour. We are inclined, somewhat in defiance of the facts, to assume that Britannia was in the habit of ruling the waves all the time; we accept too the fact that the empire did somehow grow up during that period; but we realise or attempt to realise very little about its growth, or its relation to the domestic or European events which absorb our historical interest. We become vividly

v

alive to the battle for Empire with a mighty European rival when Clive and Wolfe come on the stage; but till then our interest—though not that of our American cousins—is apt to slumber. No inclusive survey specifically of this era of birth and growth, relating its various aspects and phases to each other, has hitherto, so far as the present writer is aware, been offered to the public; hence this essay.

In a volume written on such a scale that it cannot claim to be more than a sketch of a very wide and complicated subject, anything pretending to the character of a bibliography would be out of place. It may however be useful to mention some works published during the last fifty years dealing with various branches of the subject, to which the author is most consciously indebted.

As concerns the colonisation of the American continent the first place must necessarily be taken by J. A. Doyle's *English in America* (Virginia Maryland and the Carolinas), *The Puritan Colonies*, and *The Middle Colonies*—dating from 1882. Egerton's *Short History of British Colonial Policy* (1910) is a lucid and attractive study of principles rather than a narrative. As companions to these, written from the American point of view, may be taken S. Channing's *History of the United States*, vols. i (1905) and ii, and L. G. Tyler's *England in America* (1905) on the first half of the period. G. L. Beer's *Origins of the British Colonial System* (1908), with his *Old Colonial System* (1912), correct some misapprehensions and add a valuable study of the West Indian Plantations; as also does A. P. Newton's *Colonising Activities of the English Puritans*.

The Indian Histories are apt to pass very lightly over this period as concerns the doings of the British. This deficiency was made good by Sir W. W. Hunter in his *History of British India* (1899), which ends where this volume ends. Sir H. Yule's two volumes of Appendices to his edition of *The Diary of William Hedges* (1888) throw much light on little known personalities, events, and traditions; and R. and O. Strachey's *Keigwin's Rebellion* (1916) revises popular estimates of the " *Child* " dictatorship.

On the Economic side Dr. W. Cunningham's *Growth of English Industry and Commerce* vol. ii (1903) is the leading authority; and for the Naval development after the Restoration, Mahan's *Influence of Sea Power in History* (1890). Indispensable for the whole subject is Seeley's *Growth of British Policy* (1903); and finally the latest—and admirable—summary is included in J. A. Williamson's *Short History of British Expansion* (enlarged ed. 1930).

A. D. INNES.

*Uplyme, Nov.* 1931.

# CONTENTS

## PART I. PRELIMINARY

## PART II. FOUNDATIONS OF EMPIRE. 1600–1658

ix

# CONTENTS

# CONTENTS

# PORTRAITS

# MAPS

# Part I
# PRELIMINARY

# CHAPTER I

## ANTECEDENTS

### I

In the year 1603 the first Stuart monarch, James I, was crowned King of England, in succession to the last Tudor, Queen Elizabeth. In the year 1713, fifteen months before the death of Queen Anne, the last reigning Stuart in Great Britain, was signed the Treaty of Utrecht, which assigned to Great Britain certain territories hitherto in dispute with France. Those eleven decades cover a definitely marked period in that continuous expansion of the English speaking peoples which to-day has taken the double shape of the British Empire or Commonwealth of Nations—whichever name we prefer to use—and the United States of America. For it was in those years that the British Empire began to take shape, and before they were over had fully taken shape; while the time still to come both for a further vast expansion and for the bifurcation of which the United States were the political product. In the preceding half century, the necessary condition of expansion for an island people had been achieved, and England had become an Oceanic Power, but the English had not begun to be, in actuality, a colonising people. When Elizabeth died, even as when she came to the throne, England was not in occupation of one acre of soil outside the British Isles. When the Treaty of Utrecht was confirmed, she was in actual and indisputable possession of the whole eastern seaboard of North America from Nova Scotia south to the border of Florida; of the Hudson Bay territory; of several West India islands; and of Bombay on the west coast and Madras on the east coast of India; where her great trading East India Company was also in secure occupation, by the Imperial authority of the Mogul, of a great trading centre at Fort William (Calcutta).

This, then, forms a complete and definite period distinct from that which preceded and from that which followed it; for that next period was the one in which the active rivalry of France was broken down both in America and in India, and in which the colonial system itself then broke down, resulting in the great disruption; while in it also England was established as the paramount power among several in India, owing to the disintegration of the Mogul Empire.

The Elizabethan period is familiar, by reason of the splendour of adventure which has made it the chosen theme of so many brilliant writers. The struggle with France is familiar, because most people's minds are fixed on it as the main motive of English history in the eighteenth century. But our period is not so familiar because the colonial expansion in the seventeenth century lies outside the main current of political interest which is inevitably concerned with the great constitutional conflict between Monarchical and Parliamentary sovereignty that found its final solution in the Revolution at the century's close. That is the justification—if justification there be—for what is attempted in this volume, a picturing of England's oversea development under the Stuarts.

The accession of James VI, King of Scots, to the throne of England on the death of the great Tudor

Queen, inaugurated a new era by uniting under a single crown the two countries which had hitherto been chronically hostile. Although the two kingdoms were not incorporated till another century had passed, and antagonistic domestic policies, fiscal and religious, stood in the way of co-operation, the King could not in relation to foreign powers pursue one policy in respect of England and another in respect of Scotland; and the peoples could not be in open conflict with each other unless one was in rebellion against the common sovereign. It was not, however, until after the Treaty of Union was made in 1706 that Scotland was able to take active part in the English expansion; but the change from the Tudor to the Stuart dynasty in England—the Stuart mentality—was to affect its methods materially.

National Expansion had not begun under Elizabeth; only the way had been made ready for it by the development of maritime skill and fighting power, by navigators and sea-dogs, without which the farther development would have been impossible.

The Power had come into being; but power whether on sea or on land, is not of course itself expansion. National Expansion takes four forms. The first and crudest is the conquest and armed occupation of other States, neighbouring or remote. The second is settlement, with the assumption of sovereignty, on the soil of territories where the existing occupants, whether many or few, have not attained such a degree of political organisation as is implied in the term State. The third, purely commercial in its origins, is the establishment of trading quarters without sovereignty, but by authority of the local potentate, not involving settlement on the soil at all, but almost inevitably issuing in the fourth type, the armed acquisition of fresh territory, with sovereignty, as a consequence of collision with hostile neighbours—whether the neighbours be European rivals or native powers which resent the presence of Europeans. The English expansion in the seventeenth century is all but confined to the second and third of these types; though not without the conflicts with the European rivals, specially characteristic of the fourth type, which become the prominent feature of the Expansion in the eighteenth century.

We remark farther that with the exception of a single case which occurred under the Protectorate every move that took effect was initiated and carried out by private group enterprise though with the sanction of the Government; whereas in every other country that entered the field, the Government, at least after the first inception, took over control, and the direction of enterprise was made a department of State.

Clearly, group-enterprise and Government action are the two methods by which national expansion may be sought and achieved. Individual enterprise may point the way but can achieve nothing permanent until it has set one or both of those methods in motion (though it may always operate as a factor), because it cannot work on a sufficiently large scale. Individual action was the note of the sixteenth century; it was the necessary preliminary to the group-action which was the note of the seventeenth, and led up to the Government action which was to be the note of the eighteenth.

What, then, were the incentives to the new development? For a Government, the desire for power and revenue. The Government took action only so far as, in its view, power and revenue were likely to accrue from its intervention or to suffer from its non-intervention. Expansion was an experimental process, and the less the Government could be made responsible for experimental failures the better. But for group-action, two prominent incentives present themselves—the commercial desire for personal gain by co-operative action, and the desire for relief from economic or religious embarrassments at home by removal to virgin soil, where forms of religion penalised in England might be practised. There were, of course, many other subsidiary incentives. There were visionaries to whom Ralegh's idea of a Greater England made a fascinating appeal. There were adventurers ready to gamble on the chance of either literally or metaphorically lighting upon a gold mine. There were moralists who at least persuaded themselves that the conversion of the heathen would be an acceptable reward. There were economists zealous to remove the surplus unemployed population to lands where there would be no lack of employment. There was the patriotic conception of strategic advantages accruing for the next war. None of these, however, could be called primary incentives; none of them would have induced either the maritime expansion in the East, or the trans-Atlantic settlements, without the motives of commercial gain, land-hunger, and religious emancipation; to which, nevertheless, they came in as useful adjuncts for bringing associates into one or another of the enterprises, or giving to the pursuit of gain a comforting flavour of idealism or adventure, of patriotism or public spirit or missionary zeal, which freed it from the reproach of mere self-interest; while at the same time they appealed to the benevolent consideration of the Government.

We shall therefore see the Stuart development proceeding on these three main lines: in the East, with participation in a highly profitable trade as its motive; in the West, in the Plantations, settlement under favourable economic conditions; in New England, settlement under favourable religious conditions. And in the West the favour of the Government was invited by the farther expectation that the imports from the colonies would provide goods, and particularly naval stores, for an adequate supply of which England was unduly dependent upon foreign producers. For the Government would not be in any haste to concede the privileges without which effectual development by private enterprise would be impracticable unless it expected to obtain some fairly definite advantage therefrom for itself. Such advantage would be definitely derivable from the nature of the expected products of American colonisation.

## II

This volume, then, is primarily a study of the first phase of what we may call the British Imperial Expansion, the development of an island kingdom into an Empire covering a quarter of the earth's surface; a process in certain respects unique in the world's history, because although the State took part in it, actively intervening from time to time, the moving force in it was always private enterprise, the State assuming only such responsibilities, providing only such support, and imposing only such regulation, as seemed to be demanded by its own interests. No other Empire in the world's history developed on those lines, ancient or modern; the only modern expansion akin to the British was that of the Dutch, and in that also State initiative and State control played a far larger part. In the ancient world, the nearest analogy is to be found in the Greek expansion to the west; which in fact was not an Imperial expansion at all, the Greek colony being merely a new independent City State, tied to the City State or States of which it was an offshoot only by gossamer threads of sentiment, without any sense of mutual political obligations or of interests common to both.

We shall in the next chapter survey the conditions that led up to the peculiar English development which so nearly in point of time coincides with the seventeenth century and the duration of the Stuart dynasty in England—including of course the period of Interregnum; a development which was without precedent. It may, however, be not unprofitable to touch first upon some of those Imperial expansions in the past which provide not actual precedents but points which invite comparison or contrast.

All the pre-Persian Empires may be dismissed at once, because each one was the creation of a conquering war-lord bent on subjecting to his own sway every rival his arm could reach. To conquer and despoil and exact tribute was the object; followed, if necessary, by leaving in the conquered territory a permanent garrison under arms. Empire meant simply the military subjection of the conquered, to which Nineveh added the pleasing practice, copied by the last Babylonian Empire, of transplanting subjected populations. The Persians made a great forward stride by giving their Empire a political organisation, based on a definite recognition of the different nationalities that it embraced, though under the Persian supremacy. The Macedonian conception, with the unification of the Hellenic States as its theoretical base, was the substitution of a Greco-Macedonian for the Persian supremacy; but with very much larger ideas in the mind of Alexander the Great who would seem to have contemplated a blending of the Oriental with the Occidental and an unlimited farther expansion of the Empire by force of arms. The mighty war-lord's death disintegrated his empire

B

almost in the hour of its birth; but the Macedonians had caught the idea of colonisation—of planting Macedonian settlements among the "barbarians" (i.e. non-Hellenes) which should be at once military garrisons and centres for the spreading of Hellenic culture and for trade. The farther eastward expansion on the other hand was blocked by the rise of a new military empire among the outer-barbarians.

Now every one of these ancient empires owed its creation to the sheer lust of military conquest. The empire builders were conquerors for the sake of conquest, and of the wealth to be acquired thereby, though political organisation might follow. The king and the king's officers were the empire-builders. The king—who, as in all Oriental monarchies, was the State in his own person—initiated and carried out the expansion according to his own pleasure; it was in no sense the product of private enterprise. Voluntary colonisation, the settlement of a portion of the community in alien territory at a distance from its native home, was not a preliminary to conquest; it was employed only to implement conquest already achieved. Greek colonisation, as already noted, did not mean the expansion of the parent State but the establishment of a new separate and independent State. For expansion, the continuity of a central control over the whole is an essential element; whereas the Greek peoples never accommodated themselves to that idea. The germ of it, at least, may be found in the policy of Pericles, but it did not fructify in the Greek mind, and the story of the Macedonians is in no small degree the story of its failure to do so; though with Philip and Alexander it had been fundamental.

There were foreshadowings, however, of the modern conceptions of expansion in the Carthaginian experi-

ment which was shattered by its collision with Rome;
for although the Phoenician expansion was transformed
by the personal genius of Hannibal into a battle with
Rome for the dominion of the west, it was in its
inception not militarist but maritime, its object was
not conquest but commerce, and it was operated
not by a despot in search of laurels and tribute, but
by a Republic in search of markets. Carthage was
not indeed an actual island like Britain, but she was
virtually cut off from invading, or being invaded by,
any organised State except across the sea. She planted
colonies in Sicily, but her object in doing so was not
to win territory but to secure her supremacy on the
waters of the Mediterranean. In Spain she planted
her colonies not by force of arms but by "peaceful
penetration," and treaty-making with the native tribes,
and the condition of the retention and expansion of
her Empire was the retention of maritime supremacy.
Because that maritime supremacy was lost, the Scipios,
in fact, conquered Carthage in Spain, while Hannibal
was isolated in Italy.

As in all the previous cases, Carthage alone excepted,
the expansion of Rome was effected by force of arms
in battle with peoples to whom she was superior in
armament or in discipline, or in both. But in several
respects it demands differentiation from the rest. Let
us observe its stages. In the first, the City State,
planted in a commanding strategic position astride
the Tiber, acquired a hegemony which was almost
but not quite a sovereignty among the City States of
Italy. Her triumph in the Hannibalic War started her
on the second stage of expansion oversea, because
on the west it transferred to her the Carthaginian
Empire, while to eastward it brought her into contact
successively with the minor empires or kingdoms into

which the Empire of Alexander had disintegrated since his death; and contact inevitably meant armed conflict sooner or later. These two aspects of her second stage of expansion have to be distinguished. The third stage is that of the development of what had hitherto been the Imperial Republic, as the Roman Empire, under the autocrat who bore the titles of Cæsar and Augustus; a stage in which such expansion as takes place has for its object—except in very rare cases—not the acquisition of unfruitful territories but the defence of the frontiers against gathering hosts of migrant barbarians; until the barriers are broken through, and the Roman Empire itself disintegrates.

Now in the first stage, the Roman system so limited the opportunities of even the ablest soldiers for the gratification of personal ambitions that they hardly appear as a factor. The rivalry of cities on the plains or of clan-groups in the high lands provided continual grounds for quarrels in which each side comfortably convinced itself that the other was the aggressor; the Roman practice after a victorious conflict was to plant on the soil an agricultural colony which was also in effect a military garrison, and to impose upon the defeated States a treaty of alliance which rendered them liable for military service at the call of Rome while forbidding their alliance with any State other than Rome, but was at the same time a guarantee of defence against other aggressors; and the yoke laid upon them was so far from being oppressive that Hannibal's insistence that he had come into Italy as a Liberator made no effective appeal to the "allies."

Here then we have an actual colonial expansion, but in the form of military colonies planted for purposes of State. In the second stage the eastward expansion follows the normal course of the conquest of successive kingdoms; but with the variation that it is always on the pretext at least that the conquest was forced upon the conqueror by the persistent aggression of the conquered, and on the Virgilian principle—*parcere subjectis et debellare superbos*, "sparing the humbled, warring down the proud." And here it is also to be noted that in actual fact the personal ambition of a general to be known as a conqueror or actually to play the part of a military dictator whom the State will not dare to disobey becomes an extremely active factor, though he is in name acting not as an irresponsible despot but as the servant of the Republic; and the expansion of the Roman people takes the form only of the establishment of a standing garrison under arms, largely composed of the Roman legions in which service is confined to Roman "citizens," with Roman officers, and Roman civilian officials. In the West, however, there are not organised States to be dealt with, but Celtic, Iberian, or Celtiberian tribal communities, fighters by instinct—very unlike the Eastern nations—but lacking in the military science and discipline which give the mastery to the Romans. The Roman Empire has practically already reached its limits when the revolution initiated by Julius Cæsar makes its head an Emperor—*Imperator*—removable only by rebellion in the army which has sworn allegiance to him. The Roman Empire is an expansion of the Roman dominion and influence, but not of the Roman people.

With the establishment of the Principate or Empire as distinguished from the Imperial Republic, expansion ceased, apart from the addition of Britain under Claudius and of Dacia under Trajan, and from extensions of the strategic frontier which bears a marked resemblance to the advance of the strategic frontier mainly on the north-west of India in the last quarter of the nineteenth century; which lies outside the scope of this volume. During this time, the Empire was maintained by the power of the sword, but troops, generals, and the Emperors themselves, were more and more drawn not from the Roman stock but from the warlike races in or beyond the outlying provinces. When the seat of Empire was transferred from Rome to Constantinople the west was gradually separated from the east. A new disorder arose, out of which sprang the beginnings of a new Imperial order under Charlemagne, developing as feudalism. Rivalries were not national but dynastic; there was no national expansion, but by slow degrees fresh nationalities took shape, some of which were becoming consolidated at the close of the fifteenth century at the moment when new worlds were being revealed with new possibilities of expansion: upon lines essentially different from those available in the ancient world to which, except for the Carthaginians, the sea had been not an open road but a barrier.

Only in one single respect do the Middle Ages provide us with something in the nature of a partial precedent for the new type of expansion—on the part of a northern maritime people which has supplied an invaluable element, the Scandinavian, in the British race. For the Scandinavians, the Northmen, were colonisers. They did not add new territories to the Scandinavian king-doms though there was a moment when it seemed possible that Knut, our Canute, might create a Danish Empire. Their colonisation was an affair of personal enterprise, not of national policy carried out by the State; and it was colonisation oversea. Refugees from the Norse king, Harald Harfager, planted themselves in Iceland. Viking hosts planted themselves in Scotland, in Ireland, and in the English Danelagh. A Viking host planted itself in Normandy, a Norman Duke made himself King of England, and Norman adventurers made themselves Princes in Italy, detaching themselves from the Norman dukedom as the dukedom had detached itself from the Norwegian and Danish kingdoms. Their expansion had been that of a sea-going people too few for the creation of a national empire, though their colonies exercised a dominant influence, out of all proportion to their own numbers, wherever they went, until they became an integral part of the peoples among whom they were planted, as in Great Britain and France. And it is not difficult to attribute to the Scandinavian racial element in those populations a large part of the motive force in the new expansion of which the early stages are the subject of this study.

# CHAPTER II

## PRELUDE: THE SIXTEENTH CENTURY

### I

THE revelation of the existence of new and unheard of lands and of an open route to lands which had been known to the ancients but had for many centuries been cut off from European penetration by the Mohammedan barrier, came upon Christendom with a startling suddenness and completeness in the last years of the fifteenth century, half of which had elapsed before European explorers had made their way by sea as far south as the equator; and it was only rumoured that somewhere in the far north-west, beyond Iceland, the Norsemen had come upon trans-Atlantic lands in voyages long ago. More fabulous than real, the Indies and Cathay lay beyond the blocking impenetrable lines of the Turkish empires; no civilised peoples had ever penetrated the African interior. But since the early years of the century, Portuguese sailors had been creeping down the West African coast in successive expeditions organised by Prince Henry, "the Navigator," who dreamed the dream that was to come true, of turning the flank of Islam by sea and laying the Indies and Cathay open to the Christian world. Twenty-six years after his death Bartolomeo Diaz was carried past the " Cape of Storms " (which was to be re-christened the Cape of Good Hope) into the Indian Ocean, still unconscious that he was on the clear water-way to the Indies (1486). Six years later the Genoese Christopher Columbus, in the service of the Spanish monarchy, sailed west across the Atlantic and "discovered America" that is, the West Indian islands: In 1497 an English expedition reached the North American continent, and in the following year Vasco da Gama reached India itself.

Already—after the voyage of Columbus—Pope Alexander VI, of notorious memory, had awarded all heathen lands that might be discovered to the two pioneering powers, Spain and Portugal; drawing a somewhat uncertain line from north to south down the Atlantic, to the east of which the latter should be henceforth in possession, and to the west the former; an arrangement which was ratified as between those two powers by the Treaty of Tordesillas, without protest from the rest which had not yet realised its implications; though in practice none of them recognised its validity as touching any discoveries they might make on their own account.

Now at first it was the universal belief that the explorers had discovered all but simultaneously an eastward and a westward route to the shores of India or islands adjacent, or perhaps, in the more northerly voyage, of Cathay—Empires supposed to be fabulously wealthy—and at the outset the western discoveries were painfully disappointing. There were no rich populations (though there were plenty of marvels), only naked savages; and, in the north, semi-Arctic territories, sparsely populated, which appeared most unpromising. In the quarter reached by Spain, her rights, whatever they might be worth, were indisputable. The northern maritime peoples ceased for a time to be keenly interested. But the discovery of the South American mainland, the Pacific Ocean beyond the

Isthmus of Panama, and then of a genuine Empire in Mexico, opened up new possibilities. The Portuguese Magellan rounded Cape Horn, though more than half a century passed before that perilous passage was again made, and he did not himself live to complete the voyage in person. Pizarro, in his own recklessly daring but evil fashion, repeated in Peru what Cortez had done in Mexico. The Spaniards had not reached the Indies but they had discovered a land enormously rich in precious metals and precious stones: a land whose primitive peoples were at the mercy of a mounted and steel-clad soldiery armed with guns, however crude. In other words, Spain had in her own hands the whole new world of the West to exploit as she chose, with unlimited slave-labour at her disposal, a world known to contain an enormous amount of treasure which imagination increased indefinitely. Within a few years after the conquest of Peru, it had created the myth of El Dorado, the "Gilded Prince" who dwelt in the heart of South America somewhere in equatorial regions in a land almost literally made of gold. All of this was claimed as the private personal treasury of the King of Spain, who happened also, for the time, to be "the Emperor" in Europe.

On the other hand, the Portuguese had in actual fact discovered the ocean route to the real Indies: where the States already existing could not be dealt with in the same summary fashion as Mexico and Peru. They could not be seized and exploited; but immense wealth could be drawn from them by commerce. It would appear that Henry the Navigator, though thoroughly alive to the benefits to be gained from the commerce hitherto permitted only to dribble through the Mohammedan barricade, had had for his main motive the thought of a new crusade against

Islam; which had defied frontal attack from the west but would now be enveloped on flank and rear—doubtless with the support of the mythical Christian Empire of "Prester John" which was persistently fabled to exist somewhere in the East. That dream of Henry's was dispersed promptly enough, since Abyssinia was all that could be found of the legendary empire. For the little State of Portugal to attempt the conquest of India would have been sheer futility. What she could and did do was to reserve to herself the monopoly of the new trade and to wring from the native potentates ports on the Indian and neighbouring coasts which were at once commercial depots and naval stations that gave her effective command of the Indian Ocean.

The discovery of the Pacific, however, had shown that America was not the Indies but a great land-mass lying between those realms and Europe. Other Europeans might (or might not) be debarred from tropical and sub-tropical America, but the north was still open and either by crossing or rounding it a new route might be found (or eastward past North Europe) to Cathay and India by north European explorers; apart from the chance that somewhere in North America there might be found regions as auriferous as in the southern continent. In this direction the pioneer of settlement was not an Englishman but the Breton, Jacques Cartier, though the search for the "North-West Passage" became a speciality of English explorers; while the search for the North-East Passage by the English expedition of Willoughby and Chancellor resulted in the "Discovery of Muscovy" when Mary Tudor was on the English throne, an event which may be regarded as marking the beginning of a new chapter in the story of the organised advance of England. For it turned the flank not of Islam but of the Hansa on the Baltic and procured from Ivan the Terrible free access to the Russian market; and Russia had hitherto been to Western Christendom a *terra incognita* as emphatically as Tartary or Cathay or the Indies: as indeed may be clearly enough seen from the title *The Discovery of Muscovy* given to Chancellor's adventure.

For until the sixteenth century, the Mediterranean, and especially the Italian maritime cities, had held the practical monopoly of commerce with the East, and the Hansa towns of that in the north and the north sea. Though latterly the English Merchant Adventurers had been pushing their way into European markets as competitors, their ships had occasionally penetrated to the Levant, and the English had claimed a lordship of the Narrow Seas or English Channel, their fleets had never appeared as rivals of those of the maritime cities and leagues. But now, when half the century was gone, they were on the verge of challenging all monopolies as a sea-going Power; and before the century was over, their fleets had proved themselves to be the most powerful on the seas. And it was in the character of a sea-going people that they penetrated Muscovy, though they did not thereby acquire a practicable route to the Indies either by land or by sea.

Chancellor's expedition, with the first notable voyage to the Guinea Coast, in the first year of Queen Mary, may be taken as initiating the Elizabethan development.

## II

We have spoken of the Discovery of Muscovy as the milestone marking the beginning of England's more active participation in turning to account for trading purposes the geographical discoveries of which the profits had hitherto been monopolised by the Spaniards and Portuguese. Chancellor's expedition sailed at the moment when Edward VI was dying, five years before the accession of Elizabeth. Its definite aim was the discovery of a northern route to the Indies, whether by land or sea, the Southern Ocean route being commanded by the Portuguese fleets and naval bases. The North-East and North-West "passages" were both destined to be failures as practicable routes to the Indies; but the endeavour to penetrate them was a primary motive of the English voyages of exploration under Elizabeth, which led to the colonisation of North America; and it was also a main factor in the development of English seamanship that enabled the English mariners first to challenge and then to overthrow the naval and maritime supremacy of both Spain and Portugal which at the beginning of Elizabeth's reign were apparently overwhelming. The time, however, had not yet arrived when English mariners could confidently dare to defy the might of Spain, nor had any such antagonism arisen between England and either of the Southern Powers as to excite the spirit of defiance. For the Queen who succeeded Edward VI on the English throne made the Crown Prince of Spain her own royal Consort; while Spain and Portugal were equally interested in maintaining the validity of the Papal allotment of the New Worlds.

That marriage, however, proved to be not the seal of amity but its ruin. It was intended by Charles and Philip to draw England into Spain's orbit and make her a satellite of Spain; but its effect upon Englishmen was to make them regard the Spanish connexion as a menace to their freedom, the more because it was the universal belief that the spectacular persecution of English Protestantism by Philip's wife was instigated by Philip himself; and fear bred the spirit of hostility in the English people, without blinding Mary's successor and her advisers to the necessity for a politic caution. Moreover, during those years, the Newfoundland fisheries and piracy in the Channel, between them, were making conspicuous to the eyes of English seamen the line of development, the seamanship that was to transform the sailing vessel itself into an instrument of war manœuvred by Mariners, which would, so to speak, give David a decisive superiority over Goliath, if and when the time for a definite trial of strength should come. Long before that time came the hostility had risen to fever heat, and very little was left of the fear, so that Elizabeth and Cecil had much ado to postpone the open conflict for twenty-seven years by the remarkable combination of skill and luck, of audacity and duplicity, which at last won its reward. But in point of fact, that conflict and its decisive issue were the condition precedent of the English expansion.

That conflict was inevitable, because Spaniards and Portuguese were determined to maintain their monopoly, excluding all foreigners from trading in their preserves; while the English were determined not to be excluded, being by no means satisfied to be restricted to northern latitudes in their own pursuit of wealth.

The right not to occupy but to trade was the starting point, though as the quarrel developed the English claims developed. The English claim and the Spanish–Portuguese claim were both arguable, as questions of International Law which is nothing more than a statement of established and agreed international practice. Oversea colonies were something new; there was no established practice in relation to them; on the question of what ought to be the practice there was no common authority to appeal to. Each side maintained and acted upon the view which appeared to be most to its own advantage, and since they could not come to compromise by agreement each held itself justified in applying the sanction of force. In respect of Spain, however, the English claimed that the treaties made with the Duke of Burgundy under Henry VII applied also to the territories of which his son Charles V was now Sovereign, and gave to the English treaty-right of trading therein. At the moment when Chancellor's expedition was being planned, English merchants were still hoping for freedom of trade, authorised by agreement, both in the Portuguese and the Spanish spheres, without prejudice to the claim that in those regions their trading was already in point of fact lawful.

Individual adventurers had already visited the Guinea Coast and Brazil, claimed as their own exclusive sphere by the Portuguese; Wyndham's expedition in 1553 was the venture of a group or company, though, unlike Chancellor's, it was without official government sanction. In spite of an official embargo, in deference to the wishes of Mary's husband, the English Government winked at the continuance of the Guinea expeditions during her reign. Official repudiation accompanied by secret acquiescence, not to say participation, was from the outset the well-understood policy of Elizabeth's government; the Guinea trade progressed in spite of Portuguese complaints. Moreover, English adventurers of less reputable character were beginning to take example by the French, who were already practising piracy— that is to say robbery under arms on the high seas which Spain regarded as being under her own jurisdiction.

Under these conditions, John Hawkins, in the

character of an entirely legitimate trader, recognised
nd admitted as such by the Spaniards in the Canaries,
began in 1660 that series of tentative expeditions which
culminated in the famous collision at S. Juan d'Ulloa,
the port of Vera Cruz, in the Gulf of Mexico, in 1668
—the expedition from which his young cousin Francis
Drake returned with a fixed determination to pay
himself back literally in the Spaniard's own coin.

Hawkins proposed to open up on the Spanish Main
a trade in African negroes collected by himself on the
Guinea Coast. It did not occur to anyone that there
was anything nefarious in this human traffic. He
collected his cargoes partly by purchase and partly
by capture, ignoring the Portuguese, carried them
across the Atlantic, and found a ready market for
them in the ports on the Spanish Main—the physique
of the negro made him, as a human chattel, far pre-
ferable to the South American Indian. To all intents
and purposes, the labour in the Spanish American
dominions was all slave-labour, and the Spaniards
wanted all the negroes they could get.

The project appeared promising; but it did not
please Philip. The foreign trader must be shut out.
The Spanish authorities received instructions to forbid
the traffic; but the local authorities, being anxious to
evade those instructions, found a ready excuse for
doing so in very broad hints that their visitors might
be reluctantly compelled to employ force. English
adventurers, whose claim to be legitimate traders was
a good deal more than doubtful, were already employing
force; and the Spanish ambassador was protesting
strenuously. Hawkins' fourth expedition had apparently
been brought to a successful conclusion and he was
starting for home when he was compelled by stress of
weather to run for S. Juan d'Ulloa to refit. While he

was there a Spanish squadron arrived. He could have held the harbour, but not wishing for an open breach of the peace, admitted the squadron on promise that his refitting and departure should not be interfered with. The Spaniards behaved with the utmost friendliness, but on the third day, without warning suddenly opened an attack. The two ships with Hawkins and Drake on board, respectively, escaped by hard fighting; the remaining three were lost and the survivors, as was learnt later, were handed over to the Inquisition to be dealt with as heretics.

There may or may not—the question is disputable —have been justification for the methods by which Hawkins endeavoured to procure recognition for what he regarded as the treaty-rights of English merchants, no other method being feasible. For the monstrous act of treachery (for which the Spanish Viceroy was personally responsible) no excuse could possibly be pleaded. The two Governments, neither of which desired open war, contented themselves with recriminations. Attempts at a peaceful solution of the problem ceased; open war was evaded for seventeen years more, but from that moment Spaniards and English "beyond the line"—the line, that is, which the Pope had drawn between the Spanish and Portuguese spheres of dominion—treated each other as if England and Spain were at open war. The Spaniards, though they had a strong case for dealing with the English as technically pirates and brigands, gave it away by punishing them —when they could catch them—as heretics. The fight became no longer one over the right to trade; it was a war for redress, a war of reprisals, carried on on the one side by private adventurers who if they fell were glorified as Protestant martyrs, and on the other side by the Spanish Government and the Inquisition.

c

And it was a war for maritime supremacy: a guerrilla war on the English part, in which the principal English chief was a captain of genius, Francis Drake, while the organiser of the Navy which was to come into action later, John Hawkins, was a consummate master of his business.

During the whole period of the unofficial war, the King of Spain and his agents in England were notoriously conniving at plots for the assassination of the English Queen and encouraging rebellion in Ireland; at the beginning of it Alva was grinding the Protestants of the Netherlands under an iron heel with a savagery in comparison with which any persecution ever known in England was anaemic. There was never a shadow of doubt in the mind of Drake and the rest of the "pirates" that in fighting the Spaniard, even if their own primary motive was the hope of reaping a golden harvest, they were fighting the Queen's enemies and the enemies of God, or that to rob him was a perfectly legitimate spoiling of the Egyptians.

Drake would never have dreamed of denying that in his expeditions he was working out at his own risk a personal vendetta. Up to a certain point he was a knight errant, though by no means after the pattern of Don Quixote, since he was supremely practical: one whose unfailing chivalrous treatment of the victims, upon whom he preyed with the entire approval of his conscience, the Spaniards themselves were the first to appreciate though they did not think of copying it. He was a pirate who never slew wantonly, frequently spared at no small risk to himself, thoroughly enjoyed danger, and feared nothing on earth except perhaps witchcraft. That was what we may call the romantic side of him. But on the other side, he laid fast hold of the idea of a national duel with Spain, the Power which was seeking to dominate the world, and he viewed that duel with the eye of a strategist and an empire builder—constructively as well as destructively.

Therefore Drake was by no means content to be a raider. On his raids he made it his business to explore the avenues to victory over Spain, to get knowledge of the seas, the shores, the lands, the natives, the marching routes. No audacity and no odds were too big for him; his self-confidence was indomitable, partly because it was his firm conviction that the Lord of Hosts and Francis Drake were on the same side; but his trust in Providence did not lead him into the blunder of trusting to Improvidence. He neglected no available human means to security. Before his first great raid in 1572 he had spent a couple of years in what may be called scouting. From that raid he returned triumphant (except for one seasoned old sea dog, not one of the company he took with him was thirty years old)—having seen the Pacific with his own eyes from the Isthmus, and sworn, God willing, to sail upon it. Five years later he started with four ships and the Queen's commission to fulfil his vow; though the *Pelican* or *Golden Hind* was the only ship remaining after she had passed the Straits of Magellan and discovered that Tierra del Fuego was not a continent but an island. When he had annexed all the treasure he could carry, he sailed north in the hope of finding the western end of the "North-West Passage," for the eastern end of which other mariners were persistently searching; but an Arctic voyage had not been in his original programme, and he lacked the necessary equipment. So after discovering California and making friends with the natives—his invariable custom—he sailed for home by way of the southern archipelago and so round the Cape. Even then the pretence of peace was kept up for five years more. But in 1585 the mask was dropped, and the rest of Drake's work he did as an admiral in the Queen's Navy.

Other adventurers during those years were acting on Drake's lines, sometimes successfully, sometimes disastrously, but always learning how to fight the Spaniard and increasing the country's efficiency for the struggle when the two nations should come to the grip. But while Drake and the men of his school were thinking of expansion in terms of a battle for supremacy with Spain, it was possible to aim at a solution of the problem which might escape the necessity for the appeal to arms. If Elizabeth privily encouraged the adventurers while avowedly discountenancing them, Burghley regarded them with unqualified disapproval. War might, in the long run, be forced upon England in self-defence, and she must be prepared for that contingency, but anything that could be construed as unwarrantable aggression ought to be firmly repressed. But it was sound policy to push forward experimentally in the directions which would not involve collision with Spain.

Thus during the 'sixties and 'seventies the Muscovy Company was engaged in a constant endeavour to open up a far-eastern traffic through Persia, which was only abandoned in 1580, Turkey blocking the way. Even then a "Turkey Company" was formed which hoped to achieve the same end by way of the Levant; but here too, though valuable information was obtained, it soon became clear that the overland route to Cathay or the Indies was impracticable. But there remained the North-West Passage; and in the search for it the first idea of colonial settlement appears to have germinated in the mind of Humphrey Gilbert, the elder half-brother of Walter Ralegh.

Arctic voyaging did not offer the attractions of voyaging in the tropics. Northern exploration had brought to light Newfoundland, with its cod-banks, and Jacques Cartier had planted the French on the St. Lawrence, in the first half of the century, but no promising prospects on the continent had been lighted upon when Martin Frobisher, with two vessels of twenty-five tons, sailed to tempt the Arctic seas again in 1576, a year before Drake started on his great voyage. He found Baffin Land and Frobisher Sound, the entry, as he believed, of the Passage itself. Also he imagined that he had found not indeed actual gold but ore which meant that there was gold. Angry disappointment followed when the actual worthlessness of the ore was discovered, but the ardour of belief in the Passage was only temporarily damped; and Gilbert, long a convinced believer, started his own project for combining settlement on the soil with the pursuit of the elusive passage. Gilbert's two expeditions in 1578 and 1583 both collapsed, and he himself went down in the *Squirrel* on the return journey. But his idea had planted itself in the mind of Ralegh; who forthwith began prospecting—though not in person—on the American coast, and sent out his first settlers to Roanoke in 1585. In the same year, John Davis, greatest and most modest of pilots, took up the quest for the North-West Passage in which Ralegh had not directly interested himself, and in the course of three voyages discovered Davis Strait. But it was also at this point that the private war of reprisals developed into a national duel between the English and Spanish navies.

### III

Until a generation ago, historical textbooks habitually adopted the pleasing fiction, launched by the piety of the

Elizabethans, that the victory of the English in that great conflict was in the nature of a miracle. *Dominus flavit et dissipati sunt;* how else could the little English ships have annihilated the huge sea-castles of Spain? The fiction perhaps still survives in the popular imagination, but the actual facts are now fully established. The victory at the time amazed the world, which was overawed by Spain's bulk and the prestige which had just been raised to the highest point by the destruction of the Turkish fleet at Lepanto; but it was in fact, as at Crecy and Poictiers, the victory of a new tactic over the traditional and familiar tactics hitherto universally employed; of a new scientific method in the face of which orthodox methods were obsolete: of mobility over bulk; of intelligence, initiative, and skill over inertia. So when the Armada did come, it was broken up, past hope of recovery, before the tempest arose which gave it the *coup de grâce*. To come down to details, the seamanship learnt by the English mariners in the stormy northern seas gave their sailing ships an immense advantage in manœuvre over heavy, oar-driven galleys; except in a calm, they could hold off, engage, or break away at pleasure. The English mariners, with perhaps a small complement of landsmen—fought their own ships; the galley was of far less fighting value than a true sailor of half her size, because she had to carry her crowd of galley-slaves (useless in the fighting), a few mariners, and a mass of soldiers who were never given the chance of fighting till half of them had been pounded out of action by the English gunners; until the Englishmen chose to board, they were little more than the gunner's herded victims. The Spaniard, built on the time-honoured hypothesis developed in the Mediterranean that her business was to ram or grapple the enemy, carried her guns on castles forward and aft for use in advance, pursuit, or retreat; the English guns were ranged for pouring in simultaneous broadsides at close quarters where the enemy could neither grapple them nor hit them; and while their own fire was directed upon the Spanish hulls and decks, that of the Spaniards could only be directed upon the English rigging on which it rarely took effect. And finally the English operations were directed by seamen who knew their business, while those of the Spaniards were directed by landsmen who did not.

Thus, although the overwhelming defeat of the Armada came upon the world with a mighty shock of surprise, it is clear enough that it did not surprise the English mariners themselves at all. They were perfectly confident of victory from the beginning, and were evidently annoyed by finding the task of shattering the great fleet not easier but much harder than their experience in the war of reprisals had led them to expect. It did not give them the superiority; but it was a decisive demonstration of the superiority which they knew they had already attained, though the rest of the world (English landsmen included) did not know it.

The fact, then, was revealed in 1588; but the result was not that which might have been anticipated. England did not turn her naval superiority to account for her own territorial aggrandisement at the expense of Spain. The naval war went on for another fifteen years, but the English were never in occupation of any territory claimed by Spain, though Spanish ships, unless in overwhelmingly greater force, never engaged with English ships if they could possibly avoid doing so. If the attempt had been made, it may very well be believed that it would have failed like the Plantagenet and Lancastrian adventures in France, because England's resources, more than adequate for the winning of victories, were inadequate for the retention of conquests. But the attempt at conquest was never made, because Elizabeth (in complete agreement with Burghley) did not choose that it should be made. She was willing enough to humiliate Spain, to damage Spain, to seize all the Spanish treasure she could; but she and Burghley wanted to preserve Spain as a counterpoise to, and possibly as an ally against, France, which in Europe would profit more than England by her complete ruin. If Drake and Walsingham and Ralegh could have dominated her counsels, she would have fought Spain as the elder Pitt fought France when she had been in her grave for a century and a half. But Walsingham died, Ralegh was never sufficiently trusted to be even admitted to the Privy Council, and most of the seamen, headed by John Hawkins, were more attracted—like Elizabeth herself—by the substantial rewards of raiding Spanish treasure ships in the Atlantic, and Portuguese spice-ships from the east (Philip had appropriated the Portuguese crown in 1580), than by Drake's vision of destroying the power of Spain and entering upon her oversea inheritance. The Spanish and Portuguese possessions were still intact when James I made peace in 1604. Essex, the favourite of Elizabeth's later years, was of Drake's school, but like Leicester before him he never directed his mistress's policy, while personal rivalries and jealousies made co-operation between him and Ralegh impossible; even their combined influence would never have outweighed that of Burghley, and it was not either or both of them, but Burghley's very astute son Robert Cecil, who took the old man's place when he died.

IV

We can now see what it was that Elizabeth's Government allowed Elizabeth's seamen actually to accomplish. England had not entered upon the Spanish oversea inheritance, but the mariners had made it for ever impossible for the Spaniard to interfere with an independent English expansion or for the Portuguese to prevent her from achieving supremacy in the Indian Ocean, in which she had not hitherto appeared as a rival. The rivals who were about to enter the field were the French and Dutch, both of them as hostile to Spain as the English themselves and both of them trained in the same tempestuous schools of seamanship; though the conception of Spain as the enemy persisted.

The ultra-imperialists were paralysed by the action of the Government. Drake, the popular hero when the Armada was shattered, was deliberately discredited by being allowed to undertake an expedition against Lisbon in 1589 on behalf of a claimant to the Portuguese crown, but under conditions which made, and were probably intended to make, its success impossible. A threatened revival of the Spanish sea-power forced Elizabeth so far to yield to the forward school as to sanction the final joint expedition of Drake and Hawkins to the Spanish Main, in 1595, from which neither of them returned, and the Cadiz expedition in the next year which was completely successful in its immediate object, but was followed by a reversion to the policy of hunting treasure-fleets. Ralegh was permitted in 1595 to make on his own account the expedition to the Orinoco in search of Eldorado which he described as the "Discovery of Guiana," but it was not followed up; the days when he stood high in the Virgin Queen's favour had long gone by. Not dominion but treasure was Elizabeth's maritime objective.

Ralegh, an imperialist of the most unqualified type —one, that is, who deliberately aimed at achieving empire in the New World by the strong hand if a European rival stood in the way—schemed always with his eyes on Spain. She had not found, but she claimed for her own, the mythical Eldorado. England ought to find it for herself, and hold it. It would not only bring her untold wealth; it would give her a base from which she could effect the conquest of the Spanish dominions. That this was his conception is perfectly clear from the text of the book, *The Discovery of Guiana*, in which he told the story of his forcible explorations. But conquest would have required organisation on a scale impossible for private adventure, and the design was far too speculative, and involved risks far too heavy, for Elizabeth's Government to embark on it. Nothing came of the Orinoco voyage, except occasional private ventures in pursuit of the Eldorado will-o'-the-wisp.

Neither gold-mines nor the conquest of Spain rewarded the achievement of maritime superiority, though both were part and parcel of Ralegh's dream; there is no doubt that the possession of a naval base beyond the Atlantic on the flank of the traffic between Spain and America was one of the objects Ralegh had in view when he planned the settlement at Roanoke; nor is there any doubt that both that idea and the hope of gold-discoveries were present in the minds of the men who projected and carried out the resettlement of Virginia when the first Virginia had perished and its originator was eating his heart out in the Tower. But that pioneering effort, of which was born the colonisation of North America, was itself born of a vision that embraced much more than a battle between hostile forces for a prize which lay or was supposed to lie ready to the hand of the more skilful duellist.

Ralegh saw that vision, which Humphrey Gilbert before him, and some few others inspired by Gilbert, had glimpsed; and he expended much of his private wealth, and of his care and energy, on attempting to realise it by his own almost unaided efforts in the face of repeated failures. He failed, because the vision made no popular appeal and no appeal to statesmen or politicians in whose minds there was no room for it beside the more absorbing question of the conflict with Spain; for what he saw in that vision was a Greater England, peopled by Englishmen, growing up beyond the seas, with unlimited space for development; not— apart from the accompanying dream of a Spanish conquest—an adventurer's gamble for a short cut to wealth and ease, such as was offered by looting the Spaniard, or such as had been offered to the Spaniards by the looting of Mexico and Peru. It never had a chance of realisation until war with Spain was conclusively vetoed, west of "the line" as well as east of it, by the accession in England of a king to whom the Elizabethan traditions were anathema—the king whose acceptable present to the court of Spain was the head of Walter Ralegh. But it was the vision which we shall presently watch materialising while the baseless fabric of Eldorado was melting into air. Four times Ralegh sent out his settlers; Sir Philip Sidney was to have taken part in the first expedition, but Elizabeth would not let him go; each time either the company was wiped out or a surviving remnant threw up the task. Before he made his Guiana voyage he had finally abandoned the project, which was not revived till after Elizabeth's death. Yet the vision came true.

After the third voyage of Davis, belief in the existence of the North-West Passage was strengthened rather than diminished, but the quest for it seemed too unprofitably arduous to be maintained with persistency. On the other hand, Drake's circumnavigation, followed by that of Thomas Cavendish which was concluded in the Armada year, dissipated the idea hitherto prevalent that the Portuguese monopoly of the Indian Ocean could not be effectively challenged, though their actual possession of all the ports on the West African coast gave them an immense advantage. The union of the Spanish and Portuguese crowns made their ships fair prey for the English. The disasters which attended the first voyages attempted did not destroy the conviction that the Cape route to the eastern seas was practicable and gave promise of immense profits. The conviction was confirmed by a series of Dutch expeditions and the revelation of the actual weakness of the Portuguese hold on its Maritime Empire; and the result was the formation of the East India Company—the " London Company trading to the East Indies"—and its incorporation by a Royal Charter signed on the last day of the century, December 31st, 1600. Early in the next year, its first expedition—four ships, with Sir James Lancaster in command, set forth on the very prosperous voyage which may be reckoned as the first step in the Eastward expansion of England. The first Stuart had already been King of England as well as of Scotland for some months when the squadron, which sailed in 1601, reappeared in English waters, laden with pepper and spices. The new commerce was launched.

The Elizabethans, then, had achieved the necessary condition of Expansion. Also they had done marvels in the way of exploratory and pioneering work, of which the main result was that it had taught them what was not immediately practicable, the Arctic and overland routes to India and China. Roanoke was their sole—and unsuccessful—effort at oversea settlement, unless we count Humphrey Gilbert's still more abortive attempt. The actual expansion was still to come when the great queen died. But we may append to this survey a note on another and very unfortunate type of colonisation for which the period was responsible, not in distant lands but in a province of the English Crown—the planting of English colonies in Ireland: a disastrous experiment to which we owe some of the most painful chapters in English history. It differed from all our other forms of colonisation; in that it was a planting of Englishmen not upon foreign soil, not among non-Europeans, but to serve as a garrison and to impose English law and order, upon a soil occupied by a kindred people who had long in theory acknowledged the English sovereignty which in practice had been exercised only spasmodically and ineffectively. The intention was to anglicise the Irish and make Ireland an English territory; the effect was to subject a large Catholic population to the domination of a small Protestant garrison, and to make Ireland the persistent cradle of rebellion in one form or another, open or covert, for centuries to come. But though this was in fact and in name colonisation, in the early Roman sense, it does not belong to the story of English expansion, and therefore has no further part in this volume.

# PART II

FOUNDATIONS OF EMPIRE: 1600-1658

# CHAPTER III

## THE EAST, AND THE BIRTH OF THE EAST INDIA COMPANY

### I

THE idea of colonisation, that is of establishing settled communities on the soil oversea, had been projected, attempted, and abandoned while Elizabeth was reigning: not to be renewed till after her death; but the continuous commercial expansion in the East had actually begun, though the inaugurating voyage had not yet reached completion when King James ascended the English throne. So in this survey, the early fortunes of the East India Company take precedence of the colonising movement. For the sake of continuity, some necessary preliminary details belonging to the Company's story have been postponed for examination in this chapter.

Until after the Armada, the Portuguese had held the Oceanic route to the East in their own hands, uncontested. The Indian and Pacific Oceans had been penetrated only from the east in the circumnavigatory voyages of Drake, and of Cavendish, who returned to England to find that the great victory had been already won. For this there had been two reasons. One was the apparent strength of the Portuguese in the occupation of the available ports and harbours on the route; the other, the concentration of the English upon the

discovery of a practicable Northern water-way to the
East. In a minor degree, the hypothetical possibilities
of a land-route to the Indies by way of Persia through
a friendly Muscovy or from the Levant by Turkish
concessions, had taken precedence of enterprises which
would inevitably involve collision with the maritime
power of Portugal, while relations with Spain were
still undecided.

About 1580, the Muscovy Company, while maintaining its Russian trade, ceased to attempt the overland
penetration of Asia, and at the same time the Turkey
or Levant Company was formed to make its effort by
the Mediterranean route to Syria and so to Persia.
Concessions, not very far-reaching, were obtained from
the Turks; but the Mediterranean swarmed with the
hostile ships of Spain (which commanded the entry),
of Venice, and of the Barbary Corsairs. To reach the
Levant and return from it in safety was difficult enough,
and it soon appeared that nothing more was to be looked
for through Syria than a precarious filtration. At the
same time, Ralph Fitch, of the Levant Company, was
making his adventurous journey overland to and
through India and Further India, to return in 1591
and publish a report of his travels which to the spirit
of commercial enterprise made the lure of the East
irresistible—at the same time confirming the conviction
that the way to the East must be sought by the voyage
round the Cape, in view of the impracticability both
of the North-East and the North-West passages.

For Fitch's report included an exposure of the
mythical character of the reputed effective power of
the Portuguese in the Eastern waters; a report that
was more than confirmed by that of the Dutchman
Linschoten who returned to Holland, from service
with the Portuguese at Goa—their establishment on

the west coast of India—the year after Fitch's arrival in London. Linschoten's work had already given inspiration to the Dutch before its effects reached England.

Already, however, before the appearance of Fitch's report, the spirit of enterprise had sent forth an experimental expedition into this new field under George Raymond and James Lancaster. Storms, and ultimately mutiny, brought disaster upon it; but Lancaster, who succeeded with a few of his company in reaching home after three years, was so far from being discouraged, that he was himself the chosen "admiral" under whom the East India Company dispatched its first voyage in 1601. Apart from this, the Dutch, as was previously noted, were in fact the first to enter the new field, providing us with a rival who was soon to prove a much more serious obstacle to England's commercial ambitions than the already exhausted Portuguese. But in the last decade of the sixteenth century, Dutch and English were both still fighting the common enemy, Spain. The rivalry did not develop into definite hostility until the United Netherlands, not technically but *de facto*, had won their liberty by the eleven years' truce of 1609 with Spain.

A second English expedition ended even more disastrously than the first. But the activity of the Dutch served as an additional incentive to enterprise on a big scale. And so, largely as it would seem on the initiative of leading members of the Levant Company, the new "Company of Merchants of London trading into the East Indies" was formed, and incorporated by the Royal Charter on the last day of the century. It was high time to be moving, for in the seven years, no less than fifteen Dutch expeditions had sailed, and in 1602 the various Dutch companies that had taken part therein were amalgamated in the great Dutch East India Company, with the Government of the United Provinces not passively or potentially but actively behind it.

Trade, not the acquisition of territory, was the object in view. Trade would bring wealth to the community, and the wealth of the community provides revenue, which is Power, for the State; therefore it is to the advantage of the State that it should give security to the trader, provided that his trading is not of a kind which will in other ways be injurious to the State. Also the State may legitimately demand a *quid pro quo* for its interest. These were the principles which governed the relations of the Crown to the methods of commercial expansion; otherwise the Crown did not desire to interfere with the trader in the conduct of his business of making his trading profitable. *Mutatis mutandis*, it applied the same principle to the parallel development of colonial expansion. The trader's officers were in the service not of the Government but of the Company. The Dutch, however, with the establishment of their East India Company were already adopting the principle which, in the new expansion, prevailed in all States except England, that the officers of the Company were the servants of the Government.

The English system, inaugurated by the London East India Company, was not a new invention but—like most English institutions, a normal development out of past practices, suggested by the immediate experience of the novel conditions under which they would have to work—something in the nature of a long step towards adaptation to a new environment. The steps taken by the Dutch and by the French with the same purpose did not follow the same direction and in the long run proved to be less effective; but in the seventeenth century experience had not yet provided the answer to the question which of the two schools of expansion was following the sounder track.

In the Middle Ages, commercial expansion could be effected only through organised Associations of Merchants enjoying something like monopolies by authoritative prevention of competition on the part of free traders, in face of the competition of the groups of foreign traders who were already in occupation of the markets it was sought to penetrate; since in all quarters the alien was regarded as at best an evil to be endured, necessary only because his presence brought compensating advantages; while a rival was not to be tolerated if he could be successfully suppressed. The great commercial cities of the continent were virtually mercantile corporations, which might league together and act jointly for the furtherance of their common interests and the exclusion of intruders. To force a way through such barriers was impossible for the isolated action of individuals; but a wealthy corporation could bargain with rivals, purchase privileges and guarantees, and give guarantees on behalf of its members, which would enable them to push their trade in comparative security.

Thus arose the system of "regulated" Companies; companies in which each member carried on his own trade with his own money and goods at his own risk but with the privileges conferred by membership and subject to the trading regulations of what we might call the Company's bye-laws which a royal charter gave it the legal power of enforcing on its members, while enabling it also to take preventive or penal action against non-members; membership being open to all duly qualified traders who chose to pay the authorised fees. The Government, taking its toll upon all foreign trading in the form of import and export duties, made its own profit out of the system in the first place because it increased the bulk of the trade on which the toll was taken, and secondly because it immensely facilitated and simplified the process of collecting the duties; provided that monopolistic charters were granted only to such companies as were able to work on such a scale and at such a profit that legitimate traders would prefer membership to "free" trading.

This was in itself virtually the extension to foreign trade of the working principles of internal trading which created the borough trade guilds; the various trades in each "chartered" borough being exclusively in the hands of their respective trade-guilds or companies; with the double purpose of shutting out competition and ensuring efficiency of production along with honesty in dealing; while the individual trader traded on his own account, but subject to the legally enforcible regulations of the guild, membership of which was the condition precedent of his trading at all.

The first of the new big-scale Chartered Associations was the Muscovy Company, followed by the Guinea Company which broke down, and others of which the Levant Company was the most notable until the birth of the East India Company. There was nothing essentially novel about the methods of any of them, before the last, except that the Muscovy Company introduced one innovation. It began to trade as a single body instead of as a group of Associated Merchants trading as individuals under the aegis of the Company. That is to say, it was the Muscovy Company that initiated the method of trading not with the several stocks of Richard, Henry, and Thomas on which they made or failed to make their respective profits, but on their joint stock of the collective profits of which each received his share in proportion to his original contribution. The East India Company started upon this principle from the beginning, though more than sixty years passed before it was fully organised as a Joint-Stock Company in the sense in which we now understand that term. We must not, therefore, be misled by the usual and quite justifiable habit of referring to the Company as a "Joint-Stock" because the name has acquired a specialised meaning.

For the modern Joint-Stock concern and the original East India Company are alike companies trading on a joint-stock and distributing profits in proportion to the amount of stock held by the shareholders. But the modern concern trades continuously upon a permanent capital not recoverable from the company by shareholders until the concern itself is wound up; the East India Company traded upon a capital not permanent but subscribed for each particular venture and recoverable by the shareholder upon the winding up of that particular venture from its own individual proceeds. It was a bridge between the medieval regulated company of individual traders each of whom provided his own capital and conducted his own trading, and the modern Joint-Stock Company, in which the company itself not only regulates but conducts the trading continuously, upon the permanent capital provided by its shareholders, on behalf of the shareholders; and it partook of the character both of the old type from which it sprang and of the later type into which it developed.

II

A fillip was given—if one was needed—to the design of opening up the oceanic trade with the East, by the publication, in an English translation, of Linschoten's work which had already set the Dutch so actively in motion. The promoters had given shape to their scheme and were applying for incorporation under a royal charter in 1599; but the matter was for the moment held up lest it should interfere with the prospect of a peace with Spain and Portugal. The prospect, however, faded, and it was an enlarged and more ambitious scheme that was presented for acceptance at the close of 1600.

The Charter which then received the Queen's Assent conferred upon the company the exclusive right, as against all other Her Majesty's subjects, of trading in the lands and on the seas eastward from the Cape of Good Hope as far as the Straits of Magellan, for a period of fifteen years but terminable at an earlier date by notice from the Crown; but (in relation to other powers), in such lands only as were not in effective occupation of any Christian Prince who was at amity with the Queen of England, except with consent of the Prince. Thus it explicitly assumed, first that the papal assignment to Spain and Portugal was of no effect, secondly that only effective occupation gave right of possession, and thirdly that actual possession carried with it, as in European countries, the right of barring the commercial doors as against the alien. To those principles the English Government thenceforth consistently adhered, as regards Christian though not as regards non-Christian Powers, in spite of the counter-assumption of Spain and Portugal that the papal assignment held good by the "Law of Nations"—a doctrine which was repudiated by Dutch and French as resolutely as by the English.

Further, the right of exclusive trading was reinforced by authority to grant licences to non-members, to make bye-laws, and to punish transgressions of the bye-laws by such penalties as were consistent with the laws of the realm. Moreover, the Company had authority to purchase lands, and to sue and to be sued as a body corporate; with certain privileges in respect of their exports and imports and the duties thereon. If the trade proved beneficial to the country the charter was to be renewed on the expiry of the fifteen years. Meanwhile the Company was to be entitled to dispatch annually six ships and six pinnaces, adequately armed and manned.

Finally the Company, as incorporated, was definitely organised upon the basis of joint-stock trading, but as a mercantile, not a national, enterprise. It was under the management of a Governor and a board of twenty-four Directors (officially entitled Committees, a term which had not then acquired a plural signification in common parlance), the first Governor being Sir Thomas Smythe who was also a leading member of the Levant Company. Its members were the original subscribers of the capital for the first voyage, their sons having the right of acquiring membership, while accepted subscribers to subsequent voyages also acquired membership thereby. There was no right of entry by payment of fees as with the medieval companies. Subscriptions were for the particular voyage, carried with them liability to a *pro rata* levy on all subscribers if the amount subscribed proved insufficient, and must be in cash, not in merchandise or supplies in kind. The actual subscription for the first voyage was something over £68,000—in those days, a very large sum. The trading was by the Company's servants, all private trading being prohibited except by express authority of the Company. But each voyage had to be specifically sanctioned by the Crown before it sailed. The Crown

was not trading; the nation was not trading; but the
Company's trading and its privileges were conditional
upon the Crown's approval of its proceedings, both
before and after.

Within four months after the signing of the Charter,
the first voyage set sail from Torbay; four ships under
the command of Sir James Lancaster; three years
passed before its re-appearance in English waters. Its
return is the Stuart starting point.

### III

The Portuguese were in possession, and the Dutch
were in the field against them before the English, if
we leave out of count the passages of Drake and Cavendish through Chinese and Indian waters in their
circumnavigations, and the failure of Lancaster's first
expedition. But the great trade in which Dutch and
English were both determined to participate was not
that of India so much as of the Archipelago, the Islands
beyond India; for it was primarily for the sake of the
spices there produced. There, however, the Dutch,
having taken the lead, kept it after rapidly ousting the
Portuguese. For to the United Provinces, the maintenance of that trade was an essential object of policy,
the necessary condition of winning and holding for
the small Republic so much as even a secondary position
among the European Powers. For them, it was quite
definitely a National matter, and the whole power of
the State was behind it. Their rivals were an English
trading company, paternally fostered by the English
Government, no doubt, but, except possibly in the
very last resort, dependent on its own resources in the
rivalry; coming in the track of the Dutch, it was at
an immense disadvantage.

The text within the portrait engraving reads:

VERA EFFIGIES PRÆCLARISS<sup>mi</sup> VIRI DOM<sup>ni</sup> THOMÆ SMITH IN EQVITIS AVRATI ETC.

Simon Paſſeus ſculp:

Lond: A<sup>o</sup> 1616.

Jo: Woodall exc

The honourable S<sup>r</sup> Thomas Smith Knight, late Embaſ=
ador from his Ma<sup>tie</sup> to y<sup>e</sup> great Emperour
of Ruſsie, Gouernour of y<sup>e</sup> Hon<sup>ble</sup> and famous
Societyes of Marcha<sup>nts</sup> tradinge to y<sup>e</sup> East=
Indies, Muſscovy, the French and Somer
Ilands Company: Treſurer for Virginia .etc.

SIR THOMAS SMITH [Rischgitz

First Governor of the East India Company, and first Treasurer
of the Virginia Company

[Face page 50

On the other hand, the exploiting of the islands was a comparatively easy matter, whereas India itself presented a very different problem. Consequently, while the Dutch made it their business to maintain their grip on the Spice Islands to the exclusion of all intruders, the English before long were more zealously engaged in seeking admission to India from its rulers, practically unimpeded by the Dutch, than in endeavouring to force their way through the Dutch barrier in the otherwise more attractive islands. Portuguese attempts to shut them out were a minor matter. Neither the Dutch in the islands nor the English in India took long to establish their own decisive superiority, for Portugal had completely exhausted herself in the overstrain of her heroic effort in the past; she had no reserve of strength to fall back on; and she was in the grip of Spain, which gave her no effective support. Besides which, the methods of the Portuguese had made them thoroughly detested by all the Orientals, who were ready enough to side with anyone, Dutch or English, who seemed likely to be a match for them; while in seamanship they had now been left far behind by the mariners of the north.

The Island trade had the double attraction of being much the more lucrative, immediately at least, and much the simpler; for the islands were themselves in effect a number of small chieftainships or principalities with no common allegiance (except where the princes had already been coerced or persuaded into acknowledging the over-lordship of Portugal); they could be dealt with and dominated one by one, being practically incapable of concerted self-defence, while the ejection of the Portuguese presented no serious difficulties to the very energetic Dutchmen, in the hey-day of their stubborn and finally triumphant struggle for national

and religious independence. The Dutch came in the
first instance as liberators from Portuguese oppression
and were welcomed accordingly, though as time went
on it may be doubted whether the islanders found that
their new masters were a substantial improvement on
their predecessors.

A lucrative trade with India was on the other hand
no more than a potentiality. When the Portuguese
first appeared on the western coast of the peninsula,
there was no Mogul Empire; from the Himalayas to
Cape Comorin, the land was divided into great kingdoms
and minor principalities, much as was Europe; with
a population mainly Hindu throughout, but in most
though not all of the greater kingdoms, ruled by
Mohammedan dynasties, which oppressed their Hindu
subjects, all habitually engaged in wars of aggression
against each other, expanding or contracting their
borders; the most powerful among them having been
for centuries the successive Mohammedan dynasties
which had made Delhi their capital, and held sway
over most of the north. The southern half of India
had never been effectively subjugated by the Delhi
dynasties though latterly military adventurers had
carved out great independent sultanates for themselves
in the Deccan. But between 1500 and 1530 the Mughal
conqueror, Babar, broke into Hindustan through the
passes of the north-west, overthrew the reigning
dynasties, and founded the mighty "Mogul" Empire.
In the second half of the century Babar's grandson,
Akbar, one of the world's most famous and enlightened
rulers, established and expanded that Empire over the
whole of Northern India, and began, though he did
not progress very far with, the subjugation of the
Deccan. In short during the whole period with which
this work is concerned the "Great Moguls" were at

he height of their wealth and power. Akbar's own
eign began two years before and ended two years
fter that of Elizabeth, and that of his third successor
Aurangzib—a sort of Indian Philip II, who unknow-
ngly by his fanaticism ensured the disruption of the
empire which Akbar had based upon toleration—ended
it the moment when the first united Parliament of
Great Britain was assembling. There was during the
seventeenth century no opening whatever—least of all
o a mercantile Company—in India for the forcible
methods that were so readily available and effective
n the Spice Islands. The European, if present at all,
was so only on sufferance.

## IV

From 1601 to 1612 the East India Company sent
out a series of "Separate Voyages," all upon the joint-
stock principle as explained above; reckoned variously
as Number 1 to number 9 or number 12. The second
voyage set sail in 1604, when the new king had already
been on the throne for eleven months. In 1609, when
the prospects appeared to be particularly unpromising,
it was perhaps saved from dissolution by the somewhat unexpected interest in its fortunes displayed by
King James, who granted it a new charter on terms
somewhat more favourable than Elizabeth's—though
the Company succeeded at a later date in evading
his rather dangerous suggestion that he should himself become an honorary member. James, the "wisest
fool in Christendom," did in fact combine shrewdness
with fatuity in the most astonishing manner; and
while he humiliated the Crown and the country by
such graceful concessions to Spanish prejudice as the
head of Sir Walter Ralegh, he was very wide awake

to the benefits derivable from commercial and colonial
expansion so long as they did not threaten a rupture
with the power whose good will he was so anxious to
secure. Nor did he ever by word or deed depart from
that interpretation of International Law which Elizabeth
had enshrined in the Company's charter—that only
effective occupation of oversea territory gave legal
possession; with its corollary, that exclusive possession
accompanied effective occupation—a view according to
which the total invalidity of that papal donation on
which Spain and Portugal based their extravagant
claims was too obvious to admit even of discussion.
What exactly was denoted by effective occupation was
—and remained—undefined. How James's attitude
would have been affected if Spain had troubled herself
about Portugal's moribund power in the East is an interesting question which did not in fact arise; since James
could afford to ignore a Portugal left, as she was left by
Spain, to her own resources and her own devices.

Now the English venture in the East was the following
up of the Dutch invasion of the hitherto unchallenged
Portuguese monopoly. When Lancaster sailed, Portugal
was not in the category of Christian Powers at amity
with the Queen of England, and he was at liberty to
make prize of any Portuguese ships he might have
the fortune to capture. But when the second expedition,
under Captain Middleton, sailed, peace with Spain
—and therefore with Portugal—was already in sight
and had been signed by the time that the expedition
was in Indian waters. In form, both Portugal and the
United Provinces were friendly Christian powers and
so remained generally for some fifty years. It was on
that hypothesis that the Company had to conduct its
operations in eastern waters. And as against the
Portuguese the Dutch—in addition to being first in

he field and having the National Government behind
hem—had this advantage over the English, that their
ruce with Spain was not signed till five years later,
o that conquest from the Portuguese, where they were
lready in effective occupation, was still open to them
ve years after it had been closed to the English;
he English and Dutch doctrines of the rights con-
eyed by occupation being identical.

At the same time, when actually at peace with Por-
ugal, Dutch and English traders alike could trade
nly by forcible maintenance of the legal rights they
laimed as against the Portuguese claim to exclude by
orce all rivals in Eastern waters, irrespective of " occu-
ation "; while to that end the English Government,
eyond authorising armed resistance where necessary,
ave the English Company no aid. It had to take
are of itself, arm its own ships, and fight its own
attles. And in dealing with the Dutch, the lack of an
greed definition of effective occupation was a permanent
ource of friction not unlikely to result in armed collision
—in which case again the English trading company
vould have to take care of itself—just as it had to do,
f course, in treating miscellaneous piracy.

Moreover, apart from foreign rivals, the Company
ad to face opposition at home, on two sides. Its charter
nd its monopoly were always conditional upon its
rade being advantageous to the country. The justice
f its monopoly was attacked on one side, and the
conomic benefit of the trade to the nation on the
ther.

The monopoly of the new Company differed essen-
ially from the monopolies enjoyed by the old "regu-
ated" trading companies, such as the Merchant
Adventurers, the members of which conducted their
wn trading and took their own risks and their own

profits as individuals, while the Company, as a corpora
body, did not trade at all. Membership was open
every would-be merchant whose object was legitima
trading and who chose to pay his fees. The onl
grievance of the individual was that, to be permitte
to trade, he must submit himself to regulations lai
down and generally recognised as being for the commo
good of all legitimate traders, in return for which h
obtained, as against aliens, the additional security fc
which membership of a powerful association was
guarantee. Subject to the regulations—though nc
otherwise—he could compete freely with his neighbour
and manage his own business himself or through hi
own agents. The individual who wanted legitimat
business had in effect no serious grievance at all.

The new Company on the other hand virtually elimi
nated the individual trader. He did, indeed, as a member
provide his own share of the common stock with whic
the Company traded, and received a proportional shar
of the common profits distributed; but the trading wa
done neither by himself nor by his own agents bu
by the Company's agents, over whom he had no persona
control. Once a member he remained a member, bu
he could (apart from specified exceptions) claim nc
right of admission to membership, which was in effec
open only to those who were prepared to make ai
extremely substantial contribution to the particula
joint venture in contemplation. There was a substantia
number of persons who wished to trade for them
selves with a free hand in the East but were debarrec
from doing so except under licence specially grantec
either by the monopolist Company or by the Crown
while they did not wish their trading to be done upor
the Company's terms—and all such persons were
zealous foes of the Company itself, in whose favour

they were denied the normal rights of free trading. ("Free trade" in the seventeenth century, it may be remarked in passing, was a term which had no connexion whatever with its specialised modern meaning of untaxed imports—all imports were taxed as a matter of course.) Moreover, there was an undercurrent of public opinion favouring their complaint, because legalised monopolies at large were at the time extremely unpopular; several having been granted to Court favourites who made use of them to enrich themselves by putting up prices, having no competition to face, very much to the detriment of consumers. The advantage of trading at a distance only under the authorised aegis of a company had long been recognised, but those of the new joint-stock principle which abolished instead of defending the individual trader were as yet by no means so obvious. And finally there was a growing sentiment, not economic but political, which resented the control of monopolies by the Crown to its own financial profit.

Not less menacing to the Company was the difficulty of reconciling the Eastern trade as a whole with the orthodox political economy of the day. The universally accepted doctrine was what is known as the Mercantile theory.

The trade which brings prosperity to the State is that which increases its fighting power, ensuring to it the maximum supply of the material of which it stands in need in time of war, and, above all, of "treasure," the precious metals. These the country should at any cost produce for itself to its utmost capacity, so as to be independent of foreign supplies as far as possible; what it cannot produce for itself it must purchase by the export of its own surplus productions, preferably such as will not increase the fighting power of a potential enemy, every State which is not an active ally falling under that category. Conspicuously and above all the country is strengthened by trading which exchanges her own products for bullion, but is weakened while a potential enemy is strengthened by the trading which exchanges her own bullion for foreign products—unless at least those products are material of which she stands in need for military or naval purposes; including (for England) the development of shipping, but not at that time of food-supplies of which she could and must produce a sufficiency for herself from her own soil.

Applying that test to the East Indian trade, how did the Company stand? Did its trade, however profitable it might be to its own members, increase or diminish the fighting power of the State? Was it a trade which the patriot could view with approval, or one that he was bound to denounce? *Prima facie*, there was a very strong case for its opponents. The case for its supporters was indeed actually stronger, but was at sight by no means so obvious. For there was no manner of question that the market for English products in the East was small, so that the great bulk of the products brought back from the East had to be paid for in bullion. The trade was, on the face of it, not accumulating treasure in England as a sound trade ought to do, but draining treasure out of England all the time. It required a more intelligent and a more elaborate style of reckoning to realise that the bulk of those goods for which bullion had been paid out were sold not in England for home consumption, but on the Continent in exchange for a great deal more treasure than had been expended on their purchase; so that by the time the whole transaction had been completed, the treasure-balance was very substantially in England's favour. Incidentally, it might be remarked that the treasure which came into the country came from potential enemies, whereas that which went out passed to Eastern communities whose potential hostility was of no practical account. But to combat the more obtrusive adverse view successfully was no easy matter.

Consequently we shall find that the East India Company had to gain a diplomatic footing in markets where the European was an object of suspicion, in the face of European rivals ready to resort to force to keep it out; to develop a method of conducting its trade for which there was no precedent; to protect itself from the embarrassing intervention of "interlopers"—the name applied to the recalcitrant free-traders; and to satisfy the Crown that its trade was conferring a national benefit, in face of the diatribes of the orthodox economists who denounced it as unpatriotic.

# CHAPTER IV

## THE EAST INDIA COMPANY UNDER JAMES I

### I

LONG before Lancaster's return from the first voyage, Elizabeth was scolding the company for its half-hearted sluggishness in failing to send out a second—they were throwing away their chances, while the Dutch, with all the advantages of an immense start in their favour, were going full-speed ahead. The Company, on the other hand, had taken a big risk, locked up a large capital in its venture, and was naturally anxious to proceed with caution. Not a little pressure was required before it could raise—chiefly from the same subscribers—the capital for the second venture. But prolonged delay, especially with a new King on the throne, might cost it its charter. Lancaster, when he did reappear, brought with him cargoes (including a substantial capture from the Portuguese) which represented something like a cent-per-cent profit on the capital when this voyage and the next were taken together; but the moment was inauspicious. Business was almost at a standstill, owing to a great outbreak of the Plague in London; the estimated profit, though large, would take a long time to realise and distribute (as a matter of fact the distribution was not actually completed till nearly ten years had passed); and it was not till six months after Lancaster's return that the second expedition was able to sail.

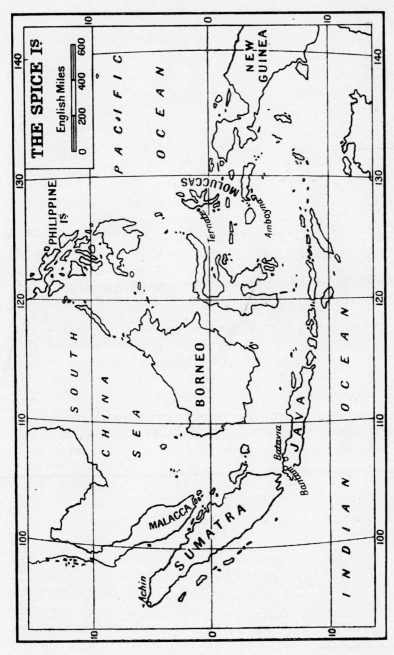

THE SPICE IS

English Miles

0   200   400   600

PHILIPPINE IS

PACIFIC

OCEAN

MOLUCCAS

Ternate

Amboyna

NEW GUINEA

SOUTH

CHINA

SEA

BORNEO

JAVA

INDIAN OCEAN

Batavia

Bantam

MALACCA

SUMATRA

Achin

[Face page 60

The methods and the difficulties of the new system are at once manifested. Lancaster had succeeded in establishing friendly relations with the young King of Bantam (in Java), and had been permitted to leave there an agency or "factory"—to adopt at once the term in universal use throughout the career of the Company until the Industrial Revolution gave it the modern meaning which has entirely superseded the old one. The second venture or voyage took over from the first the factory and its staff. It took over also the ships which had made the first voyage. In both respects this became the established practice. In raising the capital, the Company enforced upon the subscribers to the first voyage a *pro rata* levy drawn from the profits thereof, but such compulsory participation was occasional, not habitual. Incidentally, however, one Sir Edward Michelborne had been ejected from the Company for failure to pay up his subscription; and having some interest at Court he procured from King James a licence for "discovery and trade" on his own account, regardless of the Company's charter; a licence of which he made use to indulge in miscellaneous piracy and to attack the Dutch at Bantam, with whom there was as yet no quarrel; all of which was extremely detrimental to the reputation of the English, and was precisely the sort of thing which the Company's monopoly was designed to prevent. It could deal with unlicensed interlopers, but an Interloper with a royal licence to show was outside its jurisdiction.

At the same time the cargoes with which those two voyages sailed gave a handle to the enemy—that is, to the orthodox economists. For the English goods they took out were valued respectively at £6,860 and £1,142, and the specie at £21,882 and £11,160, and what they brought back was practically all in the form of goods. The subscribers got back their capital with —ultimately—a very substantial profit, but some £33,000 in the shape of treasure had gone out of the country, with only goods to show in exchange, since the return in treasure for such of those goods as were re-sold abroad was omitted from the calculation; the goods themselves being spices, mainly pepper and cloves.

Two years elapsed before the return of the second voyage, for which it had been difficult enough to make up a freight considerably less than half that of the first voyage. Meanwhile subscribers were disheartened by the prolonged delay in the distribution of the profits. Only three ships sailed on the third voyage in 1607, two on the fourth in 1608—another Interloper had been licensed, but as his route was limited to the North-West and North-East passages, no harm came of it—and only one on the fifth in 1609. The fourth was lost at sea, and the fifth was only scraped together by a compulsory levy on the subscribers to the third. But the estimated profits of the third voyage on its return were so high that hope revived and developed into confidence; and in this year, 1609, King James not only renewed the charter but did so in terms which, where they departed from those of Elizabeth's charter, added to the Company's strength instead of diminishing it.

It was the same year, be it remarked, in which the Virginia Company, almost at its last gasp, received the new Charter which gave it a new lease of life; whereof the story will presently be told.

The tide had turned. Hitherto the prospects of development had been viewed, except by the few who had faith, as an uncertain gamble; from which the cautious held aloof. For each new voyage it had been

increasingly difficult to raise funds; the four ships of
the two first voyages had dwindled to the one ship of
the fifth; year after year the men who ventured their
money had had to wait and wait without realising their
profits; but the long deferred distribution of those
profits and the assurance that the profits, as yet un-
distributed, of the later voyages, were on a still larger
scale, proved convincing. Only one peer of the realm,
the sailor Earl of Cumberland, had taken part in
the first venture; the rest of the subscribers were
for the most part merchants. When the new charter
of 1609 was granted, the list was headed by the names
of the Lord Treasurer, the High Admiral, and the
Earl of Worcester; other notables made haste to seek
membership in the Company. The growing favour of
the Crown was manifested some years later by the
King's suggestion—judiciously evaded by the Company,
as previously noted—that he should honour it by
himself becoming an honorary member. And the
subscription for the sixth voyage more than doubled
that for the first, which was itself twice as large as
any of the other four. Its commander was the same
Captain—now Sir Henry—Middleton, who had been
in charge of the second voyage.

It is not only, however, in this respect that the year
1609 stands out as a milestone or sign-post in the
progress of the Company. For in it was signed the
Dutch truce with Spain—and by consequence with
Portugal. The United Provinces (like England herself)
were no longer at war with any European Power;
Portugal stood to them in precisely the same relation
as she did to England; the three countries were
in trade rivalry with each other, but—theoretically
—were all politically in amity. Both Dutch and
Portuguese now concentrated on their antagonism to

the English penetration into their preserves, the former in the Spice Islands, the latter in Indian waters; with the result that in the course of the next fifteen years, the Dutch practically made good their monopoly, while the Portuguese had almost ceased to count. And in those years the English, ejected from the islands, acquired on the Indian Peninsula the footing, as yet precarious, which they were never to lose.

In 1609, then, the sixth voyage set sail, under better auspices than any of its predecessors. There were, indeed, only three ships, but one of them was the *Trades Increase*, the finest merchantman afloat, of 1,100 tons, specially built, since the Company had already started building its own ships. The voyage in fact proved hazardous and comparatively unprofitable; Middleton himself fell into the hands of the Arab governor at Mocha on the Red Sea, and, with others of his company, was for some time held prisoner; and the reprisals which inevitably followed bred hostility and suspicion among the Orientals, which did not simplify the business of future trading, though such contretemps were, so to speak, in the day's work.

The really significant point, however, is not the actual fortunes of this voyage but the fact that it marks the moment when the Company, strengthened though it was by the new charter, began to be conscious that some change was being forced upon it both in its methods and in the direction of its policy. Hitherto its objective had been the Spice Islands, and hitherto the antagonism of the Dutch to the English penetration had been modified by their relations with Portugal. Lancaster had taken part with them in direct conflict with the Portuguese. But now in the Spice Islands the English could be of no use at all to the Dutch, whereas

their effective rivalry would be extremely inconvenient—
so the Dutch were determined that it should not be
effective. The English did not immediately retire,
but they very soon began to be made aware that the
Dutch attitude was much more openly antagonistic
than before, that they held very much the stronger
position, and that their character made them opponents of a type far more formidable than the
Portuguese could ever be.

Wherever the English tried to go they found the
Hollanders already entrenched though their claim to
occupation in the technical sense might be challenged,
with their influence as friendly allies well established
at the native courts. When Lancaster, in amicable
association with them, was allowed to plant the first
English factory at Bantam in the course of the first
successful English voyage, fifteen Dutch expeditions,
aggregating sixty-five ships, had already sailed from
Holland; their amalgamated company had abandoned
the system of separate ventures, and was working with a
consolidated capital of half a million at its back; while
in the next seven years the English Company sent no
more than five voyages with an aggregate of thirteen
ships, and with each voyage a separate venture. In
such circumstances, English competition had little
enough prospect of being successful unless developed
on a scale which was in fact wholly impracticable; but
it was the more emphatically apparent that without a
more thorough consolidation there was no prospect
at all. Consequently—though the change may have
been more instinctive than consciously reasoned out—
the next three years (1609–1612 or 1613) witnessed the
passing of the separate-voyage system on the one hand,
and on the other increased activity in efforts to open
up trade within the Mogul Empire, a direct collision

with the Portuguese in which the English very thoroughly made good, and the actual establishment of the first English factory on Indian soil, though competition in the Spice Islands was not yet abandoned.

## II

The idea that India itself offered possibilities had been borne in upon English minds by the reports of Ralph Fitch and the Dutchman Linschoten during the decade preceding the formation of the East India Company; but with the golden promise of the Spice Islands in full glow, before it was shadowed over by rapid progress of the Dutch, the difficulties of an Indian trade more than counterbalanced its attractions. The naval stations permanently held by the Portuguese from Ormuz on the Persian Gulf down to the Malabar coast made them in appearance at least extremely formidable antagonists, however confidently the English might repudiate the legality of the claim they asserted to monopoly. Portuguese influences on the mainland were established and not easy to break through; Indian Princes or Governors of coastal dominions might detest and fear them, but were none the readier to show goodwill to other Europeans whose superiority in arms to the Portuguese remained to be proved. The Mogul at Agra was not of course troubled by similar fears; he would grant privileges if he could be persuaded that it was worth while for him to do so, but that it would be so was by no means obvious to him. And the tentative efforts that had been made so far had met with meagre success. Elizabeth had authorised a preliminary diplomatic mission to the Court of Akbar which was on the whole encouraging but nothing more. Captain

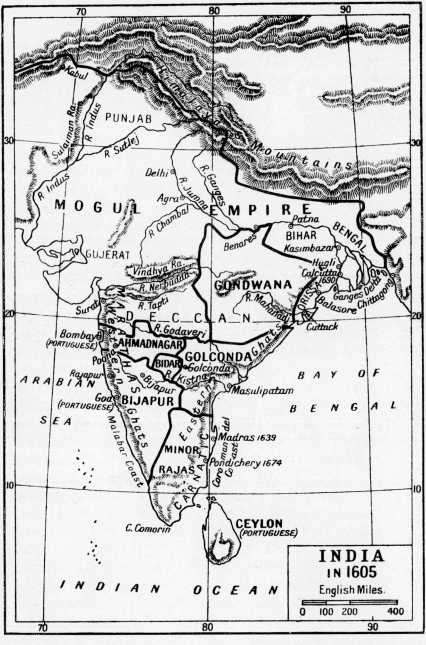

70     80     90

*Kabul*

R *Indus*

*Sulaiman Ra.*

PUNJAB

R *Indus*

R *Sutlej*

30     *Himalaya*     30

*Delhi*     R *Ganges*

R *Jumna*

*Agra*

*Mountains*

R *Chambal*

M O G U L    E M P I R E

*Patna*

BIHAR    BENGAL

GUJERAT    *Benares*    *Kasimbazar*

*Vindhya Ra.*    *Hugli*

R *Nerbudda*    *Calcutta 1690*

GONDWANA    *Ganges Delta*    *Chittagong*

*Surat*    R *Tapti*    ORISSA    *Balasore*

20    D E C C A N    R *Mahanadi*    20

R *Godaveri*    *Cuttack*

*Bombay* (PORTUGUESE)    AHMADNAGAR

*Poona*    GOLCONDA

BIDAR    *Golconda*

*Rajapur*    R *Kistna*

A R A B I A N    *Bijapur*    B A Y   O F

*Goa* (PORTUGUESE)    BIJAPUR    *Masulipatam*

S E A    B E N G A L

*Malabar Coast*

*Madras 1639*

MINOR    *Pondichery 1674*

RAJAS    *Coromandel Coast*

10    CARNATIC    10

*C. Comorin*    CEYLON (PORTUGUESE)

I N D I A N   O C E A N

### INDIA
### IN 1605
English Miles.

0   100   200     400

70     80     90

[*Face page 66*

Hawkins, on the third voyage, armed with polite
letters from Elizabeth's successor, had remained to
proceed to Agra on another diplomatic mission; but
he had failed to impress Jehan Gir who had just
succeeded Akbar on the Imperial throne. The Mogul
had indeed granted him a somewhat contemptuous
permission to plant a factory at Surat, but Portuguese
influence procured its revocation, though factors or
agents of the Company were allowed to remain. Such
was the far from promising position when Middleton
sailed on the sixth voyage. His attempt to begin the
operations of the voyage by opening trade with the
Western Moslems proved unfortunate, as we have seen,
exciting a general Moslem hostility which extended
to the Mohammedan dynasties in India, making it
the more difficult to establish friendly relations. When
he arrived at the Indian coast the Portuguese were
able to prevent him from effecting a landing, and he
continued his voyage to the Spice Islands where further
troubles awaited him—including the total destruction by
fire of his great ship the *Trades Increase* while she was
under repair in the neighbourhood of Bantam. He
himself died in the following year, 1613; his end
being probably hastened by the shock of that disaster.

The incidents, however, connected with the remaining
separate voyages, variously reckoned as from three to
six in number, are noteworthy partly for their intrinsic
importance and partly as illustrative of the prevailing
conditions. In the course of one of them, Japan,
reached by Captain Saris, of the *Clove*, in 1613,
floats into our ken. There Saris found, high in favour
with the Shogun (the *de facto* ruler of Japan, who
reigned in the name of the Mikado, while the latter,
though nominally supreme, was debarred from taking any
practical part in government or policy) an Englishman,

Will Adams, who had been stranded there thirteen years before, while serving as an officer on a Dutch ship. The Europeans hitherto known in Japan had been Jesuit missionaries and Portuguese who had taken care to warn them of the evil character of other Europeans, especially Dutch and English. But the Shogun discovered in Adams a master ship-builder, which was just what he wanted but could not get from the Portuguese. So he set Adams to work, heaped favours and estates upon him, but refused to let him leave the country at any price. Adams used his influence to procure favourable treatment for the Dutch (whom he supposed to be in close amity with England); and they had already established themselves on a friendly footing before the Englishmen arrived on the scene. He procured permission for the new-comers to set up a factory, and the Shogun could not prevent him from entering the Company's service. Had the Company been in a position to take full advantage of the situation thus created, there might have been big results, but they could not, in fact, oust the Dutch from their predominance. Dutch influence was persistently working against them, the strength of the Dutch in the China seas was much the greater, and the feeble English effort to capture even a share in the Japanese trade (to be reduced ere long to infinitesimal proportions by the self-isolating policy of the anti-foreigner Japanese government) was soon abandoned.

The Japanese excursion, therefore, is no more than an interesting episode. Actually much more importance attaches to what is sometimes called the tenth separate voyage and is sometimes treated as a bye-product of the eighth, the operations of Captain Best in 1612.

Best's instructions were to get a really effective confirmation of the very ineffective permission to plant a fully recognised factory at Surat and to trade along the western coast of India. In the previous year the Portuguese had prevented Middleton from landing, and he had been reduced to forcibly bartering his goods on the open sea. Forcible barter had been all very well on the Spanish Main under early Elizabethan conditions when Hawkins and Drake were trading with His Catholic Majesty's subjects in defiance of His Catholic Majesty's orders, at their own risk; but it was out of date and out of place for a trading Company, officially recognised by the Crown, whose business was essentially peaceful penetration. It gave the English traders a bad name, and for the Portuguese it was all to the good that they should be driven to practise it; that, however, was merely an incidental point. The main point was to baulk the English again in their endeavour to make a footing on the mainland. What the Portuguese had done in 1611, they proposed to do again in 1612; and they intended to deal faithfully with Captain Best and his two ships, the *Red Dragon* and the *Hosiander*.

Surat, Best's terminus, was not actually a port; it was prevented from being one by the silting up of the estuary of the Tapti on which it stood. But at the mouth of the estuary was the anchorage of Swally, a sheet of water plentifully provided with sand-banks and shoals, the perils whereof skilled seamanship matched against unskilled may turn to useful account; and—Best had been there before.

When the two English ships reached Swally, a Portuguese fleet was bearing down upon them; four big ships, galleons, with from twenty-five to thirty "row-galleys" or "frigates" for boarding. Best was a seaman bred in the Elizabethan heyday, when English seamen were wont to take little account of the odds against them. The approaching flotilla became entangled in the shoals with the two big leading ships separated from the rest. The *Hosiander* had anchored and could not get free; but the *Red Dragon* made straight for the space between those two big ships, poured broadsides into both of them for the space of an hour, and having so "peppered them well" (though her own long-boat was sunk and her mainmast damaged), retired for the night. Next morning the *Red Dragon* and the *Hosiander* renewed the attack together. Three of the galleons were driven aground on the sand-banks; Best himself had to draw off into deeper water lest the same thing should happen to him, as the tide was ebbing; by the time when it became practicable to renew the battle, the galleons had been floated again by the efforts of the row-galleys. The fight went on till dark; the English again retired to anchorage, and incidentally sank a fireship which the Portuguese sent down on them.

For the moment, however, Best abandoned the attempt to force his way into the Tapti. In the first definite engagement between English ships and a markedly superior Portuguese force he had taught the enemy a lesson which ensured that they would not seek a conflict in which their row-galleys would have no chance of coming into action, and he had very thoroughly shaken the reputation they had hitherto held all along that coast for invincibility on the sea. He spent the next three weeks in diplomatically culti-vating this revolutionary idea in the minds of Indian officials, the more successfully because he helped the Mogul's troops to suppress a neighbouring pirate stronghold.

And then the Portuguese challenged him again; having gathered heavy reinforcements, they came down to his anchorage to wipe him out. From daybreak to high noon he fought them, while the admiring native troops watched the engagement from the shore, and from noon till the afternoon was well advanced he chased them with his two ships. Once more they gathered to the attack, two days later, and once more he put them utterly to rout. In all the fighting, Best had lost only three men, the Portuguese (taking something less than the middle estimate between the extreme figures given), as many hundreds. The Portuguese resistance was broken, and before another week had passed, the last week of 1612, Captain Best had procured from the Governor of Surat a formal agreement, ratified in due time by an Imperial firman or decree, establishing the Surat factory and granting trading privileges.

The footing on the mainland was won, not to be lost again. The struggle with the Portuguese had ten more years to run before the English victory was finally complete. At the outset, all the odds seemed to be on their side, and it was they, not the English, who appealed to the ordeal by battle. But from the moment when Best with his two ships took up the challenge and shattered their opening attack, the English were fighting to win, whatever the odds, and the Portuguese were in fact beaten from the start, though the fight they put up lacked nothing of valiancy. The days in which the little nation could continue to do mighty deeds were already passed.

Best's great achievement gave the Company fresh vigour. The revival of 1609 had already produced some modification of the separate voyage system; a new chapter was now opened with the establishment of the second stage of the Joint-Stock idea, accompanied by a great accession of capital. The venture which was organised in 1613 and sent forth its first expedition in 1614 had behind it a subscribed capital five times as

great as the sixth, not for a single voyage but for a
series extending over four years—a step, if no more than
a step, towards the creation of a permanent joint-stock.
The commander of this first expedition of four ships
was Nicholas Downton, who had been second in
command under Sir Henry Middleton. Middleton was
dead, and the *Trades Increase* had perished in flames,
but Downton, by dint of seamanship and indomitable
pluck had succeeded in bringing his own ship home a
few months before he set sail again on the *New Year's
Gift*, the flag-ship of the new voyage. There was no
Christian Prince with whom King James was not at
amity, and Downton was under strict orders to attack
none, but he also had ample authority to defend himself
if "unjustly provoked." A most unexceptionable docu-
ment, in which his Catholic Majesty Philip III, whose
goodwill the King of England was most anxious to
conciliate, could not possibly find any ground of
complaint—except the chance of a difference of opinion
as to what did or did not constitute "unjust provocation",
a point which was left to the judgement of the
commander. Nicholas Downton adhered rigidly to his
instructions; but for the Portuguese the result was
disastrous.

Downton arrived at Swally in October 1614, with
his four ships, the largest of which, the *New Year's
Gift*, was of something over 500 tons burden; carrying,
between them, 400 men and 80 guns. The voyage had
taken seven months. The Governor of Surat was on
the point of attacking sundry Portuguese stations, and
invited Downton's assistance. To attack was against
his orders, and he refused—adding significantly that
his orders did not forbid him to fight if he were attacked;
but the Governor took umbrage and gave him clearly
to understand that since he refused his help no help

would be given to him if he should want it. The
Portuguese headquarters were at Goa, between three
and four hundred miles to the south. The lesson
taught by Best had not been lost and the Viceroy there
was preparing a great armament which should completely overwhelm the intruders. As his fleet began to
arrive, Downton could only take refuge in the Swally
waters—the angry Governor had refused supplies or
leave to land. Three months after his first arrival the
whole Portuguese fleet was on the spot—six great
galleons, ranging from 400 to 800 tons, five smaller
vessels (two of them galleys), and sixty frigates (eighteen-
oared row-galleys) with 12,000 soldiers on board besides
their crews: the whole fleet carrying 2,600 Europeans,
234 guns, and some 6,000 natives to work the ships
and do everything except the actual fighting. Whereas
Downton's 400 men had their hands more than full all
the time, whether they were fighting or not.

Downton had shown his breed before; a stern
Puritan, it would seem, who, after the fashion later
commended by Oliver Cromwell, put his trust in the
Lord of Hosts—and kept his powder dry. If the Lord
was on his side, He would none the less demand of
him that he should play his own part to the uttermost.

Downton lay among the shoals and lured the enemy
to rush upon one ship, the *Hope*, which was—inten-
tionally—parted from the other three. But the galleons
were not to be enticed into the shallows; they made
the attack with their light craft and a swarm of row-
galleys which grappled the *Hope* and strove desperately
to board her. After the third repulse, when they were
unable to cut loose, they fired the grappled craft and
swam for life—the rest were already in flight, for the
other three English ships were coming up and the
galleons were out of range. That first fight had cost the

F

English five men and the *Hope's* mainmast had been seriously damaged by the flames from the frigates. Of the Portuguese, numbers were drowned, and their loss was reported to be above three hundred.

The repulse determined the Surat Governor to await events; for the present he was deaf to appeals from either combatant. The *Hope* was out of action for manœuvring, and Downton could not in the circumstances stake everything on a pitched battle in the open. For three weeks he tried in vain to entice the Portuguese among the shoals; the Portuguese Viceroy, who was himself in command, preferred to keep him in the trap till he was starved out, since the frigates could cut off communication with the shore. During this time, Downton wrote, "it pleased God to call to His mercy my only son, when I had least leisure to mourn"; but the captain, whose crews seem to have been of the same kidney, was unshaken. At the end of three weeks, the Viceroy lost patience. Thrice he attacked, was received with a hot fire, and withdrew. Twice he sent down fireships, without result. He could not attempt to land troops without exposing them to destructive attack from Downton's ships. He dared not bring his galleons to action among the sand-banks. The first fight had been fought on January 20th (1615); on February 13th, the Viceroy recognised that he could do no more, and his fleet set sail for Goa. Best's success had been more than confirmed by Downton and the conversion of the Governor of Surat had been completed. After a few days' delay, Downton sailed for Bantam where he died a few months later.

There was no longer any real doubt of the English supremacy in the Indian waters. The Goa Viceroy's vaunted title of "Admiral of the Indian seas" was as empty as the official style which called the King of

England "King of France" also. In the years following there were collisions, but always to the advantage of the English. Still one thing was wanted to complete the overthrow of the remnant of the Portuguese power. She held Ormuz on the Persian Gulf. It was well for the English that Spain had lost all interest in Portugal's welfare in the East from her own preoccupation with America; the Crowns of Spain and Portugal were united, but their peoples were not. Had it not been so, King James would very probably have shrunk from the policy which, as against Portugal unsupported, inspired him with no qualms. In 1620 James encouraged a proposal to establish a factory near the Gulf to open up a Persian trade. As at Surat, the Portuguese tried to bar the way, and met with a smashing defeat. In consequence the Persian Governor invited English assistance for an attack on Ormuz as condition of admitting the English trade. English and Persians together captured Ormuz in 1622, the Portuguese garrison and inhabitants were shipped off to Goa— and so in that quarter too the star of Portugal set for ever, though her claims were not formally withdrawn till the days of Cromwell and Blake. Shah Abbas kept Ormuz for himself; but an English factory and fort at Gombroon transferred to the English the trade and the maritime supremacy so long held by the Portuguese.

To the prowess of Best and Downton, displayed not against Indian potentates but against European opponents, we must attribute the successful establishment of the London East India Company upon Indian soil, in friendly relations with the lords of the land, though a long time was still to pass before its development into a political and military power. Without the prestige born of the deeds of those two stout-hearted seamen, the well-meant efforts of the Scottish Solomon to establish

useful political relations by the diplomatic methods
on which he prided himself would have borne little
enough fruit. Yet those efforts were in themselves
commendable. As a diplomatic agent, Captain Hawkins,
as we have seen, had failed somewhat ignominiously,
though he cannot be held responsible for his failure;
it was through no fault of his that Jehan Gir would not
be persuaded that the King of England's friendship
was worth cultivating. But after Downton's victory,
Sir Thomas Roe was sent to Jehan Gir's Court as a
fully accredited Ambassador from the English Court;
but even then, he was aware of a latent hostility of
sentiment in the Mogul and his "Omrahs" which he
could not help reciprocating, and in his two years'
sojourn he failed to obtain the formal treaty which
Jehan Gir seemed to be always on the verge of promising.

### III

While the Company was concentrating its energies
more and more upon the new field in India, the Dutch
were devoting themselves the more zealously to blocking
its advance in the Eastern archipelago. King James,
conceiving himself to be the benign arbiter of a rational
Europe—which in act entirely ignored his advice, since
it very well understood that he would never back his
logic with cold steel—expected to reconcile the religious
fanaticisms which were leading up to the Thirty Years'
War by matrimonial alliances with the leading powers,
both Catholic and Protestant. He had married his
daughter to the Calvinistic Elector Palatine and had an
absorbing desire to marry his son and heir to a Spanish
Infanta, while his policy demanded friendly relations
with the Protestant Dutch, so far as that could be
accomplished without irritating Spain. Collisions with

Portugal did not matter, but similar collisions with the Dutch were to be avoided, almost if not quite as anxiously as collisions with Spain, a position of which the Dutch had no hesitation in taking full advantage; and when all hope of the Spanish marriage collapsed entirely and actual war with Spain was imminent, the Dutch did not hesitate to ignore James altogether, while he would venture no farther than whimpering at the treatment they meted out to him.

In plain terms, the Dutch, for whom effective possession of the Spice Islands was a primary point of National policy rather than of commercial speculation, were far too strongly entrenched to make voluntary concessions which the English traders could not compel them to grant. Ship for ship, neither English nor Dutch could ever gain a decisive superiority over the other, though, ship for ship, no other country stood a chance against either of them—and in the archipelago the English ships were hopelessly outnumbered, just as the English factories (when planted), viewed as garrisons, were certain to be overwhelmed. The Dutch were there, bent upon driving out all intruders, and confident that they could do so. The English were only striving to gain an entry, and not at all confident that they could do so without an expenditure on armament and a backing from the Crown which they had no chance whatever of obtaining from James. So the Dutch in the islands went their way, while King James played at diplomatic bargaining in London or at The Hague with an opponent who held all the trumps and never dreamed of making a bargain which secured him less than nine-tenths of the benefits. The Dutch terms for admitting the English were always quite impossible for English acceptance, while their claim that they were *de facto* in effective occupation was extremely difficult to combat. The English were driven even to such shifts as a pretence to prior occupation resting on a treaty made with the King of Ternate by Drake in the course of his circumnavigation in 1570.

Nevertheless the second joint-stock voyage, in 1617, set out with high hopes and financial backing that even doubled that of the first, which had started under Downton's command. The Dutch responded by attacking English factories, exhibiting their prisoners in chains to the natives, and seizing three English ships in waters where they declared that James had officially admitted their sovereignty. So James again opened negotiations, and in 1619 accepted a treaty which conceded extremely limited trading rights, gave no compensation for damages claimed, and, binding the two companies to joint action against other rivals, required each to maintain ten warships in the islands for that purpose, keeping the few English and many Dutch fortresses still under their several control, while the joint operations were to be under the direction of a joint Council of Defence. Practically the English were in no better position than before to resist the process of persistent squeezing; while after a grand official display to celebrate the reconciliation, Dutch and English continued to fight each other with the same obstinacy as before and the same advantage on the winning side, and each found warrant for their hostile acts in alleged breaches of the treaty by the other. Wherever they were, the English found themselves treated as subjects of the Dutch jurisdiction, which in relation to them—and, for that matter to the natives also—was exercised with a merciless tyranny which rendered their position intolerable. The end came with the black tragedy of Amboyna in 1623; a page of history shameful alike to the Dutch for their shameless brutality and to England for the equally shameless pusillanimity of her Government.

Amboyna is an island in the Moluccas group particularly rich in the most profitable spices. The Dutch, who had always claimed it for their own, were resolved to extrude the English who had specific but limited rights of trading there under the treaty of 1619. There were eighteen Englishmen on the island; there was a Dutch fortress with a garrison of 200 Dutch and 300 native troops, among them some Japanese, according to the English statement—150 Dutchmen and 50 native soldiers, according to the Dutch themselves —and there were eight Dutch ships in the harbour. Preparations were actually being made for a complete withdrawal from the island. But Van Speult, the Dutch Governor of Amboyna, who had been charged with over-scrupulousness, detected a conspiracy; that is, one of the Japanese soldiers had asked some questions which roused his suspicions. The man was seized, and under torture, made a charge against the English. They were planning to seize the fort with the aid of an expected English ship! Some of his comrades were arrested, denied his story, and then—under torture— confirmed it. Further " evidence " was procured by further tortures. The whole story was on the face of it fairly incredible. The Englishmen gave it no serious attention, but it was enough for Van Speult, the over-scrupulous. He arrested all the eighteen Englishmen.

The only evidence against them was that which had been given under torture. The gruesome details of what followed are best omitted. By admission of the Dutch themselves, twelve of the Englishmen were subjected to tortures till most of them " confessed " to the story which was put into their mouths. The wretched victims had not yet been executed when the

official English orders arrived for withdrawal from
Amboyna, nothing of course being known about the
recent proceedings. Nevertheless sentence of death
was hastily passed on ten of the Englishmen and the
nine Japanese, who were all duly and publicly executed.

When the news reached England a year later, there
was a blaze of indignation—some hopes that the King
might make a strong stand in demanding reparation
for the outrage, and even that conscience might drive
the Government of the Dutch Republic to make
amends; passionate demands for reprisals. But it was
the moment when the scheme of the Spanish Marriage
had just been shattered; James was in the act of taking
part in the formation of a general Protestant alliance
to intervene in the Thirty Years' War; in fact he dared
not face a quarrel with Holland, and the Dutch Government was not slow to realise the fact. The outrage was
denounced with sentimental fervour, and there was
big talk; but big talk from James was sound and fury
signifying nothing, and the Dutch knew it. It dwindled
down to conferences, the conferences flickered out
with nothing done; and with the old King's death and
the accession of Charles I in 1625 the country became
absorbed in domestic and constitutional problems.
Amboyna remained a lurid memory. Remained also
the bitter sentiment towards the Dutch which it had
evoked, rendering any genuine reconciliation impossible.
But it had destroyed for ever what will-o'-th'-wisp of
a chance had lingered of an effective English penetration
in the Spice Islands—at the precise moment when the
power of the Portuguese even to hinder or seriously
hamper the English penetration in India had been
finally eliminated.

# CHAPTER V

I

THE East India Company, as we have seen, was concerned not at all with colonisation in the modern sense, but with the sharing or the inauguration of a lucrative trade in lands where there was already an advanced civilisation, though not of the European type; among communities so highly organised politically that they could be recognised as States and even as Powers. The only kind of settlement in those countries contemplated, was, so far as concerned individuals, of an essentially transitory character—in the form of factories—agencies and depots—where the small European community would consist of the Company's employees wholly occupied with its trade, with no inducement to make a permanent abode. The trade was one in which the market for English goods might or might not prove considerable; but the motive to it was not export but import, the import of the valuable products of the East, whether for direct consumption at home or for re-export to other markets.

In the complex of attractions to the West, trading of this kind was only a very minor motive. Whatever the products of the soil might be, very little of them was procurable from the present occupants, and for English goods which could command a market elsewhere, there was in America no market at all—except the rigidly closed market in what were admittedly Spanish territories. The population, so far as was known, was sparse: no cities were known to exist: no community had been heard of, so organised that it could conceivably be classed as a State (though settlers, when they did go out, persistently spoke of every head-man of a village as a "king," and as often as not called the overlord of several such kings the Emperor). If there was ever going to be a substantial trade, it would be between English settlers and the mother-country. There were in short three uses to which occupation of unoccupied North America might be put: the discovery of precious metals, the discovery of a new route to Cathay and the Indies, and the settlement of permanent self-supporting colonies on the soil with a population which was for one reason or another superfluous in England.

We are a little apt—somewhat hastily—to dismiss both the first and the second of these ideas with a smile at the credulity of our ancestors; but in fact there was nothing in the least irrational about either of them. The expectation of finding that the northern land-masses of Asia and America were either in actual contact or not far apart was natural enough, as also was the alternative theory that the Western continent narrowed towards the north as well as towards the south; a practicable route by land or by water from the Atlantic to the Pacific might be improbable but was certainly not incredible. As for the gold—as a simple matter of fact it was there, though at a great distance from the Atlantic seaboard, and the gold-mines of California and Klondyke were not discovered till the nineteenth century. The fever for gold-hunting died out under the shock of repeated disappointments;

but for some years it served as a quite definite spur both to company financiers and to individual emigrants. It did not indeed cease to operate as an incentive towards the bait of the mythical Eldorado until King James used Sir Walter Ralegh to provide an object lesson in the unwisdom of infringing Spanish claims on the Southern continent.

The idea of settlement—from many and diverse motives—was the third and most potent of the incentives to Western expansion. For its creators, Gilbert and Ralegh, it had been an aspect of their vision of Empire, of an England spreading over the fruitful lands which as yet were accounted as waste places of the earth, yet remaining England still; a vision too vast and too imaginative to appeal effectively to any but kindred spirits. It did not promise the immediate wealth, either to the individual or to the country, which might accrue from privateering and preying upon Spanish treasure ships so long as England and Spain were at open—or covert—war. Ralegh could get no adequate backing for his schemes, and the successive batches of settlers he managed to send out did not find at Roanoke the Promised Land of their hopes. The Vision would never work as a generally active motive.

But when the business of privateering on a large scale was closed by the accession of a more than pacific King, the energies which had been absorbed in it wanted a fresh outlet. On the one hand colonisation might provide restless youth with new scope for irresponsible treasure-hunting and adventure; while, if the old opportunities should recur, strongholds on the flank of the Spanish waterways would certainly be useful, besides serving as a starting point for exploration which might have most advantageous results, from the national point of view. On the other hand the development of settlements should render England independent of foreigners for the supply of war-materials not produced or producible in sufficient quantity on the soil of England, but abundantly present in America, or cultivable in its virgin soil; hence the development of America would be a highly patriotic activity, developing the National power—here at least there would be no question of exporting bullion to strengthen a potential enemy in exchange for goods which had no power-value. Again, although the long displacement of agricultural labour born of enclosure for wool-growing instead of tillage had been gradually adjusting itself in the reign of Elizabeth, there was still a substantial amount of unemployment; settlement should draw off a large proportion of emigrants who in England were of no use to themselves or to anyone else.

But there remained the problem, which Ralegh had failed to solve, of financing settlement on a scale sufficient to make it effective. It was a business which the depleted Treasury would certainly not undertake on its own account. If the thing was to be done, it could be only through the combined enterprise of moneyed men who saw in it the prospect of substantial profits for themselves. Hitherto, as Ralegh had found to his cost, the prospect had not proved sufficiently attractive. But from the time when the East India Company was successfully launched, the idea would seem to have been gaining ground. On the accession of James it was taken up by Sir Thomas Smythe, the enterprising mercantile magnate who was a leading member of the Levant Company and first President of the East India Company; and we may confidently believe that the formation of the Virginia Company, of which he became Treasurer, was largely due to his influence when it was added to the advocacy of such enthusiasts as Richard Hakluyt (of *Hakluyt's Voyages*), or the rover John Smith whom we shall see playing no small personal part in the new Company's first venture—an advocacy which appealed in vain to the calculating commercial mind.

Now while Elizabeth was still living Ralegh's patent securing his monopoly was still valid; but in 1603 the Earl of Southampton sent out an exploring expedition under Bartholomew Gosnold which visited what is now the coast of Massachusetts, and in 1604—when Ralegh was under sentence of death for treason and his patent had lapsed—another under George Waymouth which lighted on what is now the state of Maine. It is likely that the glowing report brought back by Waymouth turned the doubtful scale; for in the spring of 1606 James was persuaded to issue what is known as the First Virginia Charter, appointing a Royal Council for Virginia, defined as the territory lying between the 34th and 45th parallels of latitude—in other words, the coast and the hinterland from South Carolina to Halifax. The Royal Council was to supervise colonisation in this area and retain administrative control: but the colonising was to be done by the two companies—the London Company and the Plymouth Company—which provided the capital and would enjoy commercial privileges, the southern area being allotted to the former, the northern to the latter, though by a curious arrangement the areas overlapped between the 38th and 41st parallels. As a matter of fact, no untoward collision actually resulted; for the Plymouth Company after one unsuccessful attempt which only survived its first winter abandoned further operations though it remained in being.

## II

Prominent among the heads of the London Company were the Lord Treasurer Robert Cecil, Lord Rich later Earl of Warwick, Sir Thomas Smythe, Sir George Somers, Sir Thomas Gates, and Archdeacon Richard Hakluyt.

The Charter tacitly takes for granted that all the regions described, being unoccupied by any European power, are open to appropriation—the view of international law which had been neither resigned by England nor admitted by Spain in the formal treaty of 1604 (Anglo-Spanish treaties of peace habitually omitted any express agreement on the disputed doctrines from which the recent war between the two countries had originated). The Spanish Ambassador was much annoyed, and urged his master to prevent the scheme; but James evaded the issue, doubtless stiffened by the will and aided by the diplomatic skill of Cecil, a past master in the art of managing men, who, apart from his patriotic interest in the question which would have sufficed by itself, had a personal interest in the particular enterprise. Moreover, at this stage, when Henri IV was still very much alive, Philip III could by no means afford to force England into a revival of active hostility. Cecil at least knew that such protests as Spain might make could be diplomatically shelved; though rumours, not without foundation, of Spanish plots for the destruction of the new colony, were rife during the troubled years of its infancy. No overt attempt at wreckage was ever made, nor was the profession of amity between the Powers discarded till James had reigned in England for twenty years.

The Charter was based on the patents which had been granted by Elizabeth to Gilbert and Ralegh, and it contained the clause which differentiated English colonisation from that of other countries by expressly laying it down that the settlers wherever they went would enjoy unimpaired all their civic rights as Englishmen. The actual form of government propounded was obviously clumsy, very experimental and temporary; for there were, as has been pointed out in an earlier chapter, no precedents whatever, applicable to the general scheme, to go upon; since the Dutch method was in the first place being applied under wholly different conditions and, in the second place, had not yet been put to the test of time. In this initial system, if it can be dignified by that title, control was vested in a series of Councils or committees, no individual possessing a higher authority than that attaching to his position as President of the particular Council of which he was a member.

At the head was the supreme Council of Virginia, representing the Crown and (as were the rest of the Councils) appointed by the Crown; its members were not necessarily even shareholders. Each of the two companies, the " London " and the " Plymouth," had its own Council in England to direct, and its own subordinate Council at its settlement to conduct, its administration and policy. All the Councils were nominated by the Crown, but each Council chose its own President or Governor from its own members. Thus in effect, the Government of the Colony was responsible to the directorate of the Company, which was responsible to the Crown represented by the Supreme Council of Virginia.

For this extremely experimental stage at least, the principle was sound—the interests of the State were involved in the whole enterprise, and those interests must be ultimately supreme, at least in the sense that they must not be endangered; but it was essentially a commercial venture which must be run by and in the interests of the investors; and it was a venture in a new field, under conditions of which very little was known while much was surmised, so that the immediate management on the spot must depend on the judgement of the men on the spot. If those men were of sound judgement, the less they were interfered with by the Company, the better for themselves and the Company. If the Company was guided by men of sound judgement the less they were interfered with by the Crown the better. But the power of intervention whether by the Crown or the Company must be indisputable.

But while the principle was sound, it is not surprising that the machinery, necessarily of a makeshift character, was clumsy and inefficient to a dangerous degree. Where the settlers were in the nature of things bound to be a very miscellaneous and very undisciplined body, strong and capable personal leadership, commanding general confidence, was a primary requisite, and for such leadership the supremacy of such a Council as was provided gave no guarantee whatever. A commercial Company is always apt to suffer from a fixed idea that expenditure, actually essential to its advancement, is to be condemned because its benefits are not immediately apparent in the form of dividends. In the seventeenth century, at least under the first two Stuarts, any uninvited activities on the part of the Crown—as distinguished from Parliament—were habitually regarded with extreme jealousy and suspicion. The smooth working of the machine depended on sympathetic and intelligent co-operation on the part of the three interests concerned, the Crown, the Company, and the Settlers (the term *adventurers* must be used warily since it was applied to the persons who sat at home and adventured their money as well as to those who adventured their persons); and for lack of such co-operation, the working of the machine was very far from smooth. Quarrels between Crown and Parliament, differences among directors, the short-sightedness of shareholders, indiscipline and fecklessness among the settlers, clogged co-operation, so that the infancy of Virginia was stormy. But if we feel surprise, it should not be because storms arose, but because the colony weathered them.

It proved, in fact, no easy task to collect the first batch of emigrants (some hundred and twenty, of whom one hundred and four actually disembarked on the Land of Promise) at the end of December, 1606, in three vessels under the command of Captain Christopher Newport who was to be the connecting link with England, passing to and fro, carrying reports to the east, instructions and supplies to the west, and taking personal part in the affairs of the colony when actually present. The crews under his command were not attached to the settlement. The settlers were a most miscellaneous body—gentlemen, artificers, labourers, rapscallions, who quarrelled plentifully among themselves on the way out. They had been more than four months at sea or making hasty inspection of islands or of points on the American coast, before they sighted and entered the mouth of the Chesapeake Bay, estuary of many considerable rivers, a great sheet of water stretching an immense distance inland, and giving promise that somewhere on its river banks a suitable spot would be found for the settlement.

Here they came ashore and opened the sealed instructions which had hitherto been in Newport's charge. The seven members of the Council were named therein —among them Captain John Smith who at the moment was under arrest (the fruit of quarrels on the voyage), and was consequently not at first admitted to the

G

Council. As President they elected Edward Wingfield, who would seem to have been a courageous and honourable gentleman but wholly devoid of initiative or of any qualities of leadership. Newport was an able man, but he was only a bird of passage. Among the rest, there was an admirable Chaplain but no single man of outstanding capacity except Captain John Smith, a born pioneer but a rather impossible subordinate; who being now twenty-seven years of age had already spent some eight of those years knocking about Europe, seeking—and finding—adventures, fighting the Turks, alternately fighting against and beside pirates; who was perfectly fearless, having faced death in a variety of forms scores of times without satiating his passion for perilous emergencies and for exploring the unknown; who had learnt to be infinitely resourceful, and as supremely self-confident as Francis Drake himself— though he had not learnt to abstain from riding roughshod over all opposition, while his scorn for either slackness or stupidity knew no bounds. It is not necessary to take *au pied de la lettre* all his own statements about himself, his friends, and his adversaries, who were many; but when all deductions have been made for his flamboyancy, the fact remains beyond doubt that the new Virginia would have gone the way of Ralegh's, if it had not been dominated by the invincible resourcefulness and resolution of John Smith.

The instructions contained orders, definite or vague, for the administration of the colony, and much advice as to the conduct of the settlers highly suggestive to modern ears of the words of wisdom wherewith Polonius regaled Laertes: though what are now mere platitudes were by no means so platitudinous in those days of inexperience, when the settlers were rather like a parcel of schoolboys pitch-forked into the unknown to fend for themselves. In the orders, the Council was endowed with fairly despotic powers, but without adequate provision for the control of dissensions within the Council itself. It is notable, however, that the death-penalty which in England was applied to trivial offences was sanctioned only in the case of the graver offences which threatened the well-being of the community.

It was not, however, till another fortnight had passed in pioneering that, voyaging up the James river, they came upon the place where they decided to plant their settlement, the small peninsula which they first called Fort James and finally Jamestown. It was fifty miles above the bay, out of reach of attack from the sea and easily fortified against land attack, while the water was deep enough to let the ships lie under the bank. The country was thickly wooded—a very doubtful advantage; it was not as yet realised that the spot was malarious; and the natives who had kept them company on the banks—they had never seen a white man before—on first appearance seemed disposed to be friendly.

The colonists called their new settlement Fort James or Jamestown, having named the points at the mouth of the James River, Cape Henry and Cape Charles after the young princes. The place was far enough away from Roanoke for the local Redskins to be wholly unacquainted with Europeans; most but not all of them acknowledged the supremacy of a high-chief known as Powhatan. Their villages were scattered over a wide area, and sparse as they were the number of their fighting men was overwhelming in comparison with the hundred Englishmen. To establish friendly relations with them was a prime necessity, not so much from the fear of an attack in force as of ambuscades, but much more still because the settlers would obviously be largely dependent on their goodwill for food-supplies, with which they had come insufficiently provided, at least until they could grow their own cereals. And the barbarian was naturally suspicious of the white man, however apparently friendly he might be.

The precarious character of the relations with the Indians was manifested within the next fortnight. The Red men were—provisionally—rather curious than hostile, whether parties of them came down to inspect the white men or parties of the whites went exploring among their communities. Wingfield for his part was especially anxious to avoid any activities at which they might take alarm and refused to erect fortifications or to keep his men under arms; while the " kings " of rival communities rather vied with each other in displays of goodwill. Newport, with Smith and a few others, went off on an exploring expedition up the river, were on the whole well received by Powhatan whom they visited, and reached a point where rapids made further navigation impossible. Here they set up a cross to indicate that the King of England was now in sovereign possession, and returned to the settlement, having been absent about a week.

And there they found that on the previous day one of the other " friendly " communities, not under Powhatan's sway, had made a surprise attack in force with two hundred men, had all but succeeded in rushing the very feeble stockade, and had in fact been dispersed by the fire of the ships' guns crashing at random into the cover of the woods; an experience which convinced even Wingfield (through whose beard an arrow had passed, though without hurting him) that effective fortification and systematic sentry work could no longer be dispensed with. A month later Newport and his ships took their departure, intending to be back with further supplies in twenty weeks.

## III

Before Newport's departure, there was an investigation of the somewhat preposterous charges that had been brought against Smith, who was completely cleared and was at last admitted as the seventh member of the Council. At the end of twelve weeks supplies were running dangerously short; hunting game in the forests was a very different thing from the sport to which the Englishmen were accustomed at home, apart from the prospect of being ambushed by hostile Indians; few of them were hardened to the severe manual labour the circumstances demanded, half the company were or had been down with sickness—mostly no doubt malaria—including the leader; and everyone was disposed to quarrel, grumble, and bandy reproaches. The unhappy Wingfield's conscientious ineptitude became intolerable, and at last the rest of the Council put him under arrest, deposed him from the Presidency, and elected in his place Captain Ratcliffe, the leader of the opposition; whose principal merit was that for the moment he allowed John Smith to take energetic action. It was in fact quite time to remove the illusion which was developing among the Indians that they would very soon have a famished settlement lying at their mercy.

Smith's method was simple. Food he must have, and for it he would pay fair value; what the white men wanted was honest exchange. If the Indians refused or evaded a square deal, the consequences would be more unpleasant for the Indians than for the English. When they grasped the fact that the youthful veteran was not in the least afraid of them and meant what he said, they changed their tone; there was no bloodshed, the supplies were brought in and duly paid for, and the menace of starvation was for the time averted.

Smith moreover inspired a good many of his own people with something of his own energy; they began at last to work with a will at clearing and building log-houses; he became popular with the men who were blessed with something of his own spirit, and more unpopular than ever with slackers.

But exploration was no less necessary, in his judgement, than care of the settlement, and he went off with a small party of eight on a remarkable expedition up the river in the course of which he himself was ambushed and taken prisoner and his companions were massacred. He succeeded, however, in impressing his captors with the conviction that he was a great medicine-man by the judicious display of a mariner's compass; so the sub-chief passed him on to the great Powhatan himself; who feasted him royally, asked him many questions—possibly he had not been present in person at the earlier interview with Newport—made what he could of the answers, and then ordered his captive to immediate execution. From that fate he was saved by the dramatic intervention of Powhatan's thirteen-year-old daughter Pocahontas, who claimed the captive for her own, though probably not at the risk of her own life as Smith afterwards professed to believe; an incident which has given the " princess " a distinguished place among the heroines of romance, though no mention of it was made in the published " Relation " sent home by the hero. It was, however, in complete accordance with tribal custom. At any rate Powhatan, having called off the executioners, made much of his captive, vowed alliance with the English, honoured him with a sub-chief's title, and finally, after some little delay, sent him back to Jamestown with an escort which was to leave him there and return with " two great guns " as a gage of amity. Smith was safe enough in promising the guns which,

THE PORTRAICTUER OF CAPTAYNE JOHN SMITH ADMIRALL OF NEW ENGLAND

These are the Lines that shew thy Face but those
That shew thy Grace and Glory, brighter bee,
Thy Faire-Discoueries and Fowle-Overthrowes
Of Salvages, much Civilliz'd by thee
Best shew thy Spirit and to it Glory Wyn;
So, thou art Brasse without-but Golde within.

CAPTAIN JOHN SMITH          [Rischgitz
The Virginia pioneer

[Face page 94

when duly presented, were of course impossibly heavy for carriage.

The whole story, when stripped of later fictitious embellishment for which Smith was in no sort of way responsible, is entirely credible, and is practically confirmed by the undoubted fact that the Indian maiden proved unfailingly loyal in her devotion for the Englishmen not only during the next twenty months of John Smith's stay in the colony but for eight years after his departure. More than once, the settlement was saved from possible destruction by warnings from her—Powhatan's own loyalty being at best the mask of a rooted hostility. Finally, the ' princess,' having married an Englishman, John Rolfe, was brought to London by her husband, was there fêted as " la Belle Sauvage," insisted on calling her old protégé " Father," fell into a consumption after a few months, and died.

For the next eighteen months after Smith's famous adventure, the colony had a desperate struggle for existence. Smith's reappearance was hailed with acclamation; his escort were regaled with a terrifying but harmless demonstration with the promised ' culverins ' which they found themselves unable to remove; and then Smith discovered that President Ratcliffe and ex-President Wingfield were embarking on the pinnace which the colonists had retained, intending to make off for England on their own account, seven months having passed since Newport's departure without sign of his reappearance. He and his personal adherents stopped that by training the guns of the fort onto the pinnace and threatening to sink her; whereupon he in turn was placed under arrest, tried, as having been responsible for the annihilation of his exploring party, and once more condemned to death—a consummation which was happily prevented by the belated but opportune appearance of Newport with part of the " First Supply," a second ship under Captain Nelson arriving some months later, having been driven out of its course by storms.

Newport brought with him more than a hundred fresh settlers including thirty gentlemen (one of whom, Scrivener by name, became for some time Smith's right-hand man). They were badly wanted, though by no means notably efficient, since more than half the original band were by this time dead, chiefly from malaria. Newport was the one man whose personal authority everyone respected. He effected a general reconciliation, Ratcliffe remaining the official President; but it was Newport who remained in practical control till it was time for him to depart again. The satisfactory relations established by Smith with Powhatan had excellent effect in bringing in abundant supplies, and were confirmed by a state-visit to that potentate, who stood in some awe of his former captive and of the visitor whom Smith, during his captivity, had been at pains to picture as a semi-divine personage. Newport carried off with him Wingfield and his grievances, an ingenious and troublesome gentleman named Archer, and samples of what was believed to be gold-dust, but proved in fact to be the often-deceptive mica otherwise known as fool-gold, the discovery of which had possessed most of the settlers with a fever for finding gold instead of drudging at the work which was actually essential.

Smith, who was not bitten with the gold-mania, got his men to work again, and drilled some of them up to a reasonable efficiency; Nelson's ship arrived with some more stores—it was no fault of his that he had been delayed, but they were already much needed, the management of the supply department being singularly incompetent. Smith went off with a comparatively large company on another exploring expedition up the coast; and returned to find that all the efficient men were resolved on Ratcliffe's deposition and the substitution of Captain John Smith as President; the plain fact being that whenever he was absent everything fell into disorder and the Indians naturally took every advantage of the situation. It was rash of him, in the circumstances, to go off again, leaving Scrivener in charge, but no evil results followed, and on his return he formally took office as President; a position he was to hold for one year.

Then Newport arrived once more with the Second Supply, which included seventy more settlers, some of whom proved useful and others very much the reverse, among them some foreigners referred to as Dutchmen, which probably meant Germans. Also he brought thoroughly impracticable instructions from London where the Council, though endorsing Smith's Presidency, had obviously been giving ear to Wingfield and Archer, besides being much annoyed at finding that the gold-dust was mica, that instead of making a profit they were faced with the necessity for further expenditure, that the country was not already bringing forth corn in abundance, and that the colonists had failed to find either gold-mines or a North-West Passage. To all of which complaints President John Smith replied with by no means diplomatic home-truths; while he found it needful to impress upon Newport the fact that he, John Smith, understood what was needed to be done, out of his own very practical experience, very much better than the worthy seaman, excellent though the latter undoubtedly was at his own job. When in due time Newport departed, Ratcliffe went with him, to add to the mischief making of Wingfield and Archer.

The winter that followed was exceptionally trying. The colony was in constant danger from its professed allies, Powhatan's tribesmen. Smith had the utmost difficulty in procuring provisions (what was sent out from England was always hopelessly insufficient, and on this occasion was largely consumed by a plague of rats), in the course of which he had most picturesque adventures. As the winter went on, he was reduced to quartering some of his men among the Indians who had learnt from recent experiments that treachery was not likely to prosper; others were sent down the river to live mainly on oysters.

Smith pulled through, though men continued to die off. Momentary relief was brought by an English ship commanded by Captain Argall which touched at Jamestown; but the President's task of keeping the colony alive somehow was nearly over, for in England the whole scheme was being reorganised on a much larger scale, the active influences at home were all hostile to him, and his supersession was a matter of certainty. Archer and Ratcliffe returned with the new batch of settlers that arrived in the summer; it should have been, but was not, accompanied by the officers who were to take over the government, and Smith declined to be ejected from his position by the new arrivals until the authorised officers should appear. The situation became impossible when Smith himself was so injured by an explosion that he was practically *hors de combat*, and in October 1609 he was carried on board a homeward-bound ship, leaving as temporary President George Percy; whose personal virtues and social status as brother of the Duke of Northumberland made him perhaps the only possible figurehead, though an entirely incompetent administrator where a strenuous initiative and a strong personality were of the first importance.

IV

Here, then, begins the second chapter in the life story of the colony of Virginia, if we reckon the charter of 1606 as marking the hour of its birth. It had almost perished of strangulation before the first settlers or what was left of them had been two years on American soil, a fate from which it had been saved mainly by the tenacity and resourcefulness of one man. Two facts, however, had emerged; one, that the haphazard methods with which it had started could lead nowhere, the other that the country, if rightly turned to account, contained great possibilities for the future. It is worth while again to note that in the year 1609 both the two great ventures, the East India Company and the Virginia Company were to all appearance in the very lowest of low water, both date their recovery from that year, and for both the date is marked by the issue of a new Charter giving the Company extended powers, the accession of a considerable number of persons of high rank, and of a greatly increased capital, definite indications of royal favour, and reorganisation of the management. It can hardly be regarded as a mere coincidence that Sir Thomas Smythe was the London Governor of the East India Company and Treasurer of the Virginia Company, both before and after the 1609 charters; and it can hardly be doubted that his influence, direct or indirect, was a principal factor in effecting the change.

Nor should we grudge the credit due to King James, the oddest mixture of insight, self deception, pusillanimity and generally futile cunning that ever sat on a throne—though in this case it may very well be that he was shepherded into the right way by that consummate and very astute wire-puller Robert Cecil, Earl of Salisbury and Lord Treasurer. By emphasising the royal favour to the two companies at a critical juncture in the lives of both, James made it the fashionable thing to be an " adventurer " (in the commercial sense) in at least one of them.   Yet both were notoriously resented by Spain, a power to which his fears were apt to make him cringe in despicable fashion.   Nevertheless, he was not to be turned even by Spain from encouraging the policy of expansion, and from doing so at the moment when superficially at least the omens seemed most unfavourable; when in the East India Company many of the adventurers were manifesting an inclination to throw the whole thing up and cut what they believed to be their losses; when the Plymouth Company, after one disastrous experiment, had lapsed into a state of coma; and when the Virginia settlement not only seemed to be but was in an all but desperate condition, and the reconstruction had to be boomed by pamphlets more imaginative than scrupulous in the glowing prospects they held out to " planters "—the name applied to settlers in distinction from the " adventurers " who stayed at home.

Under the new charter, the direction of affairs was placed in the hands of the Company itself, the people whose money was in it; that is to say, although the Council or Board of Management was in the first instance nominated by the Crown, they were all stockholders, and vacancies in the body were to be filled by election of the stock-holders from their own number. Their Council was to appoint a Governor and other officers for the conduct of the administration on the spot, in accordance with instructions laid down by the Council to whom they were responsible. Every " planter " became *ipso facto* the holder of one share in the Company. Though, as before, all the work was communal, the proceeds going into the common stock for ultimate distribution among the shareholders, the promise was held out that after seven years land would be allotted to the planters individually so that each would thenceforth be able to work for his own profits— the incentive to effort necessary to prevent the slacker from battening upon the toil of his industrious neighbour. Meanwhile the Company was responsible for providing all necessary supplies. Lord Delawarr was to be the first Governor, Newport, Sir George Somers, and Sir Thomas Gates the officers next in command. Some five hundred planters were collected, including as we have seen Ratcliffe and Archer. Seven of the nine ships which sailed formed the "supply" which reached the colony during the summer; but Delawarr's departure was postponed, one ship foundered, and the ninth, the *Sea Adventure*, carrying all the officers of the new Government, was wrecked by a tempest in Prospero's "still-vex'd Bermoothes," where perforce passengers and crew, who all got ashore, passed the winter as best they might, and built the pinnaces in which they succeeded in reaching Jamestown in the following May. Doubtless the news had reached England in time for a prophetic ex-Duke of Milan to introduce a topical reference to it on the stage.

They found only a starving remnant of colonists in a desolate settlement. Only sixty of them had survived the horrors of that ghastly time that followed John Smith's departure. All the food available for the entire company now assembled would be exhausted in a fortnight. There was nothing left but to crowd into the pinnaces and try to reach Newfoundland before they were all dead men; and the forlorn voyage down the river had already begun when the situation was saved by the arrival of Lord Delawarr and his ships with fresh supplies and fresh men.

Delawarr set to work vigorously; the powers conferred on the Governor were almost autocratic; discipline was restored, though fever and short commons were still to take their toll of the planters, and Delawarr himself had to return to England next year. But before he left he had succeeded in impressing on the authorities at home the necessity of sending out, yearly, provisions for twelve months. The colonists were not again in serious danger of perishing from starvation. Relapse threatened to follow his departure till the Deputy Governorship was taken up by Sir Thomas Gates who, with his colleagues Dale and Yeardley, men who had learnt military discipline in the Netherlands wars, applied the terrifically Draconic code known as Dale's laws (their own modification, leaning not towards mercy, of the code drawn up in London which Delawarr had brought with him) with relentless rigour. This, at any rate, produced the desired effect of crushing disaffection and idleness, when perhaps no methods less drastic would have succeeded. Also the old malarious position at Jamestown was abandoned in favour of healthier spots higher up the river. Dale succeeded Gates in the Governorship, and Yeardsley succeeded Dale. During the whole period friendly relations with the Indians were maintained, land was brought under cultivation, and the prosperity of the colony advanced. But perhaps the most notable feature was one not at all pleasing to the authorities at home. Tobacco, not corn, was the staple crop to the cultivation of which the planters devoted themselves; an industry condemned alike by the economists and the moralists; while the views of his Majesty King James on the subject had been set forth with some virulence in his essay, *Counterblast to Tobacco*.

Dale remained long enough to inaugurate the allotment of private estates among the planters promised at the end of seven years in 1609, giving them an individual and personal instead of only a communal interest in the product of their labours. Yeardsley was then superseded by Captain Argall, whose misuse of his powers caused such general complaints that Yeardsley was again sent out to take his place and inaugurate a new system of government with a representative House of Burgesses elected after the model of the English House of Commons (the eleven settlements into which the colony had now been divided being the electing constituencies), which with the Governor formed the legislature.

Thus in 1619, in the colony of Virginia the basic English principle, of colonial self-government within the limits prescribed by the interests of the Mother Country and consonance with the laws of England, found its first tentative expression.

In form it was intended to be a local reproduction, with appropriate modifications, of the English Con-stitutional system. In England, the Government was the King's Government, but the law could be altered only by assent of an elected legislature, and the King himself had no power to override the law, while he chose his own ministers without consulting the legis-lature. In the Colony, the Governor took the place of the King, but himself, in relation to the Crown, was the King's minister responsible to the Crown; the responsibility of ministers to Parliament had not yet become an integral part of the constitution. At this stage, however, the conditions upon which the Governor held office were laid down in the charter which authorised the Colony, and the Governor was directly responsible to the Virginia Company in London, without prejudice to the Crown's power of intervention.

Now the three leading members of the Council in London latterly had been the Treasurer, Sir Thomas

Smythe, the second Earl of Warwick, and Sir Edwin
Sandys, with the last of whom was associated the Earl of
Southampton, friend and patron of Shakespeare. The
three had differed on various questions of the Company's
commercial and administrative policy; while Sandys
and Warwick were both, then and afterwards, associated
with the parliamentarian and puritan parties in the
affairs of Church and State, which Smythe was not.
Each had his own following among the stock-holders;
Sandys is to be credited with the new departure which
sought to apply his political views in the colony.
Smythe resigned the treasurership, Sandys taking his
place and dominating the Company's policy. Smythe
and Warwick, previously at odds, united in opposition.
Then a fierce and prolonged fever epidemic broke out
among the multiplying immigrants, and—a bolt from
the blue—there came a sudden well-concerted Indian
rising. Pocahontas had died in England and the politic
Powhatan in America. Powhatan's successor Opac-
ancanough, a chief who had throughout cherished but
dissembled an undying hatred of the white man,
organised the insurrection and inaugurated it by a
massacre in which some hundreds of the settlers were
slaughtered. The long and ugly guerrilla war which
followed was disastrous to what had seemed to be
the growing goodwill between the races. The Company
was not making money; the settlers were sending home
nothing but tobacco; the King regarded Sandys personally as an obnoxious leader of sedition; and so in 1623
James took proceedings for the confiscation of the
Virginia Charter. Thus in the last year of his reign
the Company but not the colony ceased to exist. That
chapter in Virginia's history was closed; but a new and
variegated chapter of colonial development had already
opened.

# CHAPTER VI

## NEW PLYMOUTH AND ISLAND BEGINNINGS

### I

WE have seen that colonisation, in the specialised English sense of the term, was an idea without historical precedent, which only came into being during the last years of Queen Elizabeth. The dominant motives actuating the organisers of the first colony, Virginia, the story of whose early years was sketched in the last chapter, were mainly two: the commercial money-making motive and the mercantilist motive of increasing the national power. The Company, after nearly a score of years, had made no great profit, but it had succeeded in establishing overseas an English community which had at any rate a reasonable prospect of flourishing though the Company which created it was dissolved.

The parallel attempt to create another colony to the north had not been renewed after the failure of the first effort; it had not, however, been entirely abandoned, and sundry small expeditions to explore possibilities had been sent out, notably one under the redoubtable John Smith some years after his return from Virginia, in which information was collected that was soon to prove valuable.

But an entirely new factor, the factor of Religion, was now to come into play, the direct product of the ecclesiastical policy which in England enforced conformity to usages which were becoming more and more intolerable to rigid Puritanism. The New England expansion was primarily an aspect of the development of Nonconformity or Puritanism in England; not of collective or individual commercial enterprise, as was Virginia.

England on the accession of Elizabeth following the reaction under Queen Mary had definitely severed herself from that portion of the Church of Western Christendom which continued to affirm the authority of the papacy. Elizabeth's settlement of religious affairs established the continuity of the Episcopal system of Church government and laid down with a convenient latitude or ambiguity for clergy and laity the doctrines, practices and ritual to which all loyal subjects were required to conform under various pains and penalties for disobedience. The pains and penalities fell heavily upon the adherents of the papacy, commonly called Roman Catholics—mainly, so far as Elizabeth was concerned, because the Popes laid it down that Catholics owed no allegiance to a heretic prince. They also fell heavily on those advanced Protestants whose active resistance to the ecclesiastical laws was regarded as subversive of the Royal authority or as otherwise anarchical; a category which included all those who persistently set the ecclesiastical authorities at defiance in obedience to the dictates of their own consciences.

The term Nonconformist, however, was not as is now the case used to denote sects which separated themselves from the Church as by law established, but commonly those of the clergy who without feeling bound to resign their functions rather than obey the law, desired the law to be altered so that sanctioned traditional practices which were in their view "rags of Rome" should be prohibited or at least not be enjoined

Among them were zealous advocates of the Calvinistic or Presbyterian system of Church government which had prevailed in Scotland, in place of the Episcopal system as established in England. Presbyterianism was certainly not a whit less rigid and intolerant in its insistence upon uniformity than the most intolerant of the Bishops; but it was a system so democratically constituted that, in the phrase of King James, it "consorteth with a monarchy as well as God with the Devil," and in the nature of things the supporters of Presbyterianism were opponents of the monarchical theories which were a fundamental part of the Stuarts' political creed.

But the Presbyterians were only a section, though a substantial one, of those to whom the name of Puritan was properly applicable, though ultimately the term was narrowed down to the extremists; it was meant to cover those who held that religion ought to be purged of the false doctrines which had survived the severance from Rome. Puritanism was inclined to regard the Pope as the Antichrist, to stress the teachings of the Old Testament as the Word of God more than of the New, with the exception perhaps of the Apocalypse; and in course of time it particularly identified itself, being largely Calvinistic in its genesis, with the singularly joyless and narrow moral code which John Calvin had rigidly enforced as dictator of Geneva. And it covered, besides the Presbyterians, those who became known collectively as Independents or Sectaries; who, perhaps because they formed only comparatively small groups, demanded not uniformity but, at least theoretically, freedom of conscience and freedom from secular control for all groups except the followers of the Scarlet Woman.

The Calvinistic theological doctrines were not *per se* precluded by the formulae of the Church in England.

A preference for the Presbyterian system of government was compatible with conformity to the Anglican ritual. The convinced Presbyterian did not as such feel that conscience required him to break away from the Church; he remained within its fold as a protesting Nonconformist. But among the Independents there were many who could not conscientiously conform, even under protest—whose unorthodoxy would be penalised as severely under a Presbyterian system as under the Prelatical. For them escape from the existing control was the only possible course, and some of these had found an uneasy asylum in Holland. Among them the idea took shape of establishing in the New World a community of their own, where they might be guaranteed the free practice of their own religion after their own fashion, still as English subjects.

The Plymouth Company had abandoned active efforts, after its first failure, in the northern region (which Captain John Smith christened New England, in the course of his exploration in 1614) allotted to it under the Charter of 1606 which was still valid; since the prospects of a successful commercial venture in that quarter had not proved sufficiently promising. But it was not a commercial venture that these Puritans had in view. They asked only freedom to wring for themselves from the soil such livelihood as they might by their own labours, with freedom to worship God after their own fashion without interference.

Nevertheless, it was not within this New England but in the northern portion of the area included in Virginia that the English Puritans congregated at Leyden designed to seek authority to settle themselves, and even that was only after they had abandoned the wholly impracticable idea of going to Guiana, of which Englishmen continued to dream until the vision was dispersed by Ralegh's final tragic failure in 1617. Sandys, in 1619, had just gained ascendency in the Virginia Company; he was a Puritan; he may have been personally acquainted with some of the exiles in Holland; and it was doubtless through his good offices that the Company granted the concession to the Leyden congregation.

The intending emigrants themselves lacked the means for emigrating, for they had long left their English homes, with such property as they possessed, to earn a meagre and precarious livelihood among the Dutch. Sufficient funds could not be raised by subscription from sympathisers—they were all folk of humble or at least not high birth, without influence—but a syndicate was formed to finance the enterprise, out of which the financiers meant to secure a substantial profit for themselves. This little company was to consist of holders of one or more Ten pound shares; the cost of emigrating being estimated at Ten pounds a head, each emigrant was counted as the holder of one share, while the actual cost was to be borne by the company. The analogy of the Virginia Company (not, as has sometimes been suggested, that of the earliest Christian community), was followed; for seven years (as in 1609) the work was to be communal and the profits were to be the profits of the Company.

Now it was just at the time when this arrangement was taking shape that the moribund Plymouth Company was reconstructed and procured a fresh charter, under the name of the "New England Company." Ostensibly there was no connection between these two events, but the next stage gives at any rate some colour—though nothing verging on proof—that they were surreptitiously connected. The Leyden folk came from Delft to Southampton in the *Speedwell*; at Plymouth some

addition was made to their numbers; and finally on
September 6th, 1620, the company of one hundred
persons who are traditionally known as the Pilgrim
Fathers sailed from Plymouth for Delaware Bay (named
after the titular Governor of Virginia) in the *Mayflower*,
leaving the *Speedwell* behind. But when they made
land on November 11th, it was not at Delaware Bay
but at Cape Cod, 400 miles to the north of it, in the
area appropriated not to the Virginia but to the New
England Company. The Pilgrim Fathers, doubtless
convinced that the voyage had been directed by the
hand of Providence, very soon resolved to stay where
they were, though not at the precise spot where they
first made land; but it is not impossible that a mundane
pilot was in the pay of the New England Company.
They had no authority for settling in New England,
but that Company welcomed a suitable adjustment.
For the scheme of the reconstructed Company's procedure was, broadly speaking, not the financing of a
new colony but the licensing of settlements within its
territories upon conditions profitable to itself.

Adventure in one or other of its two senses, and
sometimes in both, was the mainspring for every one
who took part in the Virginia Company colonising
experiment; it did not enter at all into that of the
Pilgrim Fathers, so far at least as concerned the settlers
themselves who were men of an entirely different type
from the Virginia planters. Those planters, men of
all sorts, went out quite unconscious of what lay before
them, on the chance of making a fortune, or in search
of a career denied them at home; and such of them
as survived stayed because they preferred—or could
not avoid—taking their chance where they were to
returning home. These Puritans went out with no
light-hearted illusions, and with minds steadfastly set

on one common purpose; deliberately and consciously going—if they had not already gone—into permanent and voluntary exile for conscience' sake; yet intensely anxious to remain English however far they might be from England. Men (and women) with a lofty and over-mastering sense of duty, however narrow or even distorted their outlook might be. Practical guidance and leadership they needed, of course, for the battle of life in a natural environment of which they had no experience; but they were already a closely bound community, not a miscellaneous aggregate of individual adventurers on whom discipline must be forcibly imposed if they were to act together for the common good.

Captain John Smith's colonising zeal had made him eager to place his experience at the service of the intending settlers as their leader, but the suggestion did not appeal to them, somewhat to his annoyance. It probably did not strike him that his religious orthodoxy would scarcely have squared with their peculiar tenets or his normally unimpeachable moral standards with the abnormal standards of the Puritan conscience.

II

A special interest attaches to this first Puritan colony, which is out of proportion to its actual achievement, because in sundry respects it was unique. It initiated the Puritan emigration, and the achievement of the Puritan emigration was tremendous, but the first colony played only a minor part in it; the subsequent development was on different lines, because the type of its Puritanism was different, and it was lacking in the heroic or romantic character of the original movement.

The Pilgrim Fathers went out into the wilderness with no thought of shaking the dust of England from their feet; although the idea of transplanting themselves under the Dutch flag was mooted, it was clearly a leading desire with them to remain under the English flag, if they could be permitted to do so without violation of conscience, which was not possible for them on the actual soil of their native land. They were not bigots like so many of the later Puritan emigrants, ready not only to denounce but to penalise all who rejected their own particular tenets. They were not concerned with affairs of State at all. They had no desire to "found a community"; they were already, by force of circumstances, a community bound together by a common faith, of English exiles in a foreign land, and their desire was to transfer that community, or a portion of it, from the foreign land to English territory oversea (since they might not return to England itself), where others of like mind with themselves who sought membership in the community would be welcomed. What conscience imposed on them, that they would do at whatever sacrifice, and conscience made them tolerant of opinions not in agreement with their own; but the harmony of the community required that it should not be broken by the presence of discordant elements in its midst.

It was, of course, essential that they should go with the assent of the King, and with some guarantee that the religious liberty, which was their main requirement, should not be interfered with. The King had no sort of objection. He detested Presbyterianism on political grounds, and for like reasons insisted upon uniformity in England where Nonconformity was a nuisance, but of divergencies in religious opinion he was quite tolerant, while his own views on theology though not on Church government were Calvinistic. These people with their craze for Nonconformity would be troublesome in England, but scarcely in America. They had drawn up "the seven articles," a judiciously worded declaration of loyalty to the throne and readiness to obey " in all things lawful ", which satisfied their own conscience while it was a matter of course that in the view of the Crown all royal injunctions would be things lawful. King James would give no guarantees, but hinted that they might take it that they would be left alone unless they asked for trouble. With that they were wisely content, being aware that they would have no better security under a written guarantee which the monarch would certainly find means of evading or annulling if he had occasion to do so.

The wise and broad-minded pastor of the Leyden congregation, John Robinson, did not accompany the emigrants of his flock, though he had imbued them with his own spirit and taken active part in planning and organising the exodus.

The leading figures among the Pilgrims were William Brewster, "Ruling Elder" of the congregation, a Cambridge man, sometime secretary to Queen Elizabeth's unlucky secretary Davison and afterwards "in charge of the post" at Scrooby, on the North Road, the English home of many more of the emigrants— a man of considerable culture, who in his exile had earned his livelihood as a printer; John Bradford, a young man, son of a yeoman, but endowed with great abilities and high character, who must from the beginning have been marked out for leadership; and Miles Standish, not an original "church member," but a Puritan soldier, of a good north-country family, whose experience as an officer in the Dutch war of liberation made him an invaluable addition to a party of peaceful folk who were not unlikely to find themselves in need of a Gideon in the new surroundings of their Canaan.

Not all of the band were from Leyden; they had been joined by others from England before the *Mayflower* sailed from Plymouth; most of them but not all were from the eastern counties, the area where Independency was most active. Some brought wives and children with them; others were followed by their families later. The colony took the name of New Plymouth from Plymouth Harbour (which, like New England, had been christened by John Smith on the same voyage), the point at which after some weeks of investigation the company decided to fix its settlement. The spot was one which had been occupied and partly brought under cultivation by Indians who had abandoned it in consequence of an outbreak of some epidemic.

The Virginia planters had been provided with a governing body under the terms of the Virginia charter. This band of emigrants had a licence from the Virginia Company but it had no validity in New England territory; it did not provide them with a Government, nor had their own syndicate in England the power to do so under the agreement. The first step they took —on the day of landing—was to make the omission good by providing a Government for themselves in what is known as the "Mayflower Compact"—a mutual covenant by which the signatories, after setting forth their political loyalty, pledged themselves to obey such laws and ordinances as the community might lay down. It was not, of course, the enunciation of a political doctrine; it was simply the commonsense method of men who thoroughly trusted each other, in a situation in which mutual consent and goodwill were the essential condition of common action for the common good. Among a haphazard collection of adventurers such as the Virginia planters discipline could be enforced only by military or quasi-military methods. To this little band, accustomed to self-discipline, it was a matter of course. An official head was an obvious necessity, and they elected as Governor John Carver, who had been an active organiser, but made no further mark as he died early next year.

By the time that the settlers had fixed upon their permanent quarters, it was already mid-winter, and the immigrants had a hard time before them. Their supplies, of course, were short, and they had left behind them in the *Speedwell* the fishing-tackle they had relied on for catching fish; and though the winter was not particularly severe, game was practically not available for a party which included no experienced back-woodsmen and had more than enough to do in making the settlement habitable. Sickness broke out, and though it was not the Jamestown malaria the number of the settlers was halved in the three or four months before relief came with the spring and early summer weather. But the character of the colonists, men and women, stood the bitter test, and when they had won through that first winter, their resolution and their loyalty to each other remained unshaken.

### III

Early in May, John Carver died suddenly while engaged on the field-work to which the colony had set itself vigorously. Brewster as Ruling Elder of the congregation, was apparently regarded as disqualified for the office of Governor to which Bradford was elected for a year—and re-elected annually (except on five occasions when he absolutely refused the appointment) until 1657. Those few times, his place was taken by Edwin Winslow who was otherwise his second-in-command, while in all matters which could be described as military Miles Standish was the inevitable chief.

With the Indians of the district the best relations were established almost from the outset. Before Plymouth was fixed upon, one or two Indian attacks had been made on exploring parties, but had been dispersed by musket-fire, fortunately without loss on either side. Now there is reason to suppose that the Indians of that district were already disposed to believe that the white man's God was a dangerously powerful Being; some while before they had come into collision with some Europeans, one of whom had threatened them with a visitation from God if they dealt cruelly with the white men; they had disregarded the threat. Then the epidemic which drove them from their homes fell upon them, and they had drawn the obvious conclusion—it was the punishment sent on them by the white man's God. At any rate, when the white man reappeared, after the first harmless brush with him, and since, as the weeks passed, he showed no disposition to be aggressive, they decided to take the way of peace, being on the whole a pacific tribe with a pacific chief. They opened overtures, perceived that these English were on their guard but were people to be trusted, and then their chief, Massasoit, proposed a formal alliance which was duly made on the basis of mutual trust and fidelity, which neither party ever had reason to repent, both remaining in the fullest sense loyal to the agreement in spirit as well as in letter and scrupulously just in their dealings with each other. From the friendly Indians, the settlers not only received supplies but also valuable lessons in woodcraft and in the cultivation of the appropriate crops, and, later on, valuable warnings when dangerous movements were toward among more remote tribes. Just as the spirit of concord among the English was the main factor that enabled them to triumph over the trials and perils by which they were inevitably beset, their spirit of goodwill engendered goodwill in their barbarian neighbours, to the immense advantage of both.

It is worth while to dwell a little longer on this fundamental difference between Jamestown and Plymouth, due primarily to the difference of type between the two classes of settlers, but also between the Indian chiefs. In Virginia there was no period during the whole of the Virginia Company's career when dissensions were not raging among the settlers themselves; dissensions with which only such a masterful personality as that of Captain John Smith could cope at all until governors were appointed with virtually despotic powers which they could exercise ruthlessly. Distrusting each other, the planters acted concordantly only when under the immediate mastery of a controlling will, and in such circumstances it was impossible that they should inspire the surrounding population with confidence in them. What they could and did inspire was the fear which made the chiefs prudently careful to cloak their own hostility but only to cloak it; the planters were thoroughly aware that what they saw was a mask which might be dropped without warning. The relations between them were always those of mutual suspicion which might at any moment develop into open enmity. The treachery which in the view of the savage is legitimate cunning was always in the air; and when goodwill was apparently most prevalent, it was also most consciously superficial. The best security for the English against the dissimulation of Powhatan appears always to have been his daughter's determination to be their protectress.

In contrast, the Plymouth settlers were a united body from the beginning, with entire confidence, already long established, in each other and in the men whom they had learned to look up to for guidance as leaders of their exiled community at Leyden—men whose actual ability and integrity never in fact failed to justify the confidence reposed in them. In contact with such a folk, the instinctive suspiciousness of the savage gave place to instinctive trust, and hostility perished of inanition. With no motive to treachery, the Indian ceased to be treacherous; and when genuine goodwill was implanted, the Indian's fidelity was assured. When Indians and English visited each other, they did so unarmed, and that they could do so was the best possible guarantee that the mutual trust would not be abused. Had there been, to begin with, sharp fights and bloodshed, matters might have turned out differently; as it befell, Massasoit, unlike Powhatan, was soon ready to believe that the Englishmen were no menace to him, so that when actual intercourse began it rapidly ripened to a genuine and unbroken amity, cemented by Winslow's success in curing Massasoit of an illness which had baffled the native experts. In like manner, the Leyden community, transplanted to America, was able to adopt for itself with entire success a form of self-government by common consent which would have been quite impossible for the mixed assortment, for the most part of the rolling stone type, which quarrelled violently on the voyage out to Virginia and only at intervals could be restrained from quarrelling when it had planted itself at Jamestown.

The old Plymouth Company in England, which had been in process of reconstruction when the Leyden Congregation was preparing for emigration, received its charter as the New England Company within a few days of the landing at Cape Cod, and presently issued its patent for the new colony which lay within the limits of its territory. The "Mayflower Compact" had no legal authority behind it, but its *de facto* validity was unchallenged. The "communism" of the settlement in its initial stage was not the outcome of the Compact but was imposed by the terms of the contract with the London syndicate which had financed the enterprise. All proceeds of trading went into the common stock and all profits to the Company for proportionate distribution among the shareholders. The planters' own proposals for allotting land to individuals which they might work for personal profit had been expressly refused, and like everything else the cultivation was to be communal for seven years, as it had been in Virginia till 1616; and as in Virginia the discouraging and demoralising effect of the communal system very soon made itself felt; though not quite so acutely because communal feeling was in the nature of the case a more effective motive to energy among the band of Puritans—as no doubt it had been among the early Christians, with such painful exceptions as Ananias. But among the Puritans also it proved inadequate. Consequently they presently, in 1623, devised on their own responsibility a system of personal holdings, naturally adopted in outline from East Anglian custom, adapted to the particular circumstances. They were not lawyers or historians who troubled about precedents, but practical persons making arrangements for their own convenience; though analogies to earlier institutions may be found in some details, they were probably quite unconscious. The immediate result of the change was a rapid increase in the amount of the corn-crop.

This, however, was a breach of the formal conditions. There was, in fact, much shrewdness in the dealings of the planters with the not too scrupulous syndicate. They did not make to themselves friends of the mammon of unrighteousness, but they did not disdain the wisdom of the serpent; having indeed the characteristic Puritan faith that the God of their fathers would assuredly deliver His people, provided always that they did their best to deliver themselves. The necessary thing having been done, the syndicate would find their own interests the better served by accepting it. The Company would be automatically dissolved and the proceeds distributed among the stock-holders in 1627; so far there had been little enough promise of profit; the allotment of ground did not touch the Company's monopoly of the profits of the fur-trade which was now coming into being. When the time came the colony was able to buy out the syndicate and take upon itself the clearance of the outstanding debts; and the colony, as the grantees of the New England Company, retained the trading monopoly within its own bounds.

## IV

Meanwhile the New England Company, though occasionally projecting ambitious schemes, did not attempt to give them effect, but contented itself with securing, in spite of Parliamentary opposition, the monopoly of trading and fishing rights, and with granting patents to occasional adventurers—among them Thomas Weston who, with purely personal ends in view, had taken the lead in forming the syndicate, in which he was a principal shareholder. This worthy, who had no interest whatever in the ideals of the settlers, was foremost in complaint that they were not working profitably, quarrelled at the same time with others of the syndicate, and working behind the back of settlers and syndicate alike, procured a separate patent for himself from the New England Company, and dispatched an expedition which planted itself some five and twenty miles from Plymouth. There, in spite of warnings and protests from the Puritan settlement, they fell to quarrelling with the Indians, who were not of Massasoit's tribe and had not been in contact with Plymouth; and it was only because Massasoit sent a timely warning to his friends that Standish with a small party was in time to prevent a massacre which would probably have been followed by an attack on Plymouth itself.

That was the end of Weston's foolish design, but there were others of like character which did not make matters easier for the settlers before the new tide of Puritan emigration set in at the moment when Plymouth freed itself from the shackles of the syndicate. Of these we may be content to notice that of the extremely disreputable Thomas Morton, in the same neighbourhood. The character of his settlement may be guessed from its name, Merrymount. Plymouth was much scandalised, but when the Merrymount people began selling firearms to the Indians, it took drastic action; Standish pounced upon Merrymount and arrested Morton who was expelled from the country, though he succeeded in returning later and making more mischief.

The New England Company's actual connection with the birth of New England was, as we have seen, very slender, consisting simply in the fact that the Leyden congregation, having come ashore accidentally on its unoccupied territory, obtained from it the authority for settlement and trading. Its predecessor, the Plymouth Company, had been granted rights over a vast area by King James, but so long as that territory remained palpably unoccupied there was no legitimate method of preventing the intrusion of foreign Powers, England being committed to the doctrine that possession could only be claimed where there was effective occupation.

Even before Ralegh's earliest Virginian enterprise,

I

Humphrey Gilbert had proclaimed the Queen of England's sovereignty in Newfoundland, but no actual occupation followed. The fishing-banks were a common field for the fishing-fleets of all nations; it was long before the English became even the predominant group—so far at least as numbers were concerned—and it was not till 1610 that a Bristol merchant, John Guy, obtained from James a patent for the occupation of the Island, in which he was joined by persons so distinguished as Francis Bacon, and Northampton who as Howard of Effingham had commanded the fleet against the Armada. So there was a small official settlement; but neither Guy nor his successors as Governor succeeded in making good their authority over the seamen who frequented the shores, and before twenty years had passed the settlement faded out, though the English never abandoned their somewhat questionable claim to the sovereignty.

There were, however, two Powers whose movements at this period were to bring them before long into collision with the settlements in New England. In the first half of the sixteenth century, Jacques Cartier's explorations had established a French claim to the lower St. Lawrence basin; but no further effort for permanent settlement had been made till the matter was taken up by Champlain and Biencourt when the English were projecting the colonisation of Virginia. Champlain founded Quebec in 1608, an event which may be regarded as marking the birth of Canada proper; but three years earlier he and Biencourt had planted a settlement at Port Royal (now named Annapolis) in the district then known as Acadie, which became for more than a century a bone of contention between French and English, the latter laying claim to it as having been discovered by an English expedition under the Cabots. James in 1621 granted it to a Scottish

Company, which made some feeble pretence of occupation, and gave it the name of Nova Scotia.

The second Power was the United Netherlands. A Dutch expedition under the great English navigator, Henry Hudson, explored the coasts and the river to which (as to Hudson Bay) he gave his name, when John Smith was in Virginia. A small trading station was set up. In 1618, when the eleven years' truce between Holland and Spain was on the point of lapsing, a Dutch West India Company was formed, with the undoubted intention not so much of extending trade as in the East, as of warring on Spanish commerce after the Elizabethan fashion, while the sanction of the Dutch Government could not be regarded as claiming more than the right to occupy territory not actually in occupation by a friendly power—if at the time there was anyone in actual occupation on the Hudson, it was not the English but the Dutch; and so the colony of New Netherland was started on the lower Hudson with New Amsterdam as its nucleus, forming a wedge between Virginia and New England.

Not very much need be added in recounting the passing of the short lived dream of a Guiana empire to which Ralegh's Orinoco expedition in 1595–6 had given currency. It might be called the continued expression of the Elizabethan attitude towards Spain and the Spanish Empire in America. Spain, converted into a nominally friendly Power by the accession of James I in England, was in undeniable occupation of the Spanish Main and various West India islands; Portugal was in undoubted occupation in Brazil; but between them lay Guiana, including Eldorado if Eldorado existed, and James, with all his friendliness to Spain, was committed to the doctrine that unoccupied territory was open to occupation and possession;

consequently, while he was anxious to avoid anything that would threaten collision with Spain, he could hardly veto enterprise in Guiana. Any operations, however, on a large scale, would endanger the Spanish peace; the various experiments made were on a scale too small to lead to any permanent results. Then Ralegh was released from the Tower and sent on the last fatal expedition in search of his mythical gold-mine, with the inevitable consequence of a collision with the Spaniards who were supplied with full information; and the last of the Elizabethans returned to England that his head might be presented on a charger to Count Gondomar. Still one more experiment was made before the death of King James, by Roger North, one of Ralegh's men and a cousin of Warwick, who in defiance of the Royal disapproval (at the instance of Gondomar) attempted a settlement on the Amazon and was sent to the Tower for his pains. The Guiana idea was in fact played out, and though the Amazon scheme was revived in the next reign when England and Spain were actually at war for a time, it perished of inanition.

Guiana, then, faded out of the colonisation schemes, though when James came to the throne its imaginative appeal must still have been considerably stronger than that of the more prosaic north. But the new King's prudent attitude towards Spain—a power with which, as King of Scots, he had never known cause of quarrel —while it practically choked activity in Guiana, could not kill the latent hostility of the English people to the Spanish power, and the desire to encroach, wherever possible, on the dominions claimed by Spain. The right of the Spanish monarch to bar the door to foreign commerce with his possessions was perforce recognised under the peace-treaty; but the view that it was perfectly legitimate for the individual to evade such prohibitions at his own risk and for his own profit was ineradicable, and such eminent persons as Robert Rich (the Warwick of the Virginia Company) and the Earl of Cumberland in fact had fleets which were engaged on the illicit traffic to which the name of buccaneering was given at a later date and which was not always distinguishable from sheer piracy. For their purposes, West Indian islands would provide invaluable places of retreat, and for this more than with the ostensible purpose of legitimate commerce, the appropriation of unoccupied islands began to offer an attraction—not to the English alone. A claim to Barbados was set up as early as 1605, though actual occupation did not follow till 1624. In 1623, an English party occupied St. Christopher's Island, popularly known as St. Kitt's, got into difficulties with the Carib chiefs, but established its position in 1625 with the help of a French privateer, between whom and the English St. Kitt's was divided, remaining half French and half English. These were on the outer fringe of the Spanish islands.

It was an accident, however, that brought the Bermudas, remote from the West India Islands proper, under English sovereignty—the wreck of the *Sea Adventure*, in 1609, to which reference was made in the story of Virginia. The ship, carrying all the new officers for the colony, as reconstituted by the 1609 Charter, was driven on the rocks in a hurricane. Sir George Somers with the whole crew got ashore, wintered in the island, built themselves pinnaces, and made their way to Jamestown in the spring. The group, under the name of the "Somers Islands," was consequently attached to Virginia, but was transferred, under a separate charter, to the Somers Islands Company (mainly Virginia stock-holders) in 1615, from which time it continued as a separate colony or plantation.

# CHAPTER VII

## THE PURITAN EMIGRATION:
### NEW ENGLAND UNDER CHARLES I.

### I

THE effective motives to expansion, whether in the East or in the West, under the first Stuart King were, as concerned the Adventurers, the acquisition of wealth and (at the close of the reign) release from the shackles of the forms of religion imposed by the Ecclesiastical establishment in England. From the national or patriotic point of view it was recommended as a source of increased power provided that the wealth acquired conformed to the Mercantilist doctrine that it should bring in—without taking away in exchange—supplies of bullion, foodstuffs and war-materials, especially naval; merchant-craft being potential war-craft, the development of the mercantile marine was *per se* desirable; and settlement over seas would be a vent for surplus population. From the point of view of the Crown, it was to be encouraged on account of the aforesaid national considerations, provided always that it did not involve open collision with the Governments of either Spain or the United Provinces; while the Crown was also disposed to regard Nonconformists as a part of that surplus population whose presence on her own soil England could quite conveniently dispense with.

The Crown, however, had contented itself with encouragement. It had not taken control into its own hands, but had been satisfied to grant charters conveying territorial and trading monopolies, with rights of jurisdiction, to various Companies of adventurers, always without prejudice to its own powers of intervention, assuming that this right was within the Royal Prerogative. Although before the end of the reign this was beginning to be called in question in Parliament, one of the last acts of James was the revocation of the Virginia Company's charter, whereby the direct control of the colony reverted to the Crown.

The first settlement of heterogeneous emigrants, supplemented by successive bands of similar character, had struggled through its perilous and very experimental infancy under severe task-masters, to adolescence, reaching the stage of a society numbering over a thousand members sufficiently socialised to manage its own affairs as a body politic. The second settlement, small in number and homogeneous from the beginning, took charge of its own affairs from the moment the Pilgrims came to land, without need of the experimental period through which Virginia had passed. Self-government, in the sense at least of government by consent of the governed, was consciously or unconsciously to be the basic principle in all future developments. The communal methods and quasi-military rule required in the initial stage were not to enter into the later schemes of colonisation. Settlement in a colony or plantation took a new and more attractive aspect when personal ownership of land, with personal profit as the reward of personal exertion, took the place of communal ownership and communal profits distributed without any relation to personal effort.

This change had just become pronounced at the moment when James departed to his fathers and Charles his son reigned in his stead. The accession of the young King left the commercial motive to colonisation where it was before, but it greatly intensified the religious incentive to emigration, besides widening its basis as his ecclesiastical policy developed, while the accompanying development of the conflict between Crown and Parliament gave to the Puritan emigration—not in form but in fact—a new political character, an undercurrent at least of the anti-monarchical sentiment which permanently influenced the history of New England.

King James never summoned a Parliament if he could help it, he quarrelled with each Parliament he did summon, and throughout his reign irritation at the extravagance of his theory of the prerogative inherent in the Crown was growing, and giving birth to doctrines of the powers inherent in Parliament which were at least equally lacking in historical justification. But neither Crown nor Parliament wished to join battle, and the various minor crises which arose were tided over though without healing the fundamental causes of ill-feeling. Similarly, after the Hampton Court conference no acute religious crisis arose. James had then won a decisive victory for the prelatical establishment which he regarded as the guarantee for the effective supremacy of the Crown in matters ecclesiastical; but the bishops of his choice were as likely as not to be men of Calvinistic views in matters of doctrine, whose interpretation of the Church's formulæ practically met the more urgent demands of most of the Nonconformist clergy so far as concerned their own activities. There were Roman Catholics and Protestant sectaries whose conscience forced upon them the pains and penalties attaching to open separation from the Established Church; but it was only the latter, as yet few in number, who had been moved to seek for themselves toleration under the English flag but as permanent exiles from the land of their birth.

But with James the controlling consideration was always what he took to be political expediency except where personal favouritism or other personal whims seduced him into doing what he knew perfectly well to be inexpedient. He would never surrender a principle in words; but when matters reached the danger point, the King's grace granted the concession which saved the situation. Charles, on what he regarded as questions of principle, had no regard for expediency. When his mind was made up on a point of religion, he was quite ready to die rather than surrender. On a political question, he never realised that he had reached the danger point until he had considerably overstepped it— then he was apt to surrender with the tacit reservation that promises made under *force majeure* are not binding. And it so happened that on the religious questions of the day the views of his school and those entertained by the great mass of Puritans of all sorts were irreconcilable. James argued and bargained with his Parliaments, and snubbed the Puritans; Charles defied and then dispensed with his Parliament, straining the prerogative, and trampled on the Puritans—till the day of retribution came, when Strafford was struck down, and the issue was left to be decided by force of arms. Throughout the whole period, the Crown was in straits for money, and Charles was not too scrupulous in the use of legal trickery when money could be obtained thereby. All these were matters which told upon the colonial development while he was still the reigning King.

In the first four years of his reign, that is between March, 1625, and March, 1629, Charles summoned three Parliaments to demand supplies and dissolved each of them because each demanded the remedying of grievances as the condition of granting the supplies called for. After the dissolution in 1629, no more Parliaments were called till the "Short Parliament" of 1640, followed by the "Long Parliament" which met in November of the same year and opened the campaign against absolutism by impeaching Strafford. Before two years were passed, the Civil War had begun; in 1645 the Royalists were decisively defeated at Naseby; in January, 1649, the King was beheaded and the Commonwealth proclaimed.

The Puritan motive to emigration developed rapidly during those first four years, with the development of the King's ecclesiastical policy, which in a mainly Puritan Parliament took a foremost place among the grievances that Charles refused to remedy. In the eleven years of absolutist rule the emigration proceeded apace. With the opening of the Civil War it practically ceased. Throughout, the Puritan flow was to New England where a Puritan community was already established, while the not inactive non-Puritan flow was directed to the Virginian quarter, so that in those years the North and the South developed the special characteristics which made them two distinct types.

There is, however, still another factor to be reviewed before we embark on the main narrative, the factor of foreign relations and—associated therewith—of naval power. James, until about two years before his death, had suffered from one constant obsession—the hope of co-operation with Spain; a hope that was always futile, because Spanish aims and English aims were not only incompatible but irreconcileable. But from the final breakdown of the Spanish marriage project, Spain was either looked upon as an enemy or wholly ignored.

Europe was absorbed in the continental complications of the Thirty Years' War, and ignored England, whose domestic discords thoroughly paralysed her for European activities, though until the baleful influence of Buckingham was removed by his assassination in 1628 Charles had persisted in misdirected, costly and entirely futile interventions, to the contemptuous annoyance of Richelieu, who was doing for France what Wentworth —as soon as Buckingham was gone—tried to do for England. Charles, and even Buckingham, had genuine aspirations for the development of the navy, but the English administration had become so thoroughly corrupt under James that nothing short of an extremely drastic reform—which was not forthcoming—could have prevented its continuous decay. And meanwhile the Dutch, in the full flush of their triumph over Spain, were concentrating all their energies on establishing their own Maritime supremacy—the necessary condition of holding their own as a European Power. The Dutch expansion, however, did not threaten armed collision with the English—except for a moment, over the Amboyna affair—till England's Puritan soldiery had transformed her into the regicide republic.

From the beginning of his reign, Charles was suspect, from the Puritan point of view. In the first place the fact was conspicuous that he was entirely under the influence of Buckingham; who was the husband of a Roman Catholic wife, and was himself the incarnation of everything that most stank in the nostrils of Puritanism, except in the single point of his very recently developed hostility to Spain. In the second place, Charles immediately married the young French King's sister Henrietta Maria, the child of a zealously Roman Catholic Court, given to the forms of frivolity most offensive to rigid Puritans. In the third place he was notoriously attached devotedly to that school of Churchmanship which to Puritan eyes meant merely disguised Romanism; whereas the late King, however tolerant of Romanism he might wish to be, had never been suspected of leanings to Roman Catholic doctrine.

Puritan suspicions and denunciations only hardened Charles in his dislike of Puritans and his determination to repress Puritanism; ecclesiastical promotion and advancement to positions of authority were denied to Puritans—as they had not been under James—and were lavished on those divines who in preaching and practice were most antagonistic to Puritanism. It became quickly evident that the anti-Puritan stringency with which the ecclesiastical laws would be applied would make it impossible for all more rigid Puritans to remain much longer within the fold of the Church of England unless the King could be forced to reverse his policy. New England offered the way of escape, and the stream of emigration was beginning to flow at the moment when Charles dissolved his third Parliament and entered upon his eleven years of absolute rule.

II

The stream may be said to have started when the Massachusetts Company was incorporated by a royal charter in March, 1629. The Company itself, however, was a development from an Association originally formed in Dorchester, which had obtained from the New England Company its patent for the occupation of the Massachusetts territory in the neighbourhood of New Plymouth; several concessions having been made, as we saw, to private adventurers, on a small scale. Commerce and religion provided the mingled motive of the first enterprise, started in 1623, which met with little immediate success. The six original grantees, however, had a bolder vision of possible developments and a growing conviction of the coming tightening of intolerable ecclesiastical bonds at home, and it was clearly with intent to create a sort of religious commonwealth (though with no present idea of political separation) that their scheme took shape in the provisions of the Massachusetts Charter, the principal members of the new company being the joint partners to whom the New England Company had granted the previous patent.

The new Company also presents us with a new departure in colonial methods. The Charter vested complete authority in the Governor and Company as constituted, but for the first time it contained no clause locating the corporation in England; that is, it contained nothing to prevent the governing body itself from being located in America. The governing body consisted of a Governor, Deputy Governor and a Council of eighteen known as the "Assistants," to be elected annually by the Company, which was to hold periodical general meetings. Land was allotted at the start, on a fixed scale to emigrating shareholders, to accepted emigrants who were not shareholders, and to "old planters" already settled—since there was considerable confusion over the new grant and the existing titles under previous patents. The Company was a close body; there was no right of admission to membership, and acquisition of land as an emigrant did not carry membership with it. It forthwith delegated its absolute powers to a Governor and Council acting on the spot, and very shortly afterwards its members all either transplanted themselves or retired, so that there was left in England no body representing it. To all intents and purposes the colony was from the outset a self-governing community, apart from prerogative rights of the Crown, though its Government was of a highly oligarchical order. The Governor and Council could make and enforce laws provided that they were not at variance with the laws of England; their jurisdiction covered the whole territorial area granted under the charter; they appointed all officers; they could make provision for military defence and regulate all relations with the natives; while they were responsible only to the Crown (remotely), and to the General Assembly in respect of its powers of election. They could regulate admission to the full membership which carried the franchise, and admission to the community which did not convey the franchise; and in practice they could exercise entire control of religion. That is to say, there was nothing in the charter of "The Governor and Company of the Massachusetts Bay in New England," which precluded them from doing these things.

The organisers and leading spirits of the new colony were men of a very different type from the Independents of Leyden and New Plymouth. They had not in England severed themselves from the Church on the principle that the individual or the congregation must claim spiritual liberty from external control in the exercise of religion; they were devotees of compulsory uniformity, but of that particular type of uniformity which commanded their own approval, the type which they would—if they could—have made dominant in the Established Church. They found that they could no longer cling to the hope of doing so in England; but in a distant land, beyond the reach of Arminian bishops such as the rapidly rising Laud, and of the Court of High Commission, where they would have the moulding of the new colony in their own hands, they could hope to shape the Church to their own model of uniformity, which would be at least on Presbyterian lines. That the colony should be in effect a congregation like Plymouth, or a multitude of congregations and uncontrolled sectaries each claiming freedom of conscience and freedom of criticism, was the last thing in their

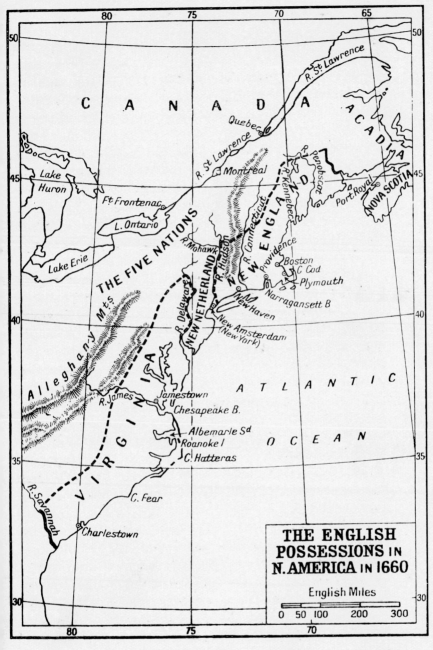

THE ENGLISH
POSSESSIONS IN
N. AMERICA IN 1660

English Miles

0   50  100        200        300

[*Face page* 134

minds. In effect, if they could carry out their intention, it would be not only a colony, but a single self-controlled Church under the direction of the governing body— and the governing body would be not a democracy but the group who organised the emigration from 1629 onward. Whether they would quite, even to themselves, have admitted that this was their aim is another question, but it was certainly the logical outcome of their methods.

These leaders, however, were not the original six partners who had laid the foundations on which the Massachusetts Company was to rise. They had already established a settlement; one of their number, John Endicott, had gone out in charge of it, and remained always a prominent and active member of its Government, but the rest retired when the Company took the definite resolution to transfer itself bodily from England to America. The stock of those who were not prepared personally to act upon that resolution was taken over by ten of the members of the enlarged company who had joined it because they intended to emigrate and to find in the colony a larger scope for their political, religious and administrative energies than England under the rule of Charles, Laud, and the "apostate" Wentworth could be expected to provide. Thus the first "governor" of the Company, appointed under the Charter, Matthew Cradock, retired, and his place was taken by John Winthrop, who from that time became the dominant figure, and the embodiment in his own person of the policy and aspirations of the Massachusetts Colony. It is clear that the old members were already prepared to acquiesce in the change when the proposal was submitted by Cradock himself to the new Company a few weeks after it received its Charter; it is clear that the new members, joining for the extension, had come in with the purpose of emigrating; and the obvious inference is that the scheme of wholesale emigration was privately understood, but not publicly avowed till after the charter had been secured, lest avowal should compromise the chances of obtaining a charter free from the usual clause pinning the headquarters of the Company to England.

The fundamentally oligarchical character of the scheme is evident in the fact that the "Governor and Company" who took over the charter on Matthew Cradock's proposition were twelve persons, in whom all the powers, legislative, administrative and judicial, were vested; the election of the governor and the appointment of the assistants were in their hands; the admission of new members was virtually in their hands. The conditions on which they acted, of admission to the "freedom of the Company" meant that they would still be able to control the appointments of Governor and assistants. Thus the whole Government for practical purposes was a close body; and the persons of whom it was composed were men of substance, of very much the same type as those of whom the English House of Commons was composed at the same period —or would have been, had it been sitting. At the moment the Company consisted of those twelve members, who elected John Winthrop their governor, and appointed the assistants.

Meanwhile John Endicott, an original member, wholly in sympathy with the new movement, having already emigrated, was, as he had been for some while, the acting governor on the spot. He had gone out with sixty companions in September, 1628, making his headquarters at Salem; the Company received its charter in the following March; it sent out a preliminary batch of emigrants at midsummer; in September the reconstruction of the Company was completed; and the

new Government with Winthrop and nine hu..
settlers arrived at Salem in June, 1630.

Endicott had been preparing the way. There were
"old planters" before him, with claims resting on
patents granted by the New England Company, which
had to be in some way compromised—among them
Morton who had returned to his Merrymount. Endicott
illustrated the quality which was to be predominant in
the new régime by his treatment of Merrymount. He
could not suppress the planters' trading rights, but he
did rigorously enforce the Puritan theory of discipline.
He hewed down and cast into the fire the ungodly
Maypole which the unregenerate settlers had raised (to
the scandal of Plymouth) and Merrymount was anathe-
matised as Mount Dagon. When the Company was
chartered, he was appointed Governor by the Company
in England, with a Council of Assistants, of whom three
were to be chosen by the Old Planters. For the spiritual
needs of the colonists, three ministers were sent out
with the first three hundred settlers. There were
instructions too for Endicott. The Old Planters were
to be confirmed in their estates and admitted to the
freedom of the Company which meant no more than
that they would have a voice in the election of the
Council. Tobacco growing was not to be suppressed
but rigidly restricted—as we have observed in relation
to Virginia, it was an industry condemned by
mercantilist economics; as well as by Puritanism, as a
pandering to demoralising carnal appetites. As to
relations with the Indians, common-sense rather than
sentiment, policy rather than Puritanism, prevailed.
Intercourse with them was not to be encouraged; firearms were not to be sold; drink might be, but "so
ordered as that the savages may not, for our lucre's
sake, be reduced (seduced?) to the excessive use or

K

rather abuse of it." Most important was the rule that land should be acquired from the Indians only by legal and formal purchase; which was not only in the nature of a safeguard for the natives, but conferred a title that was practically not to be challenged. The transfer had not yet taken place when this consignment of emigrants arrived; it included members having authority who were not of the straitest sect of the Puritans. It must be borne in mind that ecclesiastical separation was not theoretically in the programme; the Plymouth folk were avowed sectaries, but the Massachusetts Company were Nonconformists whose demand was for conformity to their own views. For most of them, but not for all, those views included disapproval of the Liturgy; and when some recalcitrants insisted on the use of the Church services, Endicott had the majority at his back in telling them that the Colony was "no place for them" if they remained obdurate. Practically the working principle was to be the exclusion from the freedom of the Company of Independents on the one side and on the other of those whose Puritanism was not sufficiently pronounced to satisfy the ruling body. The ruling body claimed in effect not only absolute secular authority but also absolute authority for the regulation of religious doctrine and moral conduct according to its own rigid and narrow but generally lofty standards.

### III

In June, 1630, Winthrop arrived, with the largest batch of emigrants that had yet been sent out to any colony; bringing the numbers (exclusive of Old Planters) up to about 1,200, many of the earlier arrivals having died. Winthrop and most of the Assistants were men of education, of good if not distinguished families,

landed proprietors at home before their exodus fr⟨...⟩
land where the prospects of the righteous were n⟨...⟩
promising. Winthrop certainly seems to have regarded
himself as fleeing from the wrath to come. He was
an Elizabethan, one of that large class of country gentlemen which had come into being with the distribution
of the monastic lands; born in the Armada year, with
a clear conviction that papistry in general and the
Jesuits in particular were the special instruments and
agents of Antichrist. He was also a lawyer who had
resigned some small office by reason of his religious
opinions; conscious, it would seem, of possessing
administrative abilities which were unlikely to find
scope in England, he had thrown himself zealously
into the new project—though we may surmise that if
he had remained at home, he might have made his
mark among the men of the Long Parliament. The
Deputy-governor Humphrey and one of the Assistants,
Isaac Johnson, were brothers-in-law of the Earl of
Lincoln, whose wife's brother was Nathaniel Fiennes,
one of the "Five Members" whom Charles in 1642
failed to arrest: another Assistant, Dudley, had been
the steward of Lincoln's estates. These names are a
sufficient indication of the home-status of the men who
founded Massachusetts.

The company who came in Winthrop's ships consisted of settlers with their wives and households, in
many cases including hired servants, gentlemen,
tradesmen, and yeomen, artisans such as would find
plenty to do in a community of the kind contemplated,
all folk who, whatever their prejudices, took a serious
view of life and its responsibilities, holding carnal
pleasures in small esteem at the best, and at worst as
temptations of the Devil; counting hard work under
the new conditions as a matter of course. They were

not in search of ease, but not a few of them found that
the new conditions were more severe than their courage
or their strength could cope with; food ran short,
though there was nothing like the starvation from which
the early Virginians had suffered, and Winthrop was
prompt to send for further supplies from England.
There was a particularly sharp winter; and though
the great majority held out with a commendable
stubbornness, there were yet many who resolved to
throw up the struggle and departed at the first opportunity, exciting the contempt of the stouter-hearted. Nevertheless, the numbers rose to 2,000 in 1631. But it was
not till 1633, the year in which Laud was translated
from London to Canterbury, that the stream of emigration began to swell into a growing tide; by midsummer of 1634 the population of the colony had risen
to 4,000; eight years later it had again quadrupled.

King Charles had been ready enough to give his
assent to a movement which seemed likely to remove
from England a number of persons who might become
actively troublesome in England, apart from the
general inclination, inherited from his father, to favour
expansion. Two considerations, however, were leading
him to a change of view. First in some quarters, alarm
was roused by the signs that a large number of
economically valuable citizens were making up their
minds to leave the country permanently. The economists
who for the last forty years had talked of colonies as
making provision for the surplus population had meant
people who were economically superfluous; now,
England had recovered from the displacement of agricultural labour under the early Tudors which had
slowly enough adjusted itself during Elizabeth's reign
and after the Poor-law enacted at the end of it. As for
the masterless adventurers and ne'er-do-weels who had

lost the outlet for their energies provided by the
maritime war, they would not find admission to Puri
settlements. The "surplus population" could not be
turned over to them; and to encourage the emigration
of an efficient and industrious population was another
matter. In the second place, Charles and Laud were
turning to the idea that it was their duty to impose
the ecclesiastical law of England upon the Englishmen
over-sea as well as at home, and to check the establishment of communities which obviously intended to
disregard the ecclesiastical authorities in England.

Hence a tendency now appears to threaten an embargo
upon Puritan emigration, and a manifest disposal on
the part of Charles to exercise the Crown's powers of
Colonial regulation actively. Four years had passed
with no Parliament to challenge arbitrary rule, when
he set up a Commission for the Plantations with Laud
as president, endowed with almost unlimited powers,
which if it had functioned would have given a different
turn to colonial and especially to New England
development. It did not as a matter of fact function
effectively, because both the King's and the Archbishop's activities were too thoroughly absorbed by
affairs in England and Scotland—Wentworth was taking
care of Ireland; so that the only practical effect of the
change of attitude was to give a fresh impulse to Puritan
emigration, more emphatically to alienate the Puritan
colonies from the Crown, and to intensify their special
character.

From the summer of 1630, the occupation of fresh
territory proceeded apace. The headquarters of the
Government were transferred from Salem to Boston.
New settlements meant new "townships," and problems
as to rights of citizenship; and the system was regulated
in 1631. Administration and taxation were in the

hands of the Governor, Deputy Governor, and Assistants, elected by the freemen of the Company in Assembly, where they were represented by three delegates from each township. Admission to the freedom of the Company was restricted to persons who were members of existing "churches,"—which meant not sects but religious communities all of which were under control of the Government; residence in the colony did not necessarily involve church-membership, admission to church-membership was conditional upon a rigid scrutiny of religious views and moral character, but only church-members could be freemen, only freemen enjoyed the franchise, while all residents whatsoever were under the jurisdiction of the Government. In 1634, however, it was successfully claimed that the power of legislation and taxation was vested not in the governing body but in the Assembly of freemen which was to meet four times a year.

It was in fact open to question how far the arrangements were in strict accord with the terms of the charter and how far the authority conveyed warranted the authority exercised—lawyers to-day will come to diverse conclusions on these questions, as they did and do over the legality of the proceedings on both sides in the contemporary conflict between Crown and Parliament. A strong and consistent Government was a necessity. The Governors were in such circumstances apt to interpret the law as the exigencies of the situation rather than a pedantic legalism demanded, and were naturally and often justifiably accused of exercising their powers in illegal and arbitrary fashion. Harmony did not always prevail among them; but though occasionally Winthrop was displaced from the governorship, he was always brought back after a brief interval. Perhaps the most interesting of these episodes was the governorship of young Harry Vane, later a prominent member of the Long Parliament and of the Rump; who on his arrival in 1636 was appointed Governor (by way of a judicious compliment to his father, the King's Secretary of State) with Winthrop as Deputy. Vane, however, was a fervent reformer, and forthwith associated himself with a remarkable lady, Mrs. Anne Hutchinson, whose peculiar religious views were causing trouble; with the result that next year Winthrop was re-elected in his place and Vane returned to England.

IV

Anne Hutchinson was one of two persons whose expulsion from the colony on grounds of religious differences led to the birth of the separate settlements which became Rhode Island, in which the settlers were off-shoots from Massachusetts. The first was Roger Williams, a preacher who came into collision with the authorities, and to avoid deportation to England went off on his own account, but, failing to make himself acceptable at Plymouth, established himself with a few followers on Narragansett Bay, purchasing his land from the Indians, and named his community Providence, in 1535. There Massachusetts left him to his own devices. Just at this time, Mrs. Anne Hutchinson, whose husband was eminently respectable but otherwise of no particular account, was developing the peculiar theories which caused the trouble in Vane's governor-ship. It was not till after his retirement that the Massachusett's Government resolved on her expulsion. With her went William Coddington (himself an Assistant) and a considerable company of her supporters. They planted themselves on an island, which they named Rhode Island, off Narragansett Bay, but did not join forces with Williams. Anne herself with her household was subsequently murdered by Indian raiders—an event which Winthrop complacently regarded as a Divine judgement. These two independent communities had in fact no legal status, but later, during the civil-war period, combined under the governorship of Roger Williams, and were ultimately recognised as the Colony of Rhode Island.

Connecticut, which takes its name from the river which flows from north to south on the west of the Massachusetts settlements, was also founded from Massachusetts by emigrants who were dissatisfied with the Government—and probably also realised that the Connecticut territory was more promising—though there was no active quarrel. The lower Connecticut was outside the area of the Massachusetts' grant, so that no serious objection could be raised. One of the principal founders, Haynes, had himself held Winthrop's place as Governor for a year. The movement began in 1635; incidentally it involved a war with the Indian tribe of the Pequods, who were in effect exterminated with the assistance of their enemies, the Mohicans and Narragansetts. A collision was also threatened with the Dutch from New Amsterdam, who had some claim to prior occupation; but this came to nothing. Yet another settlement was made at New Haven, some miles to the west of the Connecticut estuary, in 1638. This originated in England, where some Parliamentary leaders, among whom were Pym and Hampden, had obtained a grant of land from Warwick who at the time was president of the New England Council. They in fact did nothing beyond sending out a pioneering expedition, which ultimately coalesced with Connecticut; but the actual founders of New Haven, a band of Puritans who came out to Boston in 1637, transferred themselves to the new quarters a few months after their arrival, and formed a separate self-governing community.

Like Massachusetts and Plymouth, New Haven, Connecticut and Rhode Island were all intensely Puritan, though with some variation of type; but none of the three held its territory by any legal title. North of the Merrimac, however, the territories afterwards known as Maine and New Hampshire were being occupied, not by Puritans, under patents granted by the New England Council, in accordance with its habit, to miscellaneous applicants. John Mason, a friend of Buckingham and an ex-governor of Newfoundland, started settlements near the Merrimac river which were vigorously Anglican in character; but Massachusetts presently found occasion to claim that they lay within its own bounds and they were absorbed into it by a compromise which for the first time admitted a non-Puritan element into the major colony. Maine is connected chiefly with the name of Ferdinando Gorges who was always a promoter of colonisation. He had been the moving spirit in the original Plymouth Council and its reconstruction as the Council for New England; he had interested himself in the Puritan colonies; he had ideas of getting himself appointed Governor-General of all the New England settlements; and finally he procured from Charles in 1639 a charter constituting him Lord Proprietor of Maine, subject only to the powers of the Commission for Plantations (to which previous allusion has been made).

Here, however, we must turn to the relations between French and English colonists in the debatable territory on the north. As early as 1613, Argall, acting in the service of the old Plymouth Council, had attacked the French settlement at Port Royal on the Bay of Fundy.

In 1612, James I, more or less to provide an outlet for the people of his northern kingdom, had given a patent for New Scotland or Nova Scotia to Sir William Alexander. Little enough in the way of settlement resulted; but Charles on his accession confirmed the patent, instituting the Order of Nova Scotia baronets—a cash transaction in which the baronets bought their titles and a grant of land in the Colony, which otherwise hardly materialised. The whole territory, of course, was claimed both by the English crown which had granted the patents and by the French crown which had granted the French patents, while there was no established system of International Law under which either could claim an incontrovertible title. Each claimed occupation of the whole, while each had in fact occupied some fragments so far as the planting of very small trading settlements constituted occupation.

The New Plymouth colonists had planted such a trading station on the Penobscot river. In 1627, Buckingham plunged England into a war with France by intervening on behalf of the French Huguenots at Rochelle who were defying the Government of Cardinal Richelieu. In 1631, a French privateer looked in at Penobscot—which had no suspicion of his intentions and could have offered no resistance if it had—and very politely carried off everything there was to take. English privateers on the other hand reduced Quebec to surrender, and possession was taken of it; but in 1632, Charles, lacking the means to carry on the futile war, made peace, restoring Quebec, and withdrawing the English claim to Acadia, though it was ere long to be revived. New Plymouth nevertheless restored her factory at Penobscot. The French Governor claiming that it was on French soil, seized it by force in 1635, the two countries being at peace. Plymouth sent her navy—two ships—to recover it; but the commanding officer wasted nearly all his powder and shot, beginning "to shoot at distance like a madman, and did them no hurt at all." She then appealed to Massachusetts for armed support, but the application failed, and the factory was abandoned.

V

A new phase arrived for the colonies in America with the crisis of the constitutional struggle at home in 1641. Strafford fell, Laud was imprisoned, and in the next year the great Civil War began. The administrative machinery was in the hands of the Long Parliament which continued to sit at Westminster, and a Parliamentary Commission for Plantations with the Puritan Warwick (now the Parliamentary Admiral) at its head took the place of Laud's Commission—machinery which had been in the hands of the King. Hitherto, however, active intervention by the Crown in colonial affairs—though circumstances had fettered it—had always been a possibility with which the colonies had to reckon, and its authority would have been difficult to challenge however severely its action might be criticised. But now, until the definite and decisive fall of the Monarchy, it was more than doubtful whether the authority of the new Commission had legal validity, and quite certain that Parliament would have neither the means nor the leisure to enforce it. For the time being, there was no authority to which the several colonial Governments could feel themselves responsible; each was practically sovereign—and it was difficult to judge which, in the future, would prove to have been the more dangerous, acknowledgment or repudiation of the Parliament's authority.

In the second place, the flood of emigration was

stopped. It was noted above that in 1642 the sixty Salem colonists of 1628 had become approximately 16,000; but the overflow from Massachusetts, slightly supplemented from England and elsewhere, had given to Plymouth, the Rhode Island communities, Connecticut and Newhaven, and the more northern settlements, collectively, a population not much less than that of Massachusetts—all, with few exceptions, essentially Puritan in type. Non-Puritans had betaken themselves elsewhere. But now in England the battle was joined between Puritanism and Royalism; for Puritans and Royalists alike, emigration would be desertion. The tendency was rather to re-migration than to emigration. But while the sympathies of practically all New Englanders were of course with their Puritan brethren at home, they doubtless felt that they must make ready for the contingency of a Royalist victory, menacing to their own religious liberties; so the homeward stream was no more than a rivulet. This consciousness was probably, though not avowedly, the decisive factor in begetting the New England Confederation.

It had, in fact, been fairly obvious for some time past that some sort of machinery for joint action and some degree of co-operation was desirable—some recognised method of arbitration in boundary and other disputes between independent communities, a common policy in relation to the Indian tribes, and also to the French on one side and the Dutch on the other. On the other hand, there had been two standing difficulties in the way. One was the moral certainty that any recognisable attempts at combination among the Puritan groups would inflame the hostility of Laud's Commission and bring about its active intervention in colonial affairs; the other was the particularism, the dislike to surrendering any fraction of independence, on the part of each individual group, whether as a political or a religious community. The first of these had now disappeared, and with its disappearance came the sense that the colonies would be in a better position to resist its possible revival as presenting a united front than as separate units. The particularist difficulty could be overcome only by a mutual readiness for give-and-take compromises which is apt to be the outcome rather of common fears of a common menace than of such unqualified goodwill as eliminates jealousy and suspicion, the deadliest enemies of union. In 1643 the sense of mutual dependence proved strong enough to effect a union, which had actually been mooted as early as 1638, though practically it did not survive the Restoration.

The Confederation which then took shape declined to recognise the Rhode Island communities, which in the first place were not a single body and in the second were regarded by the other four—Massachusetts, New Plymouth, Connecticut and New Haven, which formed the league—as unorthodox. The first of these four was as large as the other three put together; but all were equally represented in the Federal Commission, on which each had two Commissioners. For a binding vote, six of the eight Commissioners must be in agreement. In practice, however, Massachusetts continued to act by herself if the Federal body refused to co-operate; in view of her size and her effective power, she had some right to object to being overridden by the other three. Practically the Confederation was a league of four independent States for defensive and if necessary for offensive purposes, but without powers over its separate members in any other direction. And it entirely ignored the possibility of intervention from England.

# CHAPTER VIII

## THE PLANTATION COLONIES UNDER CHARLES I

### I

ALTHOUGH Puritanism provided the leading motive for the colonisation of New England, initiated by the Leyden Independents while King James was still on the throne, the southward movement to the sub-tropical and tropical regions was almost but not altogether devoid of the Puritan element. The desire for religious freedom was in part present as a motive; but those who sought it were not Protestant Nonconformists or Independents but Roman Catholics for whom there was no place among the correct Protestants of Virginia, and still less among the New Englanders, whose views on toleration were, as we have seen, extremely limited. Yet even to this general rule we find one curious exception in an attempt of Puritan origin to organise a naval base deep in the Gulf of Mexico off the coast of the most central part of Central America. The attempt failed; perhaps it is generally forgotten; but it was not without interest—and significance. If, however, we are to reckon it in the Puritan category, it is only because its inception had a Puritan origin; the religious element does not appear to have been, as in New England, fundamental in its development.

We have seen Virginia in the troublous years of its birth and its infancy under the Virginia Company, which before its decease had introduced in practice something like the normal methods of English government, with a representative Assembly and an executive responsible to a supreme authority—the Company; their relations corresponding to those of Parliament and the Crown as commonly understood at the beginning of the seventeenth century. In the last year of James I the Company was eliminated and its delegated authority reverted to the Crown. From this time the growth and development of Virginia were continuous, because in practice they were for many years to come less liable to be interfered with by fluctuations in the policy of a supreme authority whose energies and interests were too profoundly engaged elsewhere to be actively or continuously concerned with them. For practical purposes, and for the time, the effect of the change was that the colony, like those of New England, was left to develop itself without effective intervention by a superior authority on the other side of the Atlantic. When, after the Restoration, that superior authority attempted to re-assert itself, friction arose, but the practice of self-government was too firmly established to be effectively or permanently over-ridden.

Apart from the stray settlements under the New England Council's patents, New Plymouth, with its numbers below three hundred, was the only mainland colony besides Virginia, with its twelve hundred, when Charles succeeded his father and completed the dissolution of the Virginia Company. Sir Francis Wyatt, as Governor, with the existing council was left to carry on the government—with a tacit acquiescence in, but no open recognition of, the Assembly which had come into being under the recent régime. The conflict between Charles and his successive Parliaments began forthwith; but it was one which had no Virginian repercussions. The Virginians had gone across the ocean actuated by exclusively secular motives though no doubt some of them were interested in the idea of converting the heathen. Serious Nonconformity made no appeal to them, nor were they disposed to murmur against the ecclesiastical regulations enforced in England. On their own account they were much more likely to repress than to encourage Puritan irregularities; besides, it was still some years before Charles passed from his father's attitude of tolerance towards Nonconformity so long as it was far enough away to be conveniently negligible. There was nothing which could excite the King or Buckingham to meddle with transatlantic affairs except vague visions of pecuniary profit in their financial difficulties.

This, in fact, was the only serious subject of anxiety from the Virginian point of view. Virginia had one product of great value to the planters—tobacco. The output of tobacco rose, in the ten years from 1617 to 1627, from 20,000 lb. to half a million lb. The regulation of the growth and export was for many reasons desirable. In any case it was evidently extremely profitable to the planters and exporters, but it was condemned from a national point of view by mercantilist economics, and on the other hand it offered the Crown a sort of standing invitation to annex at least a very substantial share of the profits; to the detriment of the Virginians who were already there, and of the attractions of Virginia for new settlers.

The granting of monopolies to Court favourites or through Court favourites had become during the last reign an abuse so grave that even Buckingham, who had derived much profit from it, had yielded to the outcry against them, but it was a practice which, skilfully handled, might be extremely profitable to the

Crown; and the risk of a tobacco monopoly being created was a serious one. It would, however, have provided a fresh grievance for Parliament to exploit so flagrant that if Charles ever actually contemplated it he let the project drop; and though he made sundry attempts to arrive at a bargain with the planters, they were able to hold out for terms which would have brought the Crown so little profit that no agreement could be reached.

The appointment of Wyatt to the governorship was a fortunate one. The moment was critical; for the Indian rising of 1623 had brought a rude awakening to the planters from the sense of easy security which had been prevalent, and had also brought to light the danger of exclusive dependence upon the tobacco-culture which was at once the lightest and the most lucrative occupation for the colonists. The management of Wyatt, well supported by his council, restored confidence; judicious measures for defensive con-centrations and judicious treatment of the natives restored peaceful relations though not the over-confident amity of the preceding years. Regulations were made for the tobacco-growing, which improved the quality of the crop, checked the easy habit of continuously exhausting the soil, and at the same time increased the necessary cultivation of corn, though little or no progress was made in the development of other less lucrative industries needed to make the colony self-supporting—it relied upon the export of tobacco to provide the power of purchasing the goods it did not produce for itself. When Wyatt retired in 1626 his place was again taken by George Yeardley, the Governor who had inaugurated the substitution of the representative system for the old military rule, and was well enough fitted to preside over its development,

L

as a competent and sympathetic but not otherwise
remarkable administrator. Roseate reports of the joys
of the planter's life began to be spread abroad in
England, representing Virginia as something more
like paradise than a strictly accurate attention to facts
would perhaps have warranted; but they had the
desired effect of bringing out fresh emigrants, and of
a corresponding expansion of occupied territory.
Yeardley was succeeded, on his death after a year of
office, by Harvey—a courtier who quarrelled with most
of the leading men in the colony, made himself very
unpopular without succeeding in doing serious harm,
and was in effect deposed and sent home after a stormy
scene in the Council, by the popular leaders, in 1635.
His appeal to the Crown resulted in his being sent
back as Governor for four years more, during which
he continued to quarrel in Virginia and send querulous
complaints to England, still without serious consequences.
For in 1639 the King's and Laud's ecclesiastical policy
in Scotland brought on the "Bishops' War" followed
next year by the summoning first of the Short, and then
of the Long, Parliament. So far as concerned England,
all colonial questions were in practical abeyance for
another decade.

II

The principal questions which vexed the souls of
the Virginians during Harvey's governorship were
concerned with the new Colony of Maryland and
encroachments upon territory claimed by Virginia as
falling within her own jurisdiction. On the southern
border of the premier Plantation, a colonising charter
was granted to the Attorney-General, Sir Robert
Heath, under the name of Carolana, but that infant
was still-born; Carolina actually came into being only

after the Restoration. The second Plantation colony, on the northern border of Virginia, was in its inception the work of the first Lord Baltimore, George Calvert; its execution was left to his son and successor, Cecilius. In two respects it differed from any preceding attempt since the death of Elizabeth; the grantee was not a company but an individual, and a basic principle of its government was inclusive religious toleration. For the Calverts were Roman Catholics; English Protestant sentiment, however divided, was united in this, that it put entirely out of reach the authorisation of an exclusively Catholic colony; and so, if Catholicism was to be tolerated, no form of Protestantism could be excluded. The primary object of its founders was to provide for their co-religionists an asylum where they would be free from the repressive laws enforced in England; so that it was only by the adoption of the principle of toleration that their aim could be attained.

George Calvert, one of the minor ministers of James I, was one of the few zealous supporters of the King's pet project of a Spanish marriage for the Prince of Wales. When that scheme collapsed in 1623, he retired, declaring himself a convert to the unpopular religion. James favoured him with an Irish peerage as Baron Baltimore, and with a grant of land in Newfoundland, independent of the still existing Newfoundland company. Baltimore, now debarred from political activity in England, turned his mild ambitions to the New World; but he could make nothing of Newfoundland, and in 1629 he sought to transfer himself and his colonists to Virginian territory. But Virginia would have none of him; the Virginian Assembly required him to take the Oaths of Supremacy and Allegiance, which no conscientious Catholic could do. Their legal title to exact the oaths was more than doubtful, but their action served its immediate purpose. Baltimore withdrew; but he was not to be baulked. The personal favour in which he was held by Charles procured for him a charter from the King granting him on the north of Virginia territory not in actual occupation by the colony but including a great tract covered by the defunct Company's charter, with a very inadequately defined boundary. The Maryland charter—*Terra Mariae*, named in honour of the Queen—had hardly been granted in 1632 when Baltimore died, and the rights passed to his heir; the sons, like their father being Roman Catholics, the main purpose with which the charter had been obtained remained unaltered. Cecilius Calvert was not a man of genius or an enthusiastic idealist, but he was conscientious, he was in earnest, and he was level-headed. He knew that he could not make his colony a Roman Catholic stronghold as Rochelle and other privileged towns in France had been Huguenot strongholds till Richelieu broke them; but he meant to make it a secure asylum to which Roman Catholics would, and zealous Protestants by preference would not, naturally congregate in the confident expectation of enjoying their religion undisturbed; an aggressive religious attitude would make his colony the target for Protestant zealots and even for Protestant moderates. For the rest, he intended his colony to pay. Unobtrusive but watchful moderation in all things was the condition of success in achieving the main object; it was the line of least resistance and the line of safety; and he followed it with a cool-headed persistence which at times required courage and self-sacrifice, but by no means prevented him from taking full advantage of doubtful legal technicalities when occasion served. Consequently the story of the colonisation of Maryland is not conspicuously picturesque or heroic, but it does present us with the one marked success of the principle of toleration in an age generally notable for partisan intolerance.

The second distinctive feature of Maryland is that it was the first successful "proprietary" colony, the first, that is, in which complete authority was legally vested in the proprietor to whom the Crown had granted the estate, not in a corporate body. Such had been Ralegh's charter, and such, in fact, had been George Calvert's Newfoundland Charter; but in all cases the colonising attempt had failed. Under the Maryland Charter, the proprietor's jurisdiction was virtually absolute, subject only to the regular saving clause against contravening public policy or the laws of England, and another requiring all churches to be consecrated according to the Anglican rite—doubtless inserted as security against the charge of sanctioning papistry; and there was a clause expressly providing for immunity from all taxation by the Crown. The proprietors had full power of legislation and taxation with the advice, assent and approval of the freemen; but who the freemen were and how they were to be consulted was not laid down—in practice the term was treated as equivalent to freeholder.

Virginia, of course, entered protests. The charter was an infraction of what she regarded as her own territorial rights; the powers conferred on the neighbouring colony might be embarrassing to her own Government and might jeopardise relations with the Indians which demanded expert and delicate handling. Charles had not yet set up Laud's Commission for the Plantations, and the appeal was to the Privy Council, which contented itself with recommending amicable conference and agreement between the parties, with an appeal to the Courts on disputed points of law, and enjoining the Virginians to receive their new neighbours in a friendly and helpful spirit—whereof their treatment of the late Lord Baltimore offered little promise, though obviously the advice was piously sound.

The band of settlers for Maryland, three hundred in number, under Leonard Calvert as his brother's representative—Baltimore himself remained in England —landed in the spring of 1634. Governor Harvey received them with what in other circumstances would have been no more than ordinary courtesy, the friendliness commended by the Privy Council—and thereby intensified his own unpopularity with the Virginians, whose resentment was high against the Maryland project. From the start there was hot dispute between Virginians and Marylanders, chiefly in relation to the Virginian occupation, already established, of land claimed as lying within the charter-area of Maryland; Harvey's attitude in the matter brought his unpopularity to a head and doubtless had a large share in accounting for his forcible deposition and dismissal to England next year. But the King's Government in England during the "eleven years' tyranny" was all on the side of Maryland and of Harvey; the Governor, as we have seen, was restored to his office next year, and the Maryland claim was confirmed. This friction over Kent Island, the station which a leading Virginian, William Cleburn or Clayborne (in the early seventeenth century the spelling of surnames varied indefinitely, Shakespeare and Ralegh providing particularly notable examples) had occupied as an advanced post, was decided in favour of Maryland by indisputable superior authority in England, but it continued to rankle till the royalist sentiment in both the colonies made them patch up the local quarrel, when Parliamentary and Royalist privateers began fighting each other off the American shores; but direct conflict was avoided.

Neither the unpopularity of Governor Harvey nor the advent of the Marylanders checked the expansion and development of Virginia. The sense of insecurity born of the Indian war had passed, tobacco planting continued to be extremely profitable, and corn-growing advanced so that the colony ceased to be dependent on supplies from oversea or scanty margins procurable from possibly hostile Indians. The famines from which Virginia suffered so much not only in the first pioneer days but during and following the Indian conflict, were a nightmare that had passed, and there was corn to spare for export. Tobacco culture favoured large estates, and the abundance of waterways provided by navigable rivers gave the planters easy carriage for their goods almost from their own doors without need for concentrating. The proprietor of a large estate could live as patriarchally among his dependants as the lord of an English manor; the dependants were quite as well off as the rural labourer in England, and it was not difficult —as it was in England—to become the proprietor of a large estate. Estates were sufficiently grouped to pass for townships, after the Indian war, for the avoidance of a too dangerous isolation, but a township did not mean what we mean by a town or anything remotely resembling one; whereas the life of a planter did resemble not too remotely the life of an English country gentleman. The colony in short offered agreeable openings for younger sons.

But the country could not be populated by younger sons, while it did not attract the yeomen class who, if disposed to emigration, were more likely to be drawn to the Puritan settlements. There was room, however, for a few skilled artisans, and, on the plantations, for labour—for that surplus population of which the economists had been wont to discourse. The labourer had not the wherewithal to emigrate on his own account, but there were agents who were quite willing to make a profit out of transplanting him if he could be induced to go. He went—as an indentured servant; which meant that he was bound to servitude for five years or seven years, but at the end of that time would be a free man, with a somewhat visionary prospect of acquiring a small holding of his own and a more certain prospect of taking service as a free man. Batches of such people were sent over and very easily placed; and their numbers were supplemented from the English prisons which were crowded not only with ruffians but with technical "criminals" whose offences were often of the most trivial order, for whom transportation as indentured servants was really a mitigation of a penalty much harsher than their misdoings would have earned under a criminal code less atrocious than was that of England until a century ago. It is probable that the majority of those who were thus taken from gaol and sent over were of this class; and, given the opportunity of becoming decent members of the community, they were likely to turn it to account. The time had not yet arrived for negro slavery to displace free (or indentured) white labour, though a score of negroes had been bought from the African slave-traders as early as 1619, and as time went on the numbers gradually increased. Thus the population which in 1630 scarcely exceeded 3,000 had in 1635 risen to 5,000, and increased continuously. For it does not appear that Maryland materially affected the influx to Virginia; since the Calverts demanded higher prices for estates than the Crown did in Virginia, while the special inducements offered by Maryland appealed primarily to the papists who would not in any case have been freely welcomed in the elder colony.

Generally speaking, the history of Virginia during

the fifteen years preceding the outbreak of the Civil War shows mainly that when the supreme authority had been revoked from the Company to the Crown, public opinion in the colony, represented by the leading members of the Assembly, was able to hold its own against a Governor who would have been arbitrary if he could, but, himself lacking the strength, received only lukewarm support from the Crown. If it had not been so, it is more than possible that when the shock came loyalty to the Crown would not have stood the strain as it did. The inactivity of the Crown, attributable not so much to policy as to pre-occupation with other matters, had the practical effect of sound statesmanship though it was not begotten of insight.

### III

Maryland was not in theory a Roman Catholic colony; in fact, as Baltimore very well understood from the beginning, the suspicion that it was intended to be so laid it open to a hostility on both sides of the Atlantic which it was essential to allay, if the proprietor's primary object of making it a safe refuge for the followers of his own creed was to be successfully accomplished. If they could be secured in the free exercise of their religion without being penalised as in England, the less said about it the better; they might have their liberty, without arousing active antagonism, but if they flaunted it they were not unlikely to lose it altogether. Baltimore had before him the precedent of King James's first year on the throne when the papists, under the impression that they were secure of the royal favour, by acting on the assumption that the penal laws might be ignored drove the Government into applying them with increased rigour—whereof the immediate outcome was Gunpowder Plot which in turn made Popery a popular bugbear. The premature zeal of certain Jesuits who accompanied the first batch of immigrants would probably have brought ruin on the whole enterprise if it had not been firmly and judiciously curbed. But the fact that the proprietor was a Catholic who would certainly ensure toleration for Catholics to the utmost of his power was at once an inducement for Catholics and a deterrent for intolerant Protestants to join the settlement. Hence, while it was out of the question to restrict it to Catholics, the predominance of Catholics was practically though not theoretically assured.

The economic development of Maryland differed from that of Virginia primarily in this: that Virginia was distinguished as a land of great estates and very few small holdings, while minor holdings were a feature of Maryland; and for this, one reason at least was the higher price of the land in the latter. Virginia offered the better investment for the mercantile adventurer with capital to adventure, and in Virginia the big tobacco estate was the more profitable to work, while in Maryland there was more inducement for the small man in corn-growing which in Virginia only came into active being as an adjunct to tobacco for counteracting soil exhaustion, under pressure from an intelligent Government.

Virginia after long tribulation had attained and practised what was virtual if not nominal self-government for some years before the first Lord Baltimore got his patent. Each of the Puritan colonies practised self-government from the first, adopting a representative system as its area and population made representation necessary. The Maryland patent made the proprietor an autocrat with powers limited only by the vague proviso about the advice and assent of the freemen. The Calverts—Baltimore, remaining in England, was represented by the Governor and Council who were his nominees, to whom he sent his own instructions—showed an experimental disposition to reduce the limitation to its narrowest interpretation and to treat the inevitable Assembly of freemen as existing only in a consultative capacity; but with the examples of Virginia and New England before them, the colonists were before long able to make good, without serious friction, the claims which Baltimore might successfully circumvent for a time but was too shrewd to override autocratically. In due course the Assembly became representative, passing through a curious stage in which voting by proxy was largely substituted for an attendance that was inconvenient to the persons concerned, while the proxies were apt to be placed in the hands of members of the Government. Baltimore's discretion, however, enabled him to retain in his own hands an effective direction in matters of moment, which Leonard Calvert, less politic and less shrewd, would have imperilled if left to himself. Unlike the earlier colonies, however, Maryland had plentiful precedents to guide her in the avoidance of pitfalls which had been disastrous in the pioneering days of inexperience, and the way of her development was comparatively smooth. To Baltimore, the ever-present danger was that of having his cautious religious policy upset by the over-zeal of too ardent co-religionists; which led him in 1641 to sharp dealings with the Jesuits, whom he charged with "seeking his destruction under the cloak of religion."

In 1639, the unpopular Governor Harvey was succeeded in Virginia by the same Sir Francis Wyatt who had been in charge in the first years after the dissolution of the old Company. He was followed in

1641, about the time of Strafford's fall and the height
of the Parliamentary crisis, by Sir William Berkeley, who
presently proved to be a Cavalier of the cruder kind,
hot-headed, violent, and domineering towards all
opponents, free of speech, frank and genial, a rather
exaggerated example of a familiar type of old-fashioned
country squire, accepted but not chosen by Pym, the
dominant figure of the day, and readily acceptable in
such a society as that of Virginia. There was not much
doubt about the line such a man would take if the
armed conflict between Crown and Parliament which
broke out a year later should extend across the Atlantic.
In point of fact, however, in the south as well as in
New England, the colonies did not become participants
in the struggle but remained only interested spectators
until the King had lost both his crown and his head.
Since they could not take a decisive part, and the issue
was extremely doubtful, they would not commit themselves to any course which might expose them to
severe penalisation by the ultimate victor in the strife.
And till the battle should have been fought out, neither
King nor Parliament would give much attention to
their affairs.

Baltimore, however, found the situation particularly
embarrassing. His colony was always in danger of
being made the target of intolerant religious hostility,
besides being the object of jealousy as a privileged
protégé of the court; safety required a cautious steering
which approached the ignominious. And there was
always in Virginia the Clayborne party which had
been forced to acquiesce in the loss of Kent Island,
lying in wait for a chance of recovering it. The chance
came when Leonard Calvert received from the King a
commission to suppress Parliamentary ships in American
waters. Consequently Clayborne, in alliance with a

Puritan privateer, seized the island, which Calvert recovered a year or two later; it was by a mere accident that the thing was associated at all with the big conflict in the east. Governor Berkeley did not feel called upon to interfere with Clayborne's operations; this was a private affair between the colonies, not an act of rebellion; though Royalist sentiment in Virginia not only deprived Clayborne of the support he would otherwise have received, but helped Calvert in his recovery.

But when Leonard Calvert died in 1647 the King was a prisoner, and Baltimore sought a judicious security in conferring the governorship on a Virginian Anglican, which for his Catholic colonists was doubtless the safest course he could have taken. Also he admitted into his own terationist colony a band of Nonconformists whom Virginia had declined to receive as rudely as if they had been papists. About the same time he sanctioned a change of constitutional procedure in Maryland assimilating it that of Virginia. Hitherto the Maryland Assembly had sat as one body, the elected representatives and the nominated Council together. From this time they sat as two separate chambers— like the Lords and Commons in England till the Rump abolished the House of Peers as well as the Monarchy.

## IV

Besides New England and the region of the Chesapeake, the West India Islands began during the reign of Charles I to provide a field for English colonisation. In the earlier days, Ralegh and other adventurers had contemplated the seizure of territory on the South American mainland in the region inclusively known as Guiana, but settlement on the islands offered many difficulties and no adequate attractions. Even the

Spaniards, with unlimited opportunities, had either left them alone (though always laying claim to them) or abandoned them, with the exception of the four greater islands of Cuba, Hayti, Puerto Rico, and Jamaica, with Trinidad off the Orinoco Delta, while in Jamaica their occupation was of a most perfunctory kind. There were two reasons—the obvious absence of treasure, and the dangerous character of the islanders, the Caribs from whose name the word "cannibal" derives—tribes much fiercer and more warlike than those of the main-land. It was by no means clear that the islands would repay the drawbacks, the risks and the labour of culti-vation when the inhabitants could not be exploited as slaves. To this, for Englishmen in the first quarter of the seventeenth century, was added the inconvenience of becoming involved in quarrels with the Spanish authorities as long as James chose to truckle to Spain. Only occasional adventurers, touching at islands on the way to or from Guiana, began to suggest possibilities of settlement; and it was only—as already related— in the last year of James, when he had broken with Spain, that the actual first occupation of a West India island—St. Kitt's—by Englishmen, in co-operation with Frenchmen, took place.

The English had, however, taken unchallenged pos-session of the isolated Bermudas—farther distant from the nearest West India islands than from the Virginia coast five hundred miles away—after Somers had been wrecked on them on his way to Virginia in 1609. As usual Sir Thomas Smythe and Robert Rich, not yet Earl of Warwick, were the leading members of the Company under whose charter the Somers Islands were separated from Virginia, to which they had at first been attached, in 1615. There was no "native question" there; they were sufficiently but not notably fertile; the planters were drawn primarily from Virginia, and when their own food supply was provided for, tobacco became their main product. Their development, necessarily restricted, followed the normal course of disputes between the planters and the Company's Government, and factions in the Company, leading up to the establishment of a representative system, much as in Virginia, in 1620. Their main value lay in their position in the Atlantic as a serviceable naval station out of the way of attack but providing a convenient resort—on occasion—for the roving ships employed by Warwick and the men of his school who had not discarded Elizabethan traditions. We shall presently see Somers islanders taking part in the Providence adventure; and later playing a creditable part when "sceptre and crown had tumbled down."

St. Kitt's was captured in 1629 by the Spaniards who carried off some hundreds of English prisoners. Charles let the matter drop, as in the case of Amboyna, but, as with Amboyna, Cromwell neither forgot nor forgave, and those rankling memories were among the concomitant motives of the Commonwealth's wars with the Dutch and with Spain. St. Kitt's, however, was recovered before long, and was the base from which temporary settlements were made in Nevis, Antigua, St. Lucia and elsewhere during the next ten years; temporary in the sense that very few of the islands remained permanently in the hands of the first settlers, but were lost and won more than once, changing hands as one or another of the naval Powers happened for the time being to be predominant in West Indian waters. Moreover some of the first settlements had to be abandoned while the Caribs were still strong enough to offer a fierce resistance.

This, however, was not the case with Barbados, which had been visited as early as 1605, but was not occupied

—by an expedition sent by Sir Robert Courteen under a charter actually granted by James I to the Earls of Montgomery and Marlborough—till 1625. Charles I had an unfortunate habit (as already exemplified in the case of Maryland) of granting charters with overlapping territorial rights, and in 1627 he granted such a charter to the Earl of Carlisle for the Caribbean islands generally, which was held to cover Barbados; and the hot disputes which resulted were ultimately settled by a compromise under which the principal sufferers were the planters. Barbados, however, has the two special distinctions of being the one island which has never changed hands, and the one singled out from the rest by its continuous prosperity for a very prolonged period.

Sugar-growing would seem to have been introduced in Barbados in 1640, after which it became the staple though not the sole product of most of the islands; which became as distinctively the "Sugar Islands" as those of the Eastern Archipelago were the "Spice Islands." The regular system was that of large or small estates owned by planters and worked mainly by indentured labour distinguished from slavery mainly by the fact that the indentured labourer became a free man again automatically after a fixed term of years. The practice, begun in relation to Virginia, of sending convicts to the Plantations as indentured labourers, developed; under the Commonwealth and for a long time afterwards, it was atrociously specialised for the deportation of "rebels" and other political offenders, particularly to Barbados, though as time passed the proportion of white serfs to negro slaves brought from Africa by the slave-traders in ever-increasing numbers became comparatively insignificant, the negro being far better fitted for hard toil in the tropics than the white man.

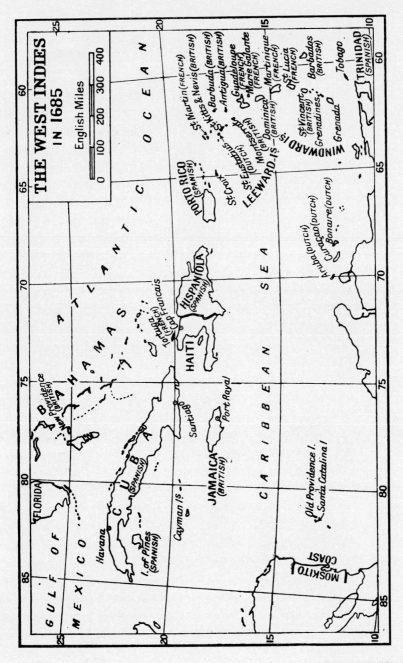

THE WEST INDIES
IN 1685

English Miles

0   100   200   300   400

ATLANTIC OCEAN

St Martin (FRENCH)
St Kitts & Nevis (BRITISH)
Barbuda (BRITISH)
Antigua (BRITISH)
Guadeloupe (FRENCH)
Marie Galante (FRENCH)
Martinique (FRENCH)
St Lucia (FRENCH)
Barbados (BRITISH)
Tobago
TRINIDAD (SPANISH)

St Croix
St Eustatius (DUTCH)
Montserrat (BRITISH)
Dominica (FRENCH)
LEEWARD IS.
St Vincent o (BRITISH)
Grenadines
Grenada
WINDWARD IS.

PORTO RICO (SPANISH)

Aruba (DUTCH)
Curaçao (DUTCH)
Bonaire (DUTCH)

CARIBBEAN SEA

HISPANIOLA (SPANISH)
Tortuga (FRENCH)
Cap Francais
HAITI

ATLANTIC

BAHAMAS

New Providence (BRITISH)

CUBA (SPANISH)

Santiago

Port Royal
JAMAICA (BRITISH)

Cayman Is.

Havana

I. of Pines (SPANISH)

FLORIDA
GULF OF MEXICO

Old Providence I.
Santa Catalina I

MOSKITO COAST

[Face page 168

One more West Indian venture in this period remains to be considered, that of the Providence Company. It originated with the Puritan leaders, and at the end of twelve years—in 1640—it was abandoned. The religious motive of Puritanism had little enough to do with it; except in so far as hostility to Spain remained part and parcel of the Puritan's religion as applied to things secular. The pursuit of religious freedom—for themselves—carried Puritans to New England in large numbers from 1630 onwards: but there were Puritan leaders who were more anxious to plant Englishmen in a favourable position for carrying on the Elizabethan tradition and breaking the Spanish monopoly of south and central American trade and territory. Even the peaceable Leyden congregation had been tempted for a moment, though a moment only. Robert Rich, who both before and after he succeeded to the Earldom of Warwick shared in every possible colonising venture—Virginia, Somers Islands, New England—appears to have maintained constantly a fleet of his own for carrying on the illicit traffic in waters claimed by Spain, with ships which did not always think it necessary to fly the English flag. In 1529 he took up the idea (suggested to him by Philip Bell, Governor of the Somers Islands, who was anxious for a change of quarters) of occupying the unoccupied island of Santa Catalina—not in the great belt from the Bahamas to the Windward and Leeward Islands which encircles the Gulf of Mexico, but in the heart of the Gulf itself, off the Moskito coast of Nicaragua. The report of the exceptional adaptability of the island for defence was not the least among the reasons for its selection. All the leaders of the party of Parliament and Puritanism, in both Houses, were in close association; and the score of those who formed Warwick's Providence Company included the names of

M

Lord Brooks, Lord Saye and Sele, Warwick's brother
Lord Holland (no Puritan, but useful as a courtier who
enjoyed the King's favour), Pym, Rudyard, and Oliver
St. John; the charter being dated November 19th, 1630.
When the Company was being formed, Winthrop had
approached them, the change in the Massachusetts
Company being then in contemplation; but he and his
whole connection were committed to New England,
whereas Warwick's objective was the West Indies. It
is to be noted, however, that when the New Haven
Colony was projected in England Providence had in
effect been abandoned, and several of the Providence
names reappear among the New Haven promoters, with
the notable addition of John Hampden, as related in
the preceding chapter; and the patent for the territory
to be taken up was granted by Warwick as Governor
of the not yet defunct New England Council.

The area of operations granted to the Company was
promptly extended by a further grant so as to include
the island of Tortuga, lying far away outside San
Domingo. The latter had just been appropriated by a
somewhat piratical rover named Hilton, who had taken
part in the occupation of St. Kitt's and of Nevis, and
now bethought himself that it might be useful to be
associated with the new Company, the island being
already a resort, for harbourage, of the rovers of all
nationalities. Tortuga, with Hilton as Governor, was
re-named Association Island. The regulations made for
Providence Island point to the desire of the projectors
to give it a really Puritan character, which in any case
would have been difficult enough; the connection with
Tortuga and its company, who were anything but
Puritans, and could not be practically brought under
control by Providence, must have made the thing
impossible. In effect it was not long before the Spaniards,

not without justification, attacked both the islands as
pirate centres. Tortuga was cleared out, but later was
recovered by the French: Providence repelled the attack,
but in 1641 the Spaniards again fell upon it, in overwhelming force: ending the English occupation, since
England was already confronted with Civil War. Yet
it remains permanently to the credit of Old Providence
settlers that during their occupation they, alone of
Europeans, gained the entire trust and confidence of
the native tribes on the coast of the neighbouring mainland, whose friendly feeling for the English was never
afterwards broken.

This "Old Providence" venture was in its inception
a serious attempt to establish a colony. The religious
motive was present. The direct mercantile motive of
profit from the soil and from trading was present. But
the primary object was a strategic position. The attempt
failed; Old Providence did not develop into a naval
base, was abandoned after a dozen years, and hardly
survived as a memory. But it has its own significance,
as exemplifying and emphasising the persistence of the
Elizabethan unofficial attitude towards Spain, the Spanish
dominions, and the right of trade with those dominions,
which had been officially abrogated by the Spanish treaty
of 1604, but was implicit in the Imperial policy of Oliver
Cromwell and of the Puritan ascendancy, degenerated,
without any survival of the Puritan element, into the
buccaneering of the Restoration, and continued to shew
itself as an active incentive in every one of the wars of
the eighteenth century.

# CHAPTER IX

## THE EAST INDIA COMPANY UNDER CHARLES I

### I

BEFORE the reign of James I was ended, the East India Company was in fact abandoning the attempt, hopeless in the circumstances, to establish itself in the Spice Islands on anything like an equal footing with what might fairly be described as the National Dutch Company. For the latter had the whole power of the Republic behind it, while the English Company was no more than a far from popular trading association for whose sake the Crown would take no risks. That, so far as James was concerned, was sufficiently demonstrated by his ignominious retreat in the Amboyna affair; a retreat followed after a little futile bluffing, by the complete and no less ignominious surrender of Charles I, which drove the lesson painfully home. Neither the Crown nor the Nation had yet learnt to think of the East India Company and its prospects as a National asset, though the insult and the disgrace of Amboyna rankled bitterly in the mind of the People.

On the other hand, the Company, if its trade east of the Malacca Straits was held up by the Dutch, had made good a footing, though a precarious one, within the borders of the Mogul Empire in India, where what survived of Portuguese rivalry was rather a help than a hindrance because of the bad odour in which the Latin power was held wherever it had penetrated. Neither the Mogul Empire itself nor the principalities of the south and east of the peninsula which had not yet been brought under the sway of the Moguls had developed anything which could be called sea-power; Portugal's sea-power had given her a detrimental hold upon them as long as she ruled the water-ways, and the power which was driving the Portuguese off the seas without showing any aggressive intent towards India might be cautiously but not effusively favoured. Nevertheless, the potentialities of the Indian trade were still very uncertain; its cultivation demanded very wary walking; the goodwill of the Indian governments was precarious; the conflict with the Portuguese must in itself be the reverse of lucrative as long as it lasted; to carry on at all required courage, prudence, and an obstinate faith, in the teeth of many discouragements.

The progress of the English traders in India could not possibly be a matter of forcible occupation and dominion, except in the particular detail of the elimination of the Portuguese power. It was a question of convincing Indian potentates, from the Mogul down, that it was good business for them to protect English traders as entirely peaceable and friendly foreigners though quite as well able—if need should arise—to defend themselves as the Portuguese, by land or sea. It may be well therefore at this point to form a somewhat clearer idea of the India in which they had to work than is usual where special and somewhat laborious study has not been devoted to the history of the Mogul Empire.

There is a rather curious correspondence with England in what may be called dynastic dates. In the first half of the sixteenth century, the Mughal Babar, the founder of the Mogul dynasty, conquered Northern India; his son Humayun lost what Babar had won, and then won most of it back. Humayun's son Akbar succeeded him two years before Elizabeth's accession and died two years after her death; having so extended and consolidated his Empire that his sway was fully established over the whole of the north, from (roughly) Bombay on the west coast to the Ganges Delta on the east. He had created a Mohammedan Empire, in which for the first time the very much larger Hindu population was treated as virtually on an equality with the Moslems: but his dominion actually included only a small portion of the northern section of the Deccan, the great plateau of southern India. In the Deccan those conquering Mohammedan dynasties reigned over populations mainly Hindu in the three great kingdoms of Ahmednagar, Golconda, and Bijapur, while in the southern quarter and both on the eastern and western coasts ruled a number of Hindu princes, sometimes and sometimes not in subjection to Golconda on the east or to Bijapur on the west.

Akbar was succeeded by his son Jehan Gir (two years after the accession of James I), who was succeeded two years after the accession of Charles I by his son Shah Jehan. Jehan Gir in his attempts to extend the Empire met with little success, some failures, one or two serious losses. Shah Jehan in a reign of thirty-one years raised the Empire to the height of its spectacular splendour and reduced both Ahmednagar and in part Golconda to subjection, sharing the former with the Bijapur Sultan; but in 1658, the year of Cromwell's death, two years before the English Restoration, he was dethroned by his son Aurangzib, who reigned till his death in 1707, the year of the Incorporating Union between England and Scotland. He, during that long reign of forty-nine years, had brought all India under his nominal sovereignty but had sown the seed of disintegration, like Philip II of Spain whom in many ways he curiously resembled, by fanatical repression and persecution of the Hindus, reversing the policy of toleration by which his great-grandfather had in part and indeed mainly built up the Empire.

The reign, then, of Shah Jehan, corresponds almost to the year with the English period covered by the reign of Charles I and the Protectorate of Oliver Cromwell. Shah Jehan is best known to most of us as the prince who built the two supreme marvels of oriental architecture, the Taj Mahal and the Moti Masjid or Pearl Mosque, and for whom was made the Peacock throne, the most costly and magnificent structure of the kind ever fashioned. But of more essential interest to us is the fact that it was in his day that the Company acquired from the Golconda Rajas its establishment at Madras and from the Mogul's Governor in Bengal on the Ganges Delta at Hugli from which its headquarters were transferred in the last decade of the century to Fort William which became Calcutta. (It may be convenient to note that Raja is not a Mohammedan but a Hindu title, borne by Hindu princes.)

It should be remarked further that from Bombay (in Portuguese possession), past Goa (in Portuguese possession), to Cape Comorin (facing Ceylon also in Portuguese possession) and from Cape Comorin along the Coromandel coast and as far north as the Mahanadi, the entire seaboard was in the hands of more or less independent Rajas throughout the period, while in its first years the Portuguese, except when they came into direct collision with English or Dutch, dominated the waters of the whole Bay of Bengal; and the Dutch were not altogether negligible, though their concentration on the much more immediately lucrative Spice Islands restricted their activities in the Indian area.

Within the Empire, the secular antagonism between the conquering Moslem overlords and the subjected Hindus had been minimised but very far from eliminated by the later policy of Akbar which was on the whole maintained by his son and grandson; though it was fatally revived by the intolerance of Aurangzib. The main preoccupation of Shah Jehan was the reconquest of the frontier provinces on the north-west and the effective subjugation of the Deccan, though there the astute Sultan of Bijapur evaded and profited by the fate of Ahmednagar and Golconda, the latter of which only escaped a harder doom by timely submission, about the time when John Hampden was refusing to pay ship money in England. Shah Jehan's attitude to Europeans was one almost of indifference, except when he was annoyed by the misconduct of the Portuguese, whose factory on the Hugli he exterminated in 1632. As official Governor of Gujerat, however, before his accession, he had learnt some respect for the English, and recognised their rivalry with the Portuguese as something that might be turned to account for policing the pilgrim-route for pious Moslems from the Indian ports to Mecca. But the very partially successful experiment of James I in sending Sir Thomas Roe as an accredited Ambassador to the Imperial Court was not repeated by his son; and Shah Jehan had no particular reason to suppose that the goodwill of the King of England— or, for that matter, of any European monarch—was worth careful cultivating. Their men were undoubtedly good fighters—the Portuguese proved that often enough; and he had seen that the Portuguese were out-classed by the English—but there were too few of them to be taken into serious account whether as friends or as enemies. It might be worth while to concede to the English merchants privileges for which they were willing to pay in some form or other, and of which, if misused, they could be deprived without a second thought; that was all. A monarch so mighty as Shah Jehan had little to gain and certainly nothing whatever to fear from the presence of the English. The doors, in short, were not closed to them—but were not thrown wide open. Only the minor coastal Rajas of the south, liable as they were to be harried on the one side by more powerful potentates and worried on the other by the Portuguese, had some direct inducement to be friendly with the English as possible allies; but then the last thing the English themselves wanted was to be involved in the political complications of the Peninsula. Their business was trade, not war.

## II

Such being the position in India, the Company had a sufficiently up-hill fight in making way there; and matters were not made easier for it by its position at home. The spreading of each joint-stock venture over a series of voyages in a period of years instead of restricting it to the single voyage as at the outset was a substantial advance in method, but it did not get rid of the necessity of raising the capital anew for each venture, before the profits of the last had been approximately ascertained, much less realised; though this was partly met by the presumption that the bulk of the previous contributors would be able to renew their contributions. The uncertainties of the trade were so great that only the stubborn persistence of the leading and most active members at home enabled the Company to carry on from one venture to the next, though in actual fact the profits continued to prove substantial. Opposition to the Company from

non-members continued to be active; its success
depended upon its holding the monopoly which was
theoretically secured to it by the Royal Charter, but
which the Crown was under very strong temptation
to infringe. Apart from the members it had few
friends; its defenders were themselves members with
large personal interests at stake, who were in consequence
suspected of misrepresenting facts and of distorting
arguments in order to hoodwink the public for their
own private gain; its opponents—sometimes honestly,
sometimes not—could pose on the one hand as patriots
denouncing a trade which was draining the life-blood of
the country, and on the other as champions of the
freeborn Englishman's right to trade anywhere on his
own account if the trade was *per se* legitimate. Consequently the public was heavily biased against the
Company, and its more unscrupulous opponents were
able to intrude serious obstacles in the way of its
successful operation.

Thus the Company had to face:—First, the problem
of raising the necessary funds for carrying on a trade
of which the costs were very heavy and the profits
though in fact large were uncertain, were at best
deferred, and had constantly to be anticipated for
fresh expenditure; secondly, the uncertain attitude
of the Crown; thirdly, the patriotic antagonism of the
prevalent school of crude mercantilist economics,
which denounced its trade as being contrary to the
public interest; and fourthly, the antagonism of the
"free-traders" who wanted to share in the trade, but
in competition with the Company—opponents who
denounced all monopoly as infringing the liberties of
Englishmen.

At a later date, the crude mercantilism of the time,
itself a medieval survival, was displaced by the much

more scientific mercantilism of which Louis XIV's very able finance-minister Colbert was the great exponent in practice; a doctrine which was largely anticipated by the Company's own champions though with little immediate success in dispelling the stereotyped prejudices. Those prejudices dominated the public mind, and were fostered by nearly all the crowd of pamphlets which in the seventeenth century performed after a fashion the functions of the Press in our own times. The pamphlets on the other side were few and far between, the voices of a small minority to which the great majority declined to listen, even though their case was set out with what should have been recognised as a quite convincing array of evidence to support it.

"The Company is every year sending out a multitude of mariners to die of disease or in useless fighting, building ships which serve no purpose, with the timber needed by legitimate shippers who have to buy their materials at enhanced prices; thus doing incalculable damage to the English marine which it is the first business of the patriot to foster. It is pouring into the East the bullion of which the accumulation is the country's most vital need, to a market where there is no demand for English goods; and it is bringing back in exchange not the gold or the war-materials essential to Power (which is the National aim of commerce), but pepper and cloves, perishable luxuries of no permanent value, serving no purpose except to enable the shareholders to sell them at a high price and fill their own pockets; diverting capital from profitable uses, and draining England of the treasure which is her life-blood. The East India trade is ruining the country, and the only remedy is, to put an end to it."

That was the gist of the economic argument. Moreover, in some respects it was *prima facie*, no more than a statement of palpable truths, and therefore convincing without farther examination, to what passed for sturdy English Common Sense. Gold went out of the country; cloves came back; to that end valuable lives and valuable ships were being wasted; the thing must be stopped. Thomas Mun, the competent spokesman of the Company, in a Memorial to the House of Commons in 1628, in the preparation of which he was assisted by Sir John Coke, repeated in more effective form the reply he had already put forward vainly in 1621 in his *Discourse of Trade*. Nothing like the supposed quantity of treasure had gone out of the country; a substantial proportion of the Indian products had been exchanged not for bullion but for English products, to the profit of English wool-growers and others; five-sixths of the goods brought home had not been consumed in England, but exported again to Europe in exchange for a great deal more bullion than had been expended upon them. The trade, in fact, instead of diminishing the store of treasure in the country materially increased it. The Company's ships and the Company's mariners, so far from weakening England on the seas, added to her strength substantially. Finally if the Company were forced to give up the trade, the wealth it was bringing in would go to the Dutch who had the wit to understand its value, or to the Portuguese—which meant much the same thing as to Spain. The facts were all on Thomas Mun's side, but still the appeal fell on deaf ears. The Company, though more than once on the verge of collapse, succeeded in pulling through, thanks mainly to the shrewdness and pertinacity of its servants in the East even more than of its chiefs in the West. But it owed nothing to popular support.

Even more troublesome, perhaps, was the hostility of the Interlopers or free-traders. The case against privilege is always a strong one; and not least against trading privilege or monopoly, primarily because it is peculiarly liable to gross abuse, but also as a grave restriction upon private enterprise, and, at least *prima facie*, an unfair interference on behalf of one competitor against all others. Moreover, at the time, the abuse of monopoly had been particularly flagrant, while the granting of monopolies by the Crown was a conspicuously dangerous method of providing it with the supplies which Parliament was bent on keeping under its own control, as the only effective check upon arbitrary government. A Company holding a monopoly by Royal favour under a Royal Charter was not likely to command the sympathies of Parliament, apart from the normal popular tendency to side with the unprivileged against the privileged few.

Nor was the case parallel to the exclusive rights of the old Regulated Companies, though even they had caused resentment; for they had not, in effect, interfered with private enterprise—rather, they had made private enterprise possible; for it was open to anyone to join them; subject only to the regulations imposed by membership, every man traded as his personal enterprise directed him; the Company did not trade as a body. Whereas the East India Company traded only as a body, giving no scope for individual enterprise; and it was a close body, membership in which could only be obtained at a big price.

To meet so strong a case as that against monopolies in general, it was necessary to make out a very strong counter-case in defence of the particular monopoly; and a very strong case there was. The risks of the trade in the East were so heavy that they could from the commercial point of view be undertaken only if there were a prospect of very substantial profits, demanding protection against competition, powers which would enable the trader to defend himself against aggressive foreign rivals, and exclusive rights as against the rivalry of his own nationals. Powers of self-defence might be entrusted to a responsible Company, whereas in the hands of the individual trader they might easily be used—in the existing conditions—as a cloak for piracy; but without those powers the legitimate private trader would stand no chance. Monopoly was practically the only security against the development of piratical practice, and piratical practice would cut the throat of legitimate commerce. Again, for the development of a national commerce with the Orientals, it was essential to establish their unqualified confidence in English good-faith and fair dealing; without monopoly there could be no security against bad faith and foul dealing on the part of private adventurers, while the English in general would be held responsible for their particular misdeeds.

## III

The soundness of the Company's contention was in fact demonstrated—though not so as to convince the free-traders—by the results of the latitude actually conceded by the Crown to Interlopers in disregard of the charter which the King himself had granted. The tacit betrayal of the Company by James and Charles over the Amboyna affair, consummated by the latter in 1628, had shown that the Crown was a very broken reed to lean upon, the sole excuse being the fear of friction with the Dutch Government at a time when its active hostility would have been extremely inconvenient. What may be called the *Civis Romanus Sum* doctrine was not in favour with the Stuarts. The Company—as distinct from the nation—had no less reason to complain of its betrayal in the interest of interlopers.

Charles again had his excuse. The Company had been granted large privileges, on the hypothesis that its trade would be of material benefit to the Nation; yet at the end of thirty years the signs of those benefits were not obvious. If it was profitable at all, why were its shares at twenty per cent below their subscription value? Its operations involved the country in diplomatic difficulties. It brought the Crown no adequate return for privileges for which, or for a share therein, others would be willing to pay a high price—and the Crown was desperately in need of money. Charles never had much difficulty in persuading himself that what other people called breaches of faith were perfectly justifiable in the particular circumstances; the courtiers and advisers who intended to reap the profits never had any qualms on the subject.

In 1628, while there was still some hope that he might take a firm stand on the Amboyna question, Charles invited the Company to lend him £10,000. The Company, much troubled by the difficulty of raising the next joint-stock, professed its inability. The King was in straits for money, since on the one hand he had just signed the Petition of Right, and on the other Buckingham was on the point of conducting his expedition to the Isle of Rhé. A month later, Buckingham was dead and Charles had surrendered to the Dutch. It was the general belief, though positive proof is not forthcoming, that they had bought the surrender for £30,000. For supplying the Royal Exchequer, the Company had proved a broken reed. Some years later, in 1640, when

Charles was at the end of his tether, he bought £65,000 worth of pepper from the Company, on credit, and sold it for £59,000 in cash. But he paid only twenty per cent of his debt at the time, and although the Company received a further payment after the Restoration, its loss over the transaction from beginning to end was not less than £30,000* For the Company, compulsory business transactions with the Crown were very bad business.

Doubtless the excuses in the King's mind were the normal one that the needs of the Exchequer must override all other considerations, and the sense that the Crown was entitled to a return, which it could not otherwise obtain, for the privileges conferred on the Company by its charter. Unfortunately for the Company, Charles applied those doctrines at the Company's expense, as a justification for authorising interlopers—people who in one form or another would pay for an independent share in the Company's privileges—since the Company was so unamenable to his demands for money. (With a prospect of deriving direct profit from the trade, the Crown, like the interlopers themselves, was deaf to the cry that the trade was *per se* injurious to the national interests.) In 1635, the year in which Charles demanded inland ship-money, he granted to Sir William Courteen and Sir Paul Pindar—wealthy London Merchants—and Endymion Porter, his own Groom-of-the-Bedchamber, a trading licence which was a flagrant infringement of the Company's Charter. The Charter was always liable to cancellation, subject to a three years' notice, on the ground of the Company's failure to make its trade profitable to the nation, but he chose instead to infringe the charter itself.

Porter was a favourite and a confidential agent of the King. Sir Paul was a man of immense wealth who

* W. W. Hunter, *History of British India*, Vol. II, pp. 31–2.

could always be relied on for a loan. Courteen, whose family was Dutch, had a finger in most of the less legitimate colonial or semi-piratical projects of the time. His place, on his death in the following year, was taken by his son. The Company was almost at its lowest ebb and would have accepted amalgamation with the new Association on terms very favourable to the latter but that was not what the Association—and therefore the King—wanted. Its methods were not to be those of the Company, to which the results of its operations were disastrous; though the King explained that Courteen and his friends were not intending to interfere with its trade, having in view a quite different object which could not at present be revealed.

The Courteen Association's ships sailed. In Chinese waters they made themselves so objectionable that the Chinese Empire proclaimed the English its enemies, and prohibited their entry into Chinese ports. In the Red Sea, they plundered an Indian ship, and roused the wrath of the Mogul; who treated the Company's factors at Surat as responsible and clapped them into prison. Everywhere they ignored the regulations by which the Company had striven to win the goodwill of the Orientals and sought deliberately to lower the Company's prestige and destroy its credit; and the Company was powerless; for when its servants protested they were met by the production of the Royal letters whose authority they could not venture to challenge. If it took legal action against the Association's servants, they were allowed to slip through the meshes of the law. It understood perfectly well that it could escape the King's pressure by accommodating itself to his wishes, but that only made it the more stubborn in resisting the pressure. When Parliament should meet once more——

N

The Short Parliament came, to be dissolved in three weeks. The Long Parliament came, and impeached Strafford. In January 1641 the Company lodged with Parliament a petition against Courteen and Endymion Porter. Charles dared not face the revelations which might ensue when the Petition came before the House. The Governor of the Company yielded to his entreaties, and just in time succeeded in withdrawing the Petition. The King in return went so far as to make a real effort to effect a reconciliation between Courteen's claims and those of the Company, but Courteen held out for impossible terms, and the despairing Company lodged its Petition.

But the Company was suspect of Parliament. It was an undeserving monopolist body created by the Crown for its own convenience. Parliament was in no haste to protect it against breaches of its monopoly, and its petition was not directed against the Crown, but against interlopers. The Grand Remonstrance and its aftermath made the appeal practically abortive, since the Company was too loyal to give prominence to the damning features of its case as an indictment against Charles himself. The Civil War broke out, and from neither Parliament nor King could the Company obtain any redress or any mitigation of its difficulties. From the beginning of the Civil War until the curtain fell on the Tragedy of Charles I, the Company was continually facing the question whether it could struggle on for one more joint-stock or even for one more single voyage on the early lines. Quartered in Roundhead London, it had no chance of support from the King and was practically at the mercy of requisitions from the Parliament seated at Westminster. But it held on year by year, till the monarchy fell and a dictator arose who took always an imperialist view of policy, and never hesitated to act upon it.

## IV

Meanwhile during all the troublous years of Charles I's reign, the Company's servants in the East, ill-supported, acting always under conditions of which their harassed masters at home had little enough understanding, doggedly maintained their slow advance. At the close of the reign of James I, after the fall of Ormuz, the Mogul had already learnt to look upon the Company's fleets as the guardians of the waterways on the west of India, and those fleets were soon effectively supplemented by the skill and energy of the chiefs of the Surat factory, Thomas Aldworth and his successors. The head of the Surat factory, who bore the title of President, became officially the President-general of all the Company's factories wherever established— even as far as the Spice Islands and the older factory at Bantam in Java—marking the fact that India had displaced the Archipelago as the main field of the Company's operations. In 1628 the Surat President on his own responsibility commissioned a fleet to fight the Portuguese, with whom England was then officially at war. In 1630 the war was officially terminated by the Treaty of Madrid; but in practice that treaty was of no effect in Indian waters. The result was constant injury to the trade of both; and in 1635 the Surat President, Methwold, again on his own responsibility, agreed with the Portuguese Governor at Goa on an armistice, developed next year into a formal convention under which British ships should have regulated access to Goa and other Portuguese ports. It was in fact a recognition, by the chiefs on the spot, of the treaty of 1630, but in form it was a remarkable assumption of authority by an officer in the service of a trading Company—the shouldering, without waiting for instructions and at the risk of repudiation, of a personal responsibility, which had been such a marked characteristic of the Elizabethans and was to be so marked a feature in the great story of the British in India. In the event, the Goa convention served its purpose. Portuguese hostility ceased to be a serious factor in our trading difficulties —the more easily perhaps because of the heavy blow Shah Jehan had recently dealt the Portuguese by the elimination of their factory at Hugli.

The confidence in the English established in India by the able conduct of the Surat Presidency is illustrated by the correspondence of the Dutch company. On Indian soil and in Indian waters there was no active hostility between the Dutch and English traders, but while the English were securing a firm foothold the Dutch were barely tolerated. The Dutch at Surat urged upon their Company's Government at Batavia that a good understanding with the English whose position was growing stronger every day was for the Dutch the condition of successful trading.* The fact was that, whereas in the Spice Islands the native potentates were at the mercy of the Dutch, in India the Europeans were at the mercy of the Mogul, and the domineering methods in which the Dutch were trained in the Archipelago were worse than futile. The English understood the situation and acted accordingly; whereas the Dutch would not learn to do so.

Yet the Englishmen met with a serious check, for which not they themselves but their fellow-countrymen were to blame. The Courteen Association began its operations in 1635—its ships being nominally on their way to the South Sea—by the piratical seizure of an Indian ship in the Red Sea, as recorded on a previous

* Hunter, II, 64.

page, and for their crime the innocent Surat officials were flung into prison in spite of their protests, and were kept there till they had promised not to do again what they never had done at all—besides being heavily fined. Armed with his letters from the King, the Courteen Captain Weddell thrust in upon the Portuguese and the Company's factories on the west coast, and procured from the Bijapur Sultan permission to establish a factory at Rajapur, a well-selected point between Goa and Surat, whence he was able to snatch much of their trade, besides inflicting other injuries upon both. No help could be looked for from the Company at home, which as we have seen was paralysed.

Nevertheless the Surat Government, left to its own resources, rose to the situation. It recovered the credit with the Mogul, which it had lost by no fault of its own. It became the successful intermediary between the Mogul Government and the Goa Portuguese with whom it had itself so recently come to terms, thereby raising the English prestige still higher. But that is not all that we have to place to the credit of those men, whose names were never familiar to English ears and would now be wholly forgotten if they were not still discoverable in the Company's archives, men who were the true pioneers of the British-Indian Empire. Surat had its indirect share too in establishing the English footing on the Coromandel Coast and in Bengal.

Attempts at settlement on the Coromandel coast, where the Rajas were either independent or unwilling tributaries of the Golconda Sultan whose fabulous wealth was proverbial, had been made before the Surat factory was definitely recognised by the Mogul government. They had failed—somewhat expensively —in part, at least, because of the opposition of the

Dutch who had been beforehand in experimenting with the petty principalities. But even then an Englishman, Captain Hippon, had gained admission farther north at Masulipatam which had long been the port of the Golconda Sultanate and its predecessor the Hindu Empire of Vizayanagar, possible havens on that coast being very few and far between. It became, in English hands, the mart of a profitable trade in the exchange of Indian fabrics for the spices of the Archipelago. The English had to contend with Dutch rivalry, but here as in other quarters where the primary necessity was not to dominate a petty chief but to placate a powerful monarch, the English were the more successful. But Golconda had not such a firm grip on its outlying territories as the Moguls had on their provinces, and the English did not always keep their hold on venal governors. The occupation of an additional station on another point of the coast was desirable, and the right position was found by Francis Day who procured the establishment in 1639, of the factory, at first named Fort St. George, which developed into Madras. At Surat, a province under full control of the Mogul central government, the traders would no more have been suffered to fortify their factories than in a European State; outside the Empire, government protection of authorised foreign residents could not be taken for granted. The right of self defence was a necessary condition of residence, at least on the seaboard where armed attacks from the sea by other foreign rivals were always a possibility. The necessity for military defences was a standing difficulty, because of its costliness, in the way of planting factories on the east coast. Day persuaded the Masulipatam Council to plant Fort St. George—the site having been granted by the local chief by leave of his Raja who was more or less a vassal of Golconda—but the depressed and anxious authorities at home, who had not been consulted, would have insisted on a complete withdrawal, had not the wisdom of the project been emphatically endorsed by the approval of the Surat Council. In 1642 the Masulipatam Council transferred its quarters to the new fort; but some years were to pass before the Company in London really laid aside its resentment at the independent action of its servants.

Masulipatam was also the base from which the Company's servants carried their enterprise into Bengal, the great Eastern province of the Mogul Empire. Bengal always stood in a somewhat exceptional relation to the whole succession of the Delhi empires, Medieval as well as Mogul. Whenever it was attached to the Delhi Empire, its Governors were in fact semi-independent viceroys, and as each empire crumbled Bengal broke away from it into complete independence, while no dynasty at Delhi was happy unless Bengal was definitely within its dominion. It was only by long campaigning that Akbar had established his supremacy in Bengal and Orissa, and the Mogul's Governors there, though by no means beyond the reach of his arm, were conveniently left to exercise there an authority much more independent than was permitted to them in other provinces, though they were not dynastic Hindu princes like the vassal Rajas of the Bijapur and Golconda Sultans, but officials of the Mogul holding office at his pleasure. In effect, the Nawab of Bengal was a powerful prince with great armies at his own command, who, if necessary, might bring into play the still greater armies of his master the Mogul.

The English had not hitherto sought an entry to the Empire through its eastern as well as its western ports.

They had been sufficiently occupied with the vain
effort of attaining an equality with the Dutch in the
Spice Islands east of Cape Comorin, and with successfully wresting the dominion of the Arabian seas from
Portugal and making secure their own footing on the
western coast. On the waters of the Bay of Bengal they
had not really challenged the Portuguese dominance
or the still active rivalry of the Dutch, and their progress
up the east coast of India was, as we have seen, slow.
The Portuguese had been established for a century at
Hugli in the Ganges Delta where they had a large
fortified settlement, and the English, far from their
own base, could not intrude upon their preserves unless
they did so in force.

But in 1630, the Portuguese suffered a crushing blow.
Reports reached Shah Jehan, which determined him
on their destruction; a great host gathered about the
Hugli settlement and in effect exterminated it; slaying,
it was said, a thousand of them, carrying away four
thousand prisoners, and capturing or destroying on the
river more than three hundred vessels, large and small—
though doubtless this native tradition is in the nature
of an overstatement. But, making every allowance for
pious exaggeration, the disaster was overwhelming. It
was just three years later that a handful of Englishmen
from Masulipatam, led by Captain Cartwright, arrived
at Harishpur, the port of Orissa, had a little brush with
a Portuguese crew in the harbour—the Portuguese were
not off the board yet—made friends with the "Rogger"
in charge of the port, visited the Lieutenant-Governor
at Cuttack, and so impressed—or amused—that dignified
person by the independent audacity of their attitude
that he granted them a formal licence for English trade
in Orissa, under Imperial protection. Within the Empire
there could be no question of the fortified posts which

so vexed the minds and the pockets of the home authorities, and the first English factory in Bengal was set
up at Balasore, with small dependent agencies here and
there.

The results were daunting. There was no market for
the goods brought by the English. They were swept
off by sickness, raided by Dutch and Portuguese pirates,
almost driven to abandon Balasore. But they held on—
till in England the Monarchy had fallen and the Commonwealth era of Imperialism dawned.

# CHAPTER X

## THE IMPERIAL COMMONWEALTH, 1649–1658

### I

ELEVEN years passed after Charles I lost his crown and his head, before the King "enjoyed his own again." The Commonwealth was proclaimed, and for four years England was under the government of a Republican oligarchy, which was then displaced by the act of a military dictator who ruled mightily till his death five and a half years later. Twenty kaleidoscopic months followed, at the end of which Charles II was recalled to his kingdom. It was an episode without parallel in English history. The Commonwealth left no mark upon the Constitution, while it implanted in the English mind a permanent hatred of military rule. Cromwell's foreign policy, based upon an obsolescent idea, perished with him, though it had helped to forward European conditions which he never suspected. But those years form a definite epoch in the history of the British expansion.

Most of us are apt to think of the whole period as if Cromwell had possessed himself of the Protectorate and ruled as an autocrat from the moment of the King's death. No doubt he was actually the foremost man in the country; but for nearly three years he was hardly in England at all; the Government was in the hands of that remnant of the Long Parliament, popularly known as the Rump, which was left sitting after Pride's Purge; and until he turned the Rump out of doors, eighteen months after Worcester fight, he was in no possible sense a dictator, and was often by no means at one with those in whose hands lay the direction of policy and the control of administration.

The novel feature of the whole period, till chaos supervened on the death of the Protector, is, from the point of view which concerns us in this volume, the Imperialism of the Government, whether it was vested in the Parliament's Council of State or in the person of Oliver Cromwell; though marked, during the period of personal rule, by special characteristics deriving from the personality of the English Cæsar. In Elizabeth's time, Walter Ralegh had been the incarnation of the spirit of Imperialism, and all Drake's activities were imbued with the same spirit; but the Government was the government of the Queen and Burghley; and what Drake and Ralegh wrought was done rather in despite of the Government than with its active support. James and Charles I both of them perhaps had inklings of the Imperialist Idea, but the former was nearly always too timid and the latter always too much embarrassed to act upon it. But Imperialism was the life-blood of the Republic in both its phases; it had to be Imperialist or to perish. The ideal was born in Elizabeth's day, when there was no English Empire at all; it was pursued by Elizabethans and Jacobeans (such as Warwick) of the Elizabethan tradition, as individuals; but it hardly became a political factor till there was a Government upon which the consciousness was forced that an English Empire had actually come into being, and that an Empire policy had become a necessity; and then Oliver Cromwell entered upon the long-deferred inheritance of Walter Ralegh.

The Commonwealth forms an epoch in our empire-building, because the prime condition of English empire building was a convincingly powerful navy. The navy had indeed become convincingly powerful when that which had hitherto been looked upon as the most powerful in the world went down before it; when the Spanish Armada was scattered in the flight from Calais Roads, irretrievably shattered in the battle of Gravelines, and its leavings devoured by the winds, the waves, and the rocks. But that great triumph was not sufficient of itself to establish England as the Mistress of the Seas. The rivalry of the southern maritime States was broken past repair; but throughout the next half century, while English administration fell to pieces, another State was developing its naval resources and devoting most of its energies to the creation of that sea-power without which it could hardly hope to maintain the independence which still hung in the balance. We saw in an earlier chapter that in their special preserve of the Spice Islands the Dutch shipping heavily outnumbered the English; the mercantile marine of both countries consisted largely of ships armed and gunned for the fighting to which merchantmen were always liable to be exposed on the high seas. The Dutch not only had a preponderance in such craft, being—besides their own commerce—carriers for half Europe; the renewal in 1620 and the prolonged continuance thereafter of their struggle with Spain imposed on them the vigorous maintenance of a fighting navy, while that of England, in spite of spasmodic attempts at reorganisation on the part of Buckingham and Charles, grew continuously weaker, though Warwick as the Parliament's Admiral had set about some improvements in the King's last years. Finally, the long Spanish struggle ended in 1648 with the full recognition of the independence of the United Provinces under the Treaties of Westphalia.

Thus at the moment when the Rump, with the Army which had won the Civil War at its back, established itself as the Government of the English Commonwealth, the Dutch Republic which might quite conceivably turn itself into a monarchy, was quite definitely the premier maritime power. England, of which no European State had for years past taken serious account, was only the second, with a commerce far outstripped by that of her rival, and a fighting fleet which, in tonnage as in training, was definitely inferior. The grand achievement of the pre-protectorate Commonwealth Government was that its fighting fleet was raised to an equality at least with that of its rival, and the advance of the mercantile marine towards drawing level began, though it can hardly be said to have done more. The men to whom above all others the credit is due were Sir Harry Vane in the Council of State and Robert Blake on the seas; what share the Navigation Act, which was the work of Parliament itself, had in the results is a much debated question. That all these things were done with Cromwell's approval need not be questioned; that any of them were due to his initiative is at best merely hypothesis. The Navigation Act had passed its second reading before he was back from the "crowning mercy" of Worcester, not having been near London but wholly taken up with his Scottish campaigns for considerably over a year.

## II

The Dutch war, begun in 1652, six months after the passing of the Navigation Act, and ended by Cromwell as Lord Protector just two years later, a twelvemonth after his ejection of the Rump, did not transfer the supremacy of the seas from Holland to England, but it shifted the balance of naval power, at first decidedly but not decisively in favour of the Dutch, so that at the end it leaned on the whole to the English side, and from that time the power of the English navy grew continuously though not without occasional alarming lapses in naval administration compensated by an unfailing capacity for recuperation impossible to a nation so small and so limited in its own natural resources as were the United Provinces. The war has an almost unique interest in our naval history, because the Dutch admirals Tromp and De Ruyter were trained seamen with a long record of naval victories behind them, whereas the English admirals pitted against them were all soldiers of distinction appointed to naval commands with no previous experience of sea-fighting. Blake himself, a civilian who was past forty when the Civil War broke out, had distinguished himself as a soldier in the defence of Lyme and of Taunton and was recalled from retirement to take command by sea against Prince Rupert in 1649, when he himself had reached the age of fifty; yet in the remaining years of his life, which ended in 1657, he won his recognised rank among English admirals as second to none save Nelson. The system had passed out of date when the century was nearing its close, but was probably a necessary phase in the evolution of the supreme navy to which, more than to any other factor, taken singly, the British Empire or Commonwealth of Nations owes its existence to-day.

We have called the Commonwealth Government "Imperialist" because it was the first which recognised the active development of sea-power as the necessary function of a Government which was no longer insular but was in control of an oversea empire with a powerful maritime rival not only in the field but actually dominant therein. Elizabeth, not in possession of an empire, had been content to permit and encourage unofficially the development of sea-power by private adventurers, winking at methods of very questionable legitimacy which were excusable only on the ground that methods no less (though in a different way) illegitimate were operated against her subjects by the dominant sea power of the day. Her Government only fostered a regular fighting navy with the specific objects of guarding England from invasion and her shores from raiders, and (when most fully developed) of crippling the power which was a menace to her throne. Even for that very limited purpose, James and Charles allowed the Navy to sink into a state of extreme inefficiency, excusable mainly on the ground that the danger of a possible invasion was non-existent; and it was only when some serious risk of raiding revived, in the uncertainties of European political complications during the Thirty Years' War, that Charles made his disastrous but well-intentioned attempt to retrieve the position by levying ship-money when he was almost at his wits' end for cash; money of which, when raised, much less than was intended though more than was commonly credited, was spent beneficially on the fleet.

Being in the hands of Parliament during the Civil War, the control of the ports by the fleet made it a useful weapon for Parliament; but when the monarchs fell, Rupert, aided by its partial defection, took to sea; his raiding of the rebel commerce and ports at once became a serious thorn in the side of the Regicide Republic; and the pressing need of dealing with the raiders was the primary incentive to naval reorganisation. But the Puritan soldier placed in command of the operations drove the Royalist cavalry captain out of British waters to temporary refuge in the neutral port

of Lisbon, whence Rupert, when the Portuguese no
longer dared to shelter him, escaped into the Mediterranean, there to be chased from pillar to post and finally
to elude pursuit by an excursion to the Atlantic and
then to the West Indies; after which the fleets of the
Commonwealth saw him no more, though he figured
again as an admiral after the Restoration.

But Blake's operations while he was in pursuit of the
elusive Rupert gave a fresh impulse to the naval reorganisation. The Government became thoroughly awake to
the fact that the restored navy was the most valuable
asset it possessed in dealing with the European Powers,
every one of which without exception looked askance
upon the Republic which had beheaded a king. None
of them had any affection for the Stuarts, or any particular desire to help them, with perhaps one exception;
but regicide had put England outside the pale. The
exiled queen-mother was a French princess; the exiled
King's eldest sister was the wife of the young Stadtholder
of the United Provinces who was undoubtedly aiming
at definitely entering the charmed circle of European
Royalties. The Puritan Republic, with never a friend,
at daggers drawn with Scotland, with a Royalist faction
kept under only by dread of the army, was in grave
danger of finding itself face to face with a foreign attack;
its one chance was to show its teeth unmistakably; and
that was what Blake did, with the whole-hearted support
of the Council of State. The foreign courts might dally
over recognising the Commonwealth's ambassadors;
Blake's warships were another matter. The Latin
Powers definitely woke up to the fact that it would not
be wise to pick a quarrel with the Maritime Republic;
even that its friendship might be worth cultivating. For
the last thirty years they had taken no count of the
navy which thirty years earlier had shattered the

Spanish dominion of the seas. Once more, suddenly, in the twinkling of an eye, it had revealed itself as something to beware of. Incidentally it had shown for the first time what might be effected by its mere appearance in the Mediterranean. Never before had English warships visited Italian ports or been seen at Toulon; such a thing had not been dreamed of. Blake had not caught Rupert; but viewed as a naval demonstration his movements were invaluable.

More than fifty years passed before England was in permanent possession of a naval base for the command of the inland sea. Ralegh indeed had dreamed in 1596 of retaining Cadiz, as legitimate prize of war, for that purpose, but the plan had found no favour with Elizabeth. It was Blake who in effect created the idea of making England a Mediterranean Power, though it was not till the War of the Spanish Succession in the first decade of the next century that the English hold was permanently established by the capture and retention of Gibraltar and Minorca.

The attitude of the Council of State to France, Spain and the other Mediterranean States was on the whole simple; each and all of them must understand that if they intervened in the private affairs of England, if they tried to outlaw the Republic, they would do so at their peril—and the initiative, if they forced a quarrel would be with the maritime power. In relation to Holland, the position was different. At the end of 1650 the young Stadtholder William II, the fourth in succession of the House of Orange which had led the Dutch for three-quarters of a century in their now decisively triumphant struggle with Spain, died suddenly. His wife was Mary Stuart, the English Princess Royal; his descendants might one day be in the line of succession to the English throne; and of all the foreign powers

o

the Dutch under his ascendency were the most likely
to take active part in a royalist restoration. But the heir
of his House was an infant, born a week after his death.
In Holland, very much the largest of the United
Provinces, there was a predominant anti-Orange party.
There was no right of succession to the Stadtholdership,
and the Republican party seized and held the reins of
government.

That party would not interest itself in a Stuart
restoration. It might be supposed that its sympathies
would be with the English republicans. A fast alliance
of the two Protestant maritime republics would hold
a position of immense strength in Europe. But the
English would profit much more by an alliance on
even terms than the Dutch, because it would involve
a harmonious sharing of the commerce whereof the
greater part was in the hands of the Dutch. The
alternative would almost inevitably be a determined
effort on the part of the English to wrest from the
Dutch their commercial and maritime supremacy. The
English Government offered the Dutch the alliance in
1651, but the Dutch were not satisfied with the terms
and declined it.

### III

In the Autumn, while Cromwell was returning from
Worcester, the English retorted by passing the Navigation Act. Similar Acts had been passed before, but
England had never before possessed a marine adequate
to their effective fulfilment. Her marine was not
adequate now—but she meant to make it so. In all
this, there was nothing to provide a technical *casus belli*;
but it created a situation in which the arising of a
*casus belli* was practically only a question of time. In
England the Royalist cause had just suffered its decisive

ROBERT BLAKE *[Rischgitz*
The Commonwealth Admiral

*[Face page 202*

overthrow at Worcester. Blake was back from the Mediterranean. Tromp was in command of the Dutch fleet. In April, 1652, though the countries were at peace, the two commanders attacked each other, each claiming that it was the other who broke the peace; each Government declared its own admiral in the right, and for two years the two navies battered each other with alternating successes and defeats till the Lord Protector ended the war on terms which were a good deal more satisfactory to the English than to the Dutch but could be honourably accepted by the latter. For the balance of fighting force was evidently turning in favour of the English, while the strain upon the Dutch, far the more dependent on their sea-borne commerce which they were less and less able to protect, was much the more severe. The Anglo-Dutch war may be said to have opened the era of great fleet-actions which were the standing feature of England's maritime wars thereafter.

Now let us observe that the Navigation Act—popularly but erroneously known as Cromwell's; " old Oliver entertained this law but coldly," says a contemporary —was, like the Government's organisation of the Navy, an imperialist extension of what had been a merely insular policy on the part of previous governments. In the past, the island State had required a navy to protect her shores from invasion and to bridle piracy in the Channel, and shipping to carry her own commerce to Aquitaine, Flanders, or even the Baltic. Government action had never gone beyond fostering those ends. Even Elizabeth's navy had not been raised above the point where in emergency it required, even for those limited ends, to be supplemented from local and personal sources. The Navigation Acts, passed at intervals since the reign of Richard II, had in fact aimed either at shutting out the alien or at nothing more than giving English shipping what we might now call a "preference" in English ports to encourage the multiplication of English ships and mariners essential to an island Power. And each of those Acts in succession had very soon become a dead letter. The Commonwealth Navigation Act had a new intention—the transference of the world's carrying trade from Holland to England. Holland had been offered the choice between co-operation and competition. Having had very much the best of it in competition so far, she rejected co-operation. The new Act, coupled with the new naval organisation, was the mobilisation of the English forces of competition; and the first Dutch War was the opening campaign of what from one point of view might fairly be called the "Hundred Years' War" for Imperial ascendency, though in its later stages France took the place of Holland as England's rival, and the actual stake was not always kept in view.

All "Navigation" Acts had a common starting-point —that imported goods must be brought into English ports, for unloading, either in English bottoms or in the ships of the exporting country. Thus if the foreigner had not enough ships to do his own exporting he would have to hire English ships to carry his goods to the English market and would find it convenient to make them his carriers to other markets as well; English shipping would increase and multiply to meet an ever-growing demand for its services. In the fifteenth and the beginning of the sixteenth centuries, the scheme always broke down, partly because political exigencies demanded the admission of the German Hansa, and partly because the demand for foreign goods exceeded the English carrying-power. The restriction if observed would merely have kept the wanted goods out of England,

and consequently it was tacitly set aside. The Hansa had been the carriers; the Dutch, not the English had taken their place in the seventeenth century. Now England was to make her bid for ousting the Dutch. Whether she would have done so with equal or greater success by relying entirely on open competition is a hotly debated question; but that success did follow in the wake of the Navigation Act, and that England was drawing level before the end of the century, is indisputable. For three-quarters of a century, that fact was attributed as a matter of course to the Navigation Act; or rather to the Act as reinforced after the Restoration, since it was the one measure of the Republic which was whole-heartedly endorsed under the Monarchist reaction. It is to be noted however that the Commonwealth Act imposed no new restrictions upon colonial exports and imports, and under it "English bottoms" included Colonial shipping. The direct subordination of the commercial interests of the Colonies to those of the mother-country was no part of the Puritan Imperialism.

## IV

The robust Imperialism of the Council of State gave place to the Imperialism of the Protector, which was no less robust, but took a somewhat different colour from his personal idiosyncrasies. In Elizabeth's day, as we have said, Ralegh incarnated the idea of England as not merely "this sceptred isle" but an Imperial world Power resting on her might as mistress of the seas. In Elizabeth's reign, Francis Walsingham incarnated that side of national sentiment which always craved that England should stand forth as the uncompromising champion of the Protestantism which was fighting for life against Philip of Spain and the

Guises in France. For both Ralegh and Walsingham,
Spain was the arch-enemy, for both the necessary
weapon was a supreme navy. Their policy did not
fit in with the statecraft of the Queen and Burghley.
But Oliver Cromwell was the heir of that policy in
both its aspects, though Walsingham was dead before
he was born and Ralegh was in the Tower throughout
his boyhood. In its Protestant aspect, it was no doubt
an obsolete policy when Oliver became Lord Protector
at the age of fifty-four, but it was the root of the foreign
and imperial policy of the Protectorate. Like Gustavus
Adolphus, he had ever in his mind the ideal of a *Corpus
Evangelicorum*, a Protestant Union, though with England
instead of Sweden at its head, ready to draw the sword
in defence of Protestants anywhere and everywhere.
We can see now that the armed conflict between the
religions had worn itself out as a primary factor in
international relations, but the fact was by no means
obvious in the decade after the Peace of Westphalia.
Papistry was to Cromwell still the supreme menace.
And therefore, in spite of Holland's maritime rivalry
he desired reconciliation—though he had been willing
enough that she should be taught a sharp lesson—and
he brought the war to an end before he had been
Protector for six months. And therefore, before
another six months had passed, two English fleets
were in preparation for very active service, though
what precisely that service might be was still uncertain.

It proved in the course of the next year to be the
unprovoked renewal of the maritime war with Spain.
France and Spain were at war with each other and
each was anxious by this time for the Protector's goodwill. Both were Catholic powers and Cromwell trusted
neither of them. He was prepared to fight either or
both, or to join either against the other, on a sufficient

guarantee that the Protestant cause would profit thereby. Guarantees were not forthcoming and he would make no alliance. But France was at least not aggressively hostile to Protestantism, while Spain flatly refused to give up at Cromwell's demand what the Spanish ambassador called his Master's two eyes—the jurisdiction of the Inquisition and the exclusion of the English and other foreigners from what Spain claimed as her dominions in America and the West Indies. With Penn and Venables in naval and military command respectively, one great expedition crossed the Atlantic with an unknown objective. The other expedition, under Blake, was despatched to the Mediterranean to argue decisively with the corsair Barbary States who were the common enemies of Christendom—but with the Spanish treasure fleets as the second objective, when Penn and Venables had opened war with Spain in the West Indies.

Blake, after accomplishing the unprecedented feat of sinking the pirate fleet of the Dey of Tunis under the guns of the land-batteries which he blew to pieces, though they were supposed to make the harbour impregnable, at the cost of less than seventy casualties, crowned his naval career by the triumph still without parallel in naval annals of sinking a Spanish war-fleet with the treasure fleet it was convoying, in the still more impregnable harbour of Teneriffe. But the West Indian expedition accomplished no more than the acquisition of Jamaica, an island of which the value was not recognised till many years later.

V

Until the closing years of the Interregnum when a new charter from the Protector placed it upon a new footing, the East India Company was continuously in very troubled waters; always, we may say, in doubt whether it could keep itself afloat for one year more, while its servants in India, virtually left to their own resources, struggled along on their own responsibility.

On Indian soil, the notable event of the period was the establishment of an English factory at Hugli, the main fort of the Ganges Delta, where a few years earlier the Portuguese factory had been extirpated. It was not, as we have seen, actually the first factory in Bengal, since Orissa was officially a department of that province, but it very soon superseded Balasore as the centre and depot of the Bengal trade. The first appearance of the English traders—on a tentative expedition from Balasore —and their first permission to trade occurred in 1650; and the licence to trade was obtained by an English surgeon, Gabriel Boughton, who was already established in high favour as official "Chirurgeon" to the Nawab or Viceroy of Bengal. The picturesque tradition runs that he cured Shah Jehan's daughter who accidentally had been so badly burnt that her life was despaired of; that the Mogul bade him name his own reward for that inestimable service, and that all he asked in return was the grant of this favour to his countrymen. There are no known documents confirming in its details the established tradition; in some respects the information upon which it was based was certainly inaccurate; but enough of it is actually possible to warrant us in accepting it not indeed as undeniable history but as admissible legend. *

The east coast establishments were all subordinate to Madras, which found itself so little able to control

---

* See Sir Henry Yule's study of the evidence in the *Diary of Sir William Hedges*, Vol. III, p. 167. But it is not easy to see how the tradition could have become established unless its essentials had a substantial foundation in fact.

the Hugli factory and its off-shoots that the abandonment of Bengal was seriously entertained; but courage
revived with the new charter of 1657 which brought
in an unprecedented influx of capital; it became at
once possible to take matters in hand with vigour,
and four separate factories were staffed—the first
station at Balasore, Hugli as headquarters, Kasimbazar
higher up the river near Murshidabad the usual
Vice-regal capital, and Patna, still higher, actually
not in Bengal proper but in Behar.

Both from Charles before and from Parliament
after the outbreak of the Civil War, the Company had
failed to obtain redress or security against the destructive
competition of the Courteen or Assada Company, so
called because it had set up a station of its own at
Assada in Madagascar, on the flank of the trade-route
to the East Indies. Its appeals against the Dutch in
the early days of the Commonwealth met with more
consideration, as adding to the just grounds for war
with the United Provinces, and compensation for the
still rankling grievance of Amboyna was among the
peace terms most rigorously demanded when the Dutch
War was brought to an end.

Incidentally, Cromwell in the same year intervened
decisively to end the troubles with the Portuguese
which had survived the Goa Convention. Surat in
India and the Company in London had been endeavouring to settle these difficulties by negotiations on their
own account, as Government neglect had taught them
to do in the past; the Protector, however, took up the
question as an international matter, and though he
snubbed the Company for its pains, he imposed upon
Portugal a definite treaty, abrogating on her part all the
exclusive claims to which she had hitherto made pretence.
Portugal was now—in her own view—once more an

independent kingdom under the House of Braganza, though her independence was as yet by no means assured, since the King of Spain still claimed the crown; in dealing with her, the Commonwealth was no longer, as in the past, dealing with Spain but with a Government hostile to Spain, a fact which was soon to become a very important factor in England's foreign relations. But at the moment of which we are speaking, Blake had very recently shown her by the broadest of hints that she could not afford to challenge the ill will of the English Republic—therein only anticipating Cromwell's cardinal principle of emphasising in every quarter the danger of forcing a hostile attitude upon England. English Governments had not hitherto sought to impress actively upon foreign Powers the consciousness that they regarded English trade as an Imperial interest; the Dutch War was the first indication of the new Imperialism; of which Cromwell was now to develop a new aspect.

It was Cromwell's habit to deal trenchantly with problems as they arose, rather than to pursue what could be called a settled scheme of policy. The development of the country's commerce was a national necessity, which the pre-Protectorate Commonwealth Government had recognised as demanding the development of the national navy to guard it against national rivals. Now, the prevailing conditions of the Eastern trade demanded that it should be brought under national control. The rights and wrongs of the East India Company in relation to its domestic trade rivals were a minor matter, but to place the Eastern trade on a permanently secure footing presented itself now as a major matter. Cromwell set on foot a series of enquiries; and their outcome was the charter of 1657.

Clearly the existing system was unsatisfactory and

unworkable. There were in actual fact two chartered companies, one of which had been promised a monopoly upon which the second had been authorised to intrude, with disastrous results. One was perpetually on the verge of winding itself up, and the other of bankruptcy. Rival companies could not subsist side by side. The two must be reduced to one, either by accommodation or dissolution, if the monopolist system, trading on a joint-stock, was to be retained at all. Alternatively there was a wide and powerfully supported demand for the total abolition of monopoly, and complete freedom of trade for the adventurer. There remained, however, a third alternative which had powerful advocates within the Company itself.

This was, in effect, reversion to the medieval company system, the monopolist Company of which all traders must be members and all who wished to trade could without difficulty become members, but all traded as individuals, not on a joint stock, on their private capital at their own risk for their personal profit, subject only to observance of the Company's regulations.

Enquiries, efforts at adjustments which mainly showed that in the desperate confusion of the last few years justice in the allotment of claims could by no possibility be ascertained, dragged on, and still the Council of State could reach no decision. But the Protector reached his own conclusions by the aid of the man on whose judgement in this matter he placed a merited confidence, Colonel Philip Jones, whose report was adopted by the Council of State and issued in "Cromwell's Charter" of 1657. Free trading was ruled out; it would demand for defence the constant presence in Indian waters of a Government fleet for which there was more than enough occupation elsewhere. Competitive quasi-monopolies were ruled out.

A "Regulated" Company of the medieval type would not have sufficient control over its members. It was inadvisable to turn the whole trading business into a State department, as had practically been done by the Dutch in the Spice Islands. The monopolist company trading as a corporation must remain, but with a larger capital, a stronger sense of Government backing, larger powers and larger responsibilities, than the old Company had ever enjoyed. It had tried temporary joint-stocks for single voyages, and then for series-voyages; latterly, to carry on, it had been forced back on single voyages, for lack of funds, and the entanglement of the successive joint-stocks had become inextricable. In its new shape, the Company must have not only security of tenure from the Government but a continuous and permanent joint-stock to trade on. It was to emerge at last into what modern nomenclature means by a Joint Stock Company.

The effect of the promulgation of the charter was immediate. Delays, difficulties, and uncertainties to which there seemed to be no end or prospect of one had reduced the Company to such depths that at the moment when the report was laid before the Council of State it was actually preparing to close its career. The charter gave it a new lease of life and a big subscription of capital; from that time it went forward vigorously. Nevertheless it still had before it a hard fight with the hostile forces in England, which was not finally ended till the first years of the next century; besides its difficulties in India, where a new European competitor was about to appear on the scene, and the accession of Shah Jehan's rebel son Aurangzib to the throne of the Moguls, in the year of Cromwell's death, heralded an era of revolt and disintegration within the Empire itself.

The charter provided the Company with the new constitution which remained as the basis of every reconstruction for the two hundred years—1657 to 1858—of life which remained to it; the two centuries during which, by overthrowing the French rivalry, it became first the leading and then the paramount power in India, till it finally disappeared with the extinction of the great Sepoy revolt and the full assumption of the Indian sovereignty by the English Crown.

The charter itself has disappeared, but its practical outcome in the organisation of the company can be summarised from the records connected with it.* The minimum subscription was for a £100 share; five shares qualified for a shareholder's vote, ten for two votes, and so on; small shareholders could combine to acquire a vote between them. The shareholders formed the body of "Proprietors." There were to be periodical valuations (the first at the end of seven years) when shareholders who wished to retire could claim to be paid out at the current price of their stock. Profits were to be distributed in cash—not, as had often been done in the past, in merchandise. Membership was open, for a nominal fee. The subscribed capital, of which, however, only half was called up, was close on three-quarters of a million. The management, as before, was in the hands of an elected Governor, Deputy-Governor, Treasurer, and Committee or Board of twenty-four members; to which only holders of not less than £1,000 were eligible, while one-third of their number retired annually in rotation. The new company took over the old company's factories, as each joint-stock in the past had taken them over from its predecessor; all were now placed definitely under the presidency of Surat. Private trading was forbidden to

* Hunter, II, 134 ff.

members, on pain of forfeiting their shares; external interlopers were liable to confiscation of their ships with the contents thereof. The Company's servants and factors in the East were forbidden to trade on their own account, while in addition to their salaries they drew dividends as shareholders to a proportionate amount; but this legitimate remuneration was so obviously inadequate that the non-trading regulation was practically allowed, by a universal connivance, to become a dead letter, or rather was applied only to the trade between India and Europe. Officials who habitually broke it themselves could hardly enforce it with any rigidity upon subordinates.

## VI

We have just seen Cromwell treating the Eastern trade from a point of view which was not local or sectional but Imperial: as something, that is, which must be developed in the manner most beneficial to the Nation, the Common Weal, the *Res Publica*, the Empire—call it by what name you will—the great body of English or British citizens (for in his theory he included Scots and Irish, however they might kick against the pricks) regarded as a whole wherever they might be. His charter was granted as giving to the trade as a whole the only available form of security which would enable it to be carried on in the manner most likely to be beneficial to the Commonwealth at large. That form happened to involve the guarantee of the East India Company's monopoly. If unrestricted trading had seemed in Oliver's judgement to give the better security, he would have blown the monopoly to the winds. The prevailing anarchy compelled the Government to intervene in order to enforce certain principles, and to make the Trade feel that if well conducted it would have the power of the nation at its back, that its prosperity was regarded as a national concern. But the Government would intervene further only when intervention was imperative. The difference between his attitude and that of the pre-Protectorate Government was not one of principle; it lay simply in the fact that he recognised immediate and decisive intervention by the Government as a necessity of the moment.

Similarly his attitude in relation to the existing colonies and to Colonial expansion was in principle that of his immediate predecessors, though he did, (as they did not,) take Government action with extension of dominion as his immediate object when he dispatched Penn and Venables on the West Indies expedition.

The Commonwealth Government took no action which differentiated between the mother country and the colonies as such. It did take action against those of the colonies which revolted or threatened to revolt against its authority as the supreme Government of the Commonwealth, not because they were subordinate provinces but because they were members of the Commonwealth within which no community could be permitted to be in a state of rebellion. It made no claims to control which had not been asserted by the Crown. It issued no trade regulations which were intended to restrict colonial trade for the convenience of traders at home. Its Navigation Act made no distinction between home and colonial shipping and manning of ships; the purpose of it was the development of the Imperial navy, which was as necessary to the outlying parts of the Empire as to its centre, though the outlying parts might not be equally conscious of its urgency or of the security they derived from it. Its provisions hampered

commerce in general in order to develop Empire shipping
in particular at the expense of the hostile rival who
was even more dependent upon his shipping and his
commerce than England herself; economically unsound,
as economist critics pointed out, it was nevertheless
politically sound, according to the theories of the day
(reproduced in our own time in the doctrine of retaliatory
tariffs) because it told more to the injury of the rival
than of England. The Colonies only shared the advantages and disadvantages of it in precisely the same way
as the mother country, though they were more
directly sensitive to its inconveniences.

We may see then that the determining factor in the
Empire policy of the Crown, the Commonwealth, and
the Protector respectively was their attitude to the
Dutch and finally to Spain. Throughout, the Dutch
were the obstacle in the way of expansion. Charles
quailed before that obstacle; he desired expansion
for itself, but not if it should involve him in a quarrel
with the Dutch; so expansion went to the wall. The
Commonwealth was willing to co-operate with the
Dutch, but failing co-operation it was equally willing
to fight them; the fight opened with the Navigation
Act, was continued by Blake's cannon, and was stopped
by the Protector. The Protector stopped it at the stage
when the continuance of the Navigation Act was
assured and the effective superiority of the English
fleet was at last becoming apparent, while he wanted
Dutch co-operation in other schemes; since he was
possessed with the conviction that Spain was the
enemy, so that Blake's guns were to be directed against
the Spaniards instead of the Dutch. When Cromwell
had gone, and with him his belated conception of a
Protestant League, Holland again took her former
place as the rival, till the menace of French ambitions

overpowered all other rivalries. The policy inherited by the Restoration was a reversion to that of the Long Parliament rather than to Cromwell's.

The domestic conflict in England was only rather mildly reflected in the American colonies. Viewing it as a constitutional struggle, they were onlookers not directly affected by it, and with no motive to take sides; the issue was one which could hardly be influenced by anything that they might do. Viewing it in its religious aspect, Puritanism in the West would no doubt regard the decisive victory of the king with uneasiness. New England being solidly Puritan, its sympathies were solidly with Parliament, but since all Puritan emigration had gravitated to New England, the southern colonies from Maryland to Barbados leaned rather to the other side; the more when, after the decisive defeat of the Royalists at Naseby, a considerable number of Royalist refugees betook themselves thither. But opposing sympathies did not issue in armed conflicts except when Clayborne turned the presence of a Puritan privateer in American waters to account for the recovery of Kent Island—the loss of which had always rankled—from Maryland. The one point upon which every colony alike would seem to have made up its mind was that it would resist any encroachment, by whomsoever made, upon their rights under their respective charters or those which they regarded as already established by custom. And none of them wished to challenge the penalising intervention in their affairs which would inevitably result if they took sides against the side which should prove victorious at home.

The position, however, was somewhat changed when the constitutional struggle culminated in regicide, to the horrified amazement of the world at large. In

P

England the acceptance of the new régime was imposed
by the presence of the irresistible Army which had set
it up, and in Ireland and Scotland by the campaigns
of Oliver Cromwell; but across the ocean it soon became
clear that the acquiescence of the plantation-colonies
was by no means assured. Virginia where Berkeley
was still governor, Barbados (to which one of the
Royalist leaders, Lord Willoughby, had betaken
himself) and Antigua in the Islands, and the faction
in Maryland which was at the moment predominant,
all repudiated the authority of the Republican Government in England. Having on its hands Prince Rupert's
Royalist fleet, rebellion in Ireland, and defiance from
Scotland, the Government replied first only by forbidding
trade with the revolted Cavalier colonies—an ordinance
to which foreign countries paid no attention. In 1651
however, when Cromwell had just finished the Worcester
campaign and the Navigation Act was on the point of
passing, a strong Commonwealth squadron under Sir
George Ascue appeared at Barbados—where he found
6,000 men under arms, led by the redoubtable Lord
Willoughby, ready to oppose his landing; the first
rumour of the battle of Worcester having brought a
report that it was a decisive Royalist victory. When,
however, it became known that the Royalist cause had
been decisively shattered, the futility of defying the
Commonwealth became obvious. The *de facto* Government on the other hand was bound to insist on
unqualified recognition of its authority, but it had no
vindictive intent, and the "moderate" party in Barbados
had no difficulty in obtaining terms of capitulation
which rather increased than curtailed their liberties.
The die-hards, however, were required to leave the
island. It is curious to note that the very capable leader
of the moderates, Colonel Modyford, made the very

remarkable suggestion—in relation to the question of taxation—that the Colony should be represented in the Parliament at Westminster; an idea which, if its realisation had been practicable, would have averted the claim put forward a century later that the imposition of taxes on the colonies by the Parliament in England contravened the fundamental doctrine of "no taxation without representation." And the Commonwealth commissioner did not at once reject the suggestion but reserved it as a matter for subsequent consideration.

The islands—Antigua, the Bermudas and others—which had followed the lead of Barbados in declaring against the Republic, followed it again in submitting upon the favourable terms which the commissioner was quite willing to concede. About the same time, Virginia submitted, though Berkeley was disposed to fight; the moderates, who were in the majority, were not seriously troubled about the theory of monarchy, provided that the interests of the colony itself were safeguarded, especially against Puritan domination. Berkeley himself, the most zealous of the Royalists, was allowed to remain in the Colony, but in retirement from public affairs. New England had accepted the Republic without demur.

In Maryland there were complications, following upon its acceptance, after a slight show of resistance, of terms somewhat more restrictive than those conceded to Virginia. Maryland, unlike the rest, was a proprietary colony, and though it was not definitely Roman Catholic, it was predominantly so, while tolerant of all religions including Independent Puritanism; the proprietor, Lord Baltimore, in England was a member of that body which the Puritan Commonwealth hardly tolerated at all; the Commonwealth was by no means disposed to consider favourably the exceptional rights claimed by or on behalf of a Catholic proprietor who had acquired his privileges by personal favour of the King who had just been beheaded; the Marylanders were bent on retaining or increasing the popular control of the Government which they had so far extracted from Baltimore who claimed that under the charter it was vested in himself, on resisting the imposition of a Puritan domination, and on submitting to no encroachments on the part of Virginia; and finally Baltimore, relying wholly upon political astuteness, was bent on recovering in his own person the lost control which was to the liking neither of the rulers of England nor of the popular party in Maryland. Baltimore, sitting at home in England, withdrawn from public affairs as a Catholic, had an unfailing skill in adapting himself to circumstances while missing no opportunities, and in providing himself with an unimpeachable legal justification for each step he took before taking it; he was admirably served by his agents in the spirit as well as in the letter; it was always impossible, technically, to convict him of illegality in any of his measures; he slipped through between his Scylla and Charybdis—and ended as proprietor in fact as well as in name. The whole performance was an amazingly clever piece of successful steering under extremely adverse conditions; but there were times when its intelligence was more convincing than its honesty; and during the process there were periods of considerable disturbance.

PART III

THE EMPIRE IN BEING

1660-1714

# CHAPTER XI

## THE NAVAL DEVELOPMENT: 1660–1713

### I

THE English Empire came decisively into being in the years when the historic English Monarchy was in suspense; because it was in those years that the National Government first realised its Imperial character, provided itself with the essential instrument of oversea empire, an Imperial instead of a merely national Navy, and set itself to develop a mercantile marine on an Imperial scale. The fleets with which Elizabeth fought Spain were largely composed of privateers, and since her death, her Royal Navy had been allowed to dwindle —during the very period when England was setting up her oversea settlements and competing for the commerce of the East. In the first three years of its existence, the Commonwealth created the navy which could without hesitation challenge the Dutch for the fighting supremacy of the seas, and passed the Navigation Act which, whatever we may think of its economic soundness, was definitely directed to depriving the Dutch by Government action of their maritime commercial supremacy. In the course of the next half century the Imperial policy inaugurated by the Commonwealth came to full fruition; the fighting supremacy and the commercial supremacy both passed definitely from the Dutch to the English, while the new competitor, whose rivalry for a moment threatened both, had failed to make good.

During the first half of the seventeenth century, the Empire was coming into being; not by a national effort, but by private enterprise, only so far fostered by the State as it gave a degree of security to the adventurers by the Crown's grants of charters to groups formed into Companies, or in two or three cases—Gorges in Maine and Baltimore in Maryland—to individuals, conveying to them exclusive rights of trading, jurisdiction over their memberships, authority for self-defence, and privileges balanced by restrictions in favour of the Crown. The Crown, in short, took a paternal interest in its subjects who for their own ends sought to venture their capital or their persons in oversea enterprise, being conscious of possible benefits to its own purse or to the national strength which might accrue from their energies; but farther than this it did not go in developing the expansion. It recognised no obligation on its own part to the adventurers beyond the fulfilment of definite promises under the charters—and even those it did not hesitate to break on occasion. In any case, the interests of the adventurers must not embarrass the Crown in its relations with foreign powers.

On the other hand, the Crown had no desire to burden itself with the business of control; the Companies or proprietors shaped their own governmental systems under Governors appointed by themselves—until the Crown resumed for itself the powers granted to the Virginia Company after the governmental system had already taken shape. Even then the fact that the Crown in England instead of a body of directors in England sent out the Governor made no material difference to the colony.

Nevertheless, Charles I, within a few years of his accession, did resolve to tighten the reins at the expense of the liberties of the settlers, because he was conscientiously convinced that it was his duty to regulate their religious practices into conformity with his own school of churchmanship. With that object in view he set up Laud's Commission for the Plantations, the purpose being unmistakably manifested in the appointment of Laud as its head. Its activities, however, were practically paralysed by the political situation; but when the Long Parliament was coming to grips with the Crown it substituted the authority of Parliament for that of the Crown and set up its own committee in place of Laud's Commission; doing so more for the purpose of overriding the claims of the Crown than with a view to active interposition on its own part. Virtually it interposed its authority only when interposition was invoked by the colonists themselves, or demanded by inter-colonial differences, or by the need of checking Royalist activities. But those very circumstances prepared the ground to receive the seed of the idea which began to show itself when the Long Parliament had been "purged" by Colonel Pride and the remnant thereof assumed the sovereign authority; the idea of a British nationality, Imperial because not confined to the British Isles, whose common interests it was the business of a National Government to safeguard; an idea which only somewhile after the Restoration degenerated into the doctrine that the interests which lay outside England must be not merely reconciled with but kept subservient to the interests of England itself.

Cromwell supplemented this Imperial policy, while making it his own and emphasising it both in East and West, by adopting an aggressively Protestant policy for the Empire, in relation to Europe. That Protestant policy died with him; but the Imperial policy, with the Imperial fleet, was the main legacy inherited by the restored Stuart monarchy from the Commonwealth and the Protectorate.

To summarise the "Argument" (in the eighteenth century use of that term):—The condition of oversea empire and commercial ascendency was the development of oceanic sea-power. The Elizabethans developed sea-power so far that at the end of the great Queen's reign Spain and Portugal had definitely lost to England the supremacy of the seas, but the development had been State-organised only up to the point necessary for the defeat of Spain which lacked the power of recuperation, while Portugal was already exhausted past recovery. At that point the English organised development was not only suspended but was actually allowed to decay, for about half a century. On the other hand during that half century another State, much smaller but of the same nautical calibre as England, a State, however, which had only just shaken itself free from the bondage of Spain, set itself to the organisation of sea-power and commerce as a national concern of transcendent importance, and had achieved the position which at the beginning of the century had apparently been destined for England. Then with the fall of the monarchy in England came a sudden awakening of the Government to the nature of the change which had taken place. The paramountcy which at Elizabeth's death lay easily within the reach of the English they had allowed the Dutch to grasp with both hands, whereby the Dutch instead of the English, and much at their expense, had attained wealth and power absurdly disproportionate to their numbers. That paramountcy was England's birthright, which she must recover—if not by peaceful competition, by the arbitrament of battleships. Within five years' time, that arbitrament had established parity at least—not yet in commerce, but in fighting. But parity was not ascendency; to achieve ascendency was the business of the Commonwealth's successors; and it was not won till the last decade of the seventeenth century. During the forty years that followed the Restoration, Holland was striving to hold her own against heavy odds; England was forging ahead; but France, inspired by Colbert, was entering the field she had hitherto neglected, and made her bid for parity if not actual leadership. Her success would have been more menacing to the English or British expansion than that of Holland could possibly become. She failed, and the English won the ascendency which ultimately broke the French rivalry both in America and in India.

The story of the establishment of this ascendency is the prologue to the stories of the Colonies and of India, in the same period.

## II

Between the Restoration of 1660 and the Revolution of 1688, there were two naval wars on a large scale; in both the hostile navy was again that of the Dutch. In the first, the rumoured approach of a French fleet in alliance with the Dutch gave the latter a Pyrrhic victory in a tremendous four-days' battle, without otherwise materially affecting the outcome of the war. In the second, the presence of a French fleet in alliance with the English gave the English a Pyrrhic victory in the battle of Southwold Bay or Sole Bay—though the French omitted to take part in the engagement— also without materially affecting the outcome of the war. With the Revolution came a new phase. The Dutch were no longer the enemy; the Stadtholder of

Holland was king of England, and France was the common enemy. In two battles, victory over the English fell to France; in the third, her fleet in the Channel was overwhelmed and her navy never recovered, or indeed attempted to recover, from the blow. From 1689 to 1697 and from 1702 to 1713, England and Holland in alliance were at war with France; but after La Hogue in 1692, France was permanently out of the naval race, though she developed and maintained a very active privateering war on English and Dutch commerce. Holland had already reached the limit of her capacity for expansion; and in the second period of war with Louis XIV, England by her seizure of Gibraltar and Minorca established her own domination in the Mediterranean, at the moment of her union with Scotland. From that time Great Britain held in her own hands not only the ascendency but the supremacy of the seas.

The Navy which the restored Monarchy took over from the Commonwealth was one hundred and fifty per cent larger than the Royal Navy when the monarchy of Charles I fell ; and the primary purpose of that increase was to make it more than a match for the most powerful navy then afloat. When, after the Protectorate, Cromwell's obsolete Protestant policy, which had not been shared by his predecessors, was dropped, and the menace of Louis XIV's aggressive designs was not yet apparent, the Anglo-Dutch antagonism revived in full vigour, nor was there any disposition on the part of the Crown to reverse that part of the Commonwealth's policy which was dictated neither by Puritanism nor by hostility to the claims of the Monarchy. Charles II had no goodwill to the Republican Dutch Government which had shown no goodwill to him in his exile and was holding his own youthful nephew in virtual captivity. Covering his own remarkable political astuteness with the cloak of irresponsible frivolity, no man was more thoroughly alive than he to the uses of expansion, though he was ready enough to let them go to the wall when they stood in the way of his other projects and predilections. Holland stood in the way of English expansion, and he had nothing to lose by quarrelling with the Republic; so when national sentiment grew bellicose, war followed.

This second Dutch war, like the first, was definitely Imperialist in its motive—Dutch Imperialism was explicitly hostile to English Imperialism. English and Dutch were in each other's way everywhere; in the West where the Dutch colony on the Hudson had planted a wedge between New England and the Plantation colonies; in the East, where the Dutch had choked the English out in the Spice Islands; on the African Guinea Coast, where Dutch and English were rivals in the slave-trade; and it is not unfair to say that of the two the Dutch had always been the more aggressive until the first Dutch war. Another and a very different motive entered, as we shall see, into the third Dutch war, though ostensibly the Imperialist motive was still the one that was put forward and accepted, not without questionings after a very short time, by the English people and by some of its most zealous supporters.

Here, then, we may pause to examine the personal policy of Charles II and his brother James Duke of York, who succeeded him as James II, in relation to maritime ascendency and Imperial expansion, on which both exercised an important influence though in very different ways; the one having a very acute brain which was denied to the other. Stupid though James undeniably was, he had an absorbing passion for the Navy. Until his devotion to the Church of Rome compelled his resignation of the position of official chief of the

Navy he devoted himself with single-hearted fervour
to its welfare, nor did his attachment to it diminish
when he ceased to be officially responsible for it. That
fact must always weigh heavily in his favour, however
severely we may condemn his melancholy failure as a
king. Moreover, he was keenly interested in new
colonisation. But the point to be emphasised here is
that of the three objects of his devotion,—Divine Right,
the Roman Church, and the Navy, devotions between
which there was no conflict or none of which he was
conscious—the third was hardly, if at all, less strong
than the first and second. The Navy definitely benefited
by his share in its administration during the first half
of his brother's reign, and he is entitled to the credit
for those benefits though doubtless their initiation was
due to shrewder men than himself; while the grave
defects in that administration cannot be laid at his
door. He had an almost infallible instinct for doing
the thing which was most certain to thwart his own aims,
and selecting the worst possible moment for doing it,
but in this particular relation it was an instinct which
happily failed him, so that in fact he left the Navy
appreciably indebted to his service.

The contrast between James and his amazingly clever
brother is remarkable. Charles II all his life played a
lone hand and played it with unfailing skill, while no
one, until Shaftesbury's suspicions were aroused, guessed
what he was about. It took him over twenty years to
accomplish his object, but in the end he achieved it.
He himself—but no one else—always knew what he
was doing. He took big risks, but with his eyes open,
like Elizabeth trusting his own ingenuity to evade disaster
if things went wrong.

Charles had no devotions, but he kept one aim, consistently in view, to the furthering of which minor ends

however desirable in themselves must give way. Expansion was certainly to be fostered, but its claims were to be tacitly but ruthlessly subordinated to the interests of the Crown as understood by the King. He meant to be a King secure against rebellion and free from Parliamentary control. Any attempt to play the tyrant would be fatal, but he had no sort of wish to play the tyrant.

The suspicion that he was working for absolutism would be fatal. Personal popularity would be helpful. Puritanism was happily played out in England—if it had not been so, the business would have been much more difficult and irksome for a man of his temperament. It would always pay to follow the line of least resistance, at least if it could be diverted into the right direction —and the less other people understood the direction in which it was leading, the better. But in any case he must have more money than he could hope to extract from a Parliament whose suspicions were likely to be easily aroused; though where it was to come from was by no means clear at the beginning of the reign. Meanwhile, the line of least resistance was to leave the conducting of the Restoration Settlement to the judicious management of the Royalist Edward Hyde, now Lord Clarendon, and the Cromwellian soldier and admiral, George Monck, who on his own responsibility had so successfully engineered the Restoration and was now made Duke of Albemarle. Both desired a settled England, a Government resting upon the widest general assent attainable, a powerful monarchy (though Cromwell's particular brand of powerful monarchy had not rested upon general assent), a powerful navy, and a firmly independent attitude towards the foreign Powers. In all of which the King was in complete agreement with them—as yet.

Hostility to Holland was an inheritance common to

Charles, Clarendon, Albemarle, and the nation at large. Cromwell, choosing between France and Spain, had ultimately made alliance with France, to further his project of a Protestant Union. That project had passed, leaving no specific reason for allying with either the one or the other except that the theory of maintaining the "balance of power" in Europe (which Cromwell's Protestantism had deliberately ignored) suggested a preference for the weaker Power. The Restoration Government attached itself to neither—but the restored King married the Portuguese princess Catherine of Braganza. That marriage was most agreeable to the King of France and offensive to the King of Spain who was still hoping to recover the Portuguese crown which his grandfather had stolen eighty years before from the house of Braganza, but he himself had been vainly trying to retain for twenty years past. The marriage meant that as between Spain and France Charles was giving the preference but nothing more to France, as Cromwell had done, though without Cromwell's reason.

The development of that policy may be held to account for the immense predominance which France was very soon to attain in Europe; because in the hands of Charles II it presently became a policy of deliberate subservience to France in the interest of his own monarchy—when Charles had decided to make Louis instead of Parliament his paymaster. But when the Portuguese marriage was made, he had not yet formed that design, nor was England in any way committed to a French alliance. Even from the orthodox "Balance of Power" point of view, it was not as yet by any means clear that the Bourbon power was a more dangerous menace to the European equilibrium than the Hapsburg powers acting in concord. And on the

EDWARD HYDE, EARL OF CLARENDON
The first Minister of Charles II

[Face page 232

other hand, from the specifically English Imperialist point of view, the Portuguese alliance proved to be of first-rate value. For it gave England a much-needed naval base at the gate of the Mediterranean, in Tangier, and full and independent possession of the island of Bombay which in a few years was to become the head-quarters of the English in India; both being included in the dowry of the royal bride.

Charles very well understood the possible value of Bombay and the certain value of Tangier, though at a later stage of his reign it suited his personal policy to let it go. But at this stage he recognised its value so thoroughly that, having to choose between its effective retention and that of Dunkirk since the cost of main-taining both would be too great a strain, he chose to retain Tangier; wherein he had the very emphatic support and approval of Albemarle. Dunkirk, in the Spanish Netherlands, had been won by Cromwell's Ironsides in the last year of the Protector's life, to take the place of Calais—lost a hundred years before—as the gateway to the Continent for English armies; so that popular sentiment was outraged when Charles sold it to France; but a naval gateway to the Mediter-ranean was for England of far higher value than a military gateway to Flanders.

### III

In 1664 then, England and Holland drifted into the war which was declared openly at the beginning of the next year and was ended by the Treaty of Breda in 1667. While it was in progress England (particularly London) was smitten by two great catastrophes, the Plague and the Fire. The paralysing effect of those two calamities was partly responsible for the folly

Q

which in the last few months of the war laid up half the fleet, so that the Dutch were able to sail into the Thames and the Medway, bombard Chatham, and create a panic in London itself by the booming of their guns, when peace negotiations were already in progress. Disgraceful as the episode was, it did not mean that the English fleet had lost its equality with that of the Dutch, but only that a particularly short-sighted Government order had deliberately put the greater part of it out of action for the time being.

So it was that under the peace-treaty which was signed in the following month, England, not Holland, was the substantial gainer by the war. Captures made on either side during the war were retained, and what fell to the English included the Dutch New Nether-land on the Hudson. Thus England was in possession of the whole sea-board from the border of Florida to Maine. On the other hand King Louis, besides enjoying the spectacle of the two maritime Powers battering each other's fleets, secured some pickings for himself at the expense of England. He was able to do so, because he was under treaty obligations to support Holland as her ally—obligations which he fulfilled up to the precise point which suited his own convenience; so that it was the threat of a movement of the French fleet which forced Albemarle to face De Ruyter with half the English fleet instead of the whole of it when the Four Days' Battle began, though the French fleet did not actually move at all; and by a like interpretation of his obligations to Holland he was able to effect some captures on his own account on the other side of the Atlantic, among them Acadie, which had been resigned by Charles I but restored by Mazarin as part of his bargain with Cromwell. Thus was initiated in the Dutch war the practice followed in subsequent wars of the maritime Powers filching from each other, whenever hostilities were afoot, "sugar islands" which might or might not be restored when hostilities ended.

Blake had died as he was coming into port, in the year before Cromwell's death; but the fleet with which the English fought the Dutch in 1664–7 was the Commonwealth fleet which he had done so much to make, and its admirals and captains were for the most part the Commonwealth admirals, Monck himself, Montague, now Lord Sandwich, William Penn and others; to whom, however, must be added that most valiant adversary of Blake and of the Commonwealth, Prince Rupert, and his cousin James Duke of York, the Lord Admiral, who himself held the supreme command with credit (and with conspicuous courage) when he defeated the Dutch at Lowestoft. Apart from the fact that Blake could not be replaced, there was no falling off in the personnel, the courage, or the seamanship of the Royal Navy. The mismanagement in the service was the doing of the landsmen. Even the strategic blunder which sent Albemarle in one direction and Rupert in another on the eve of the Four Days' Battle, when concentration was all-important, was imposed upon the admirals by positive orders from Whitehall.

There was no ostensible change in the policy of the Government following upon the Dutch war, but there was a fundamental change in the unsuspected policy conducted by Charles behind the backs of his ministers. Clarendon could never have been brought into line, but there was an excellent opportunity for getting rid of Clarendon. He had served the particular turn Charles wanted him to serve; he was unpopular with the court and unpopular both with the vindictive section of the old Cavaliers and with the Puritans for precisely opposite reasons; and now the whole country had persuaded itself that he was responsible for everything that had gone wrong in the Dutch war. Under pressure from Charles, Clarendon reluctantly withdrew into exile instead of remaining, as he himself wished, to face his impending impeachment which might have been extremely inconvenient for the King.

The country—and the Protector himself—had never been at ease with the French alliance under Cromwell, who would have broken it off without hesitation if Mazarin showed signs of evading the terms and understandings on which it had rested. The alliance had not been renewed under the restored monarchy, and Louis had taken part with the Dutch in the war. At the moment when the war ended his movements on the Continent were suspiciously aggressive. They were, in fact, the opening moves in the great game of aggression which he was going to play for the rest of his life, the game in which young William of Orange was to be his most stubborn opponent, and which was finally to be wrecked by Marlborough and Eugene. Suspicion of France, growing by degrees into a profound hostility, was rooting itself in the English mind. And at that precise moment Charles was making up his own mind that his French cousin should be his own purse-bearer. An incredible scheme as matters stood! Louis, unless he believed it to be in his own interest, would certainly not give him money. If the country knew that Charles was trying to get money from Louis, he would certainly be sent either to the scaffold, or, if he escaped that, on his very uncomfortable travels again. To carry out the scheme, he would have to hoodwink the nation, hoodwink his ministers, hoodwink finally King Louis himself. But his chance lay precisely in its incredibility.

Nation, ministers and King, would never suspect, and for that reason they might all be hoodwinked—and hoodwinked all of them were, until Shaftesbury began to suspect. Then for ten years there was a duel of wits between Charles and Shaftesbury—and Charles was able to deliver the decisive thrust at the exact moment when the ex-minister had made sure that the King was at his mercy.

Very conveniently for himself, Charles was able for some time to come to give his policy the appearance of continuity; that is, of an anti-Dutch policy which might be modified by the necessity for combining with the Dutch to check the aggression of a Catholic Power whose activities were creating uneasiness. Hostility to the Dutch as rivals was deep-seated in the popular mind and was aggravated by the final humiliating episode of the war just ended, but was over-ridden for the moment by the development of Louis XIV's aggressive activities. Charles fell in cheerfully with Sir William Temple's project of a triple alliance between England, Holland, and Sweden for the restraint of that aggression; but this made it the more imperative to provide material reasons which should induce Louis to regard the personal support of Charles as worth buying. It was, however, at the same time a very broad hint that France might find the national opposition of England decidedly embarrassing. National opposition would carry the day unless the King of England was provided with the necessary means for over-riding it—financial independence of Parliament, and the military force at his own disposal which would enable him to nip in the bud any attempt at armed rebellion. Given those conditions, Louis might rely upon Charles to help him to the full extent of his power, but without those conditions, Charles would be powerless to aid him and would probably find himself forced to act against him. Moreover, there was another inducement which would appeal strongly to Louis' sentiments. Charles as yet believed that if he had a free hand he could reinstate the Roman Catholic Church in England, not being conscious that the dominant Anglicans were as hostile to the claims of the papacy as to those of the Protestant dissenters.

We may then summarise, in the order of their importance in his eyes, the aims which Charles definitely set before himself when, having freed himself from Clarendon, he began to rule through the group of ministers known as the Cabal. First, he must retain his personal popularity with the public at large, who must continue to attribute not to him but to his ministers the responsibility for anything that went wrong. Second, Louis was to be cajoled into making him independent of Parliament. Third, the Roman Church was to be restored if the thing could be done without a too violent disturbance of public feeling. Fourth, the interests of the nation generally should be fostered, so far as they did not collide with his dominant aims. Fifth, the depression of Holland under its Republican Government would be agreeable alike to the English people, to the King of France, and to the King of England. To these had presently to be added a stubborn determination to secure the succession to the throne for his unpopular brother James. Presently also his attitude to Holland was changed by the fall of the Republican oligarchy, and the raising of his nephew William to the Stadtholdership as the indomitable champion of Dutch liberties.

The Triple Alliance was signed six months after the Treaty of Breda. When two years had passed, the secret compact of Dover was made between Charles and

Louis, accompanied by a secret Treaty which the ministers were allowed to regard as their own work, directed to joint action against Holland by France and England; but the ministers were not privy to the personal agreement between the two monarchs, which made at least partial provision for what were in their view the fundamentals. Even the formal treaty was unknown outside the confidential circle. The issue of the Treaty was the wholly unexpected joint declaration of war against Holland by the two Powers two years later (March, 1672).

As in the two previous formal Dutch wars, and in the informal engagements between Dutch and English in waters where their fighting with each other did not involve an open breach between the two Governments, the battles in the third Dutch war were desperate ding-dong conflicts in which both sides fought to the bitter end whatever the odds, and victory, usually dubious, went sometimes to the one and sometimes to the other, with the balance on the whole in favour of the English. Nevertheless, the war is a landmark. In the first or Commonwealth war the predominance of the Dutch was challenged by the English, who may be said to have drawn level. In the second the Dutch, who suffered the more, were hard put to it to maintain a very doubtful equality at the cost of a heavier strain. In the third they were fighting with their backs to the wall, to preserve not an equality but their existence as a first-class naval Power, while the position of their rivals in the front rank was never threatened. They had reached the limit of their naval resources, whereas England's were growing. Unless through her own fault, England's ultimate ascendency was assured. By sheer indomitable tenacity the Dutch did to their eternal honour hold their own alone by sea against the most powerful navy on the seas, and on land against the most powerful army in Europe, though not alone, since Louis' aggression had brought a European coalition into action against him. When it came to exchanging blows, the English fought as stoutly as the Dutch, but they went into the war and conducted it half-heartedly, and they dropped out of it without decisive victory but without reluctance, because they were doubtful not of their own power but of their Cause—since France was their official ally.

The Dutch and English fleets were not again to be pitted against each other till more than a hundred years had passed. Fifteen years after the Peace of Westminster in February, 1674, ended the war, so far as England (but not France) was concerned, the Dutch Stadtholder accepted the throne of England vacated by the flight of James II. The Peace itself was an acknowledgement, in no way humiliating, of defeat on the part of the Dutch in the sense that they could not hope to hold out much longer against the combined powers of England and France. But it signified that they had lost, and England had won, a position which they could never recover.

Charles had plunged the country into the war primarily in fulfilment of his secret bargain with Louis, and secondarily with intent that the restoration of the House of Orange should be part of the peace-terms. The gratitude of his nephew might be useful— might in fact be more useful to him than to Louis who undoubtedly intended to make Holland a French dependency. The scheme went to pieces when the Dutch rose against the rulers who had failed to avert the war, murdered the de Witts, and made William Stadtholder. Charles saw that he had taken a false step, if William was to learn to look upon him as a friend. Then, England was uneasy. To fight Holland was natural—but there had been no *casus belli*, and the alliance with France was suspicious. It became all the more suspicious when, as it seemed at Sole Bay, the French fleet limited its co-operation to looking on at a distance while Dutch and English were at deadly grip. If the enemy's trade was suffering, so was that of the English. France was making England her catspaw! Public opinion demanded that the war should be ended on reasonable terms. So Charles explained to a much-annoyed Louis that he could not stand out against the national sentiment. He must make peace. It was not his wish; but it all showed how impossible it was for him to help France as he desired—until he should be made independent of Parliament. And for the same reason the reinstatement of the Roman Church must wait—the only result of a tentative movement in that direction had been that Parliament passed the Test Act, excluding Catholics from the public services, the Duke of York had been obliged to resign his naval command as a declared Roman Catholic, and Shaftesbury was organising an Opposition.

Here, however, we may also note that the third Dutch war marked the close of the chapter in our naval history in which the most notable commanders were soldiers who had exchanged the field for the quarter-deck. They had been needed to give that touch of military organisation and combination in which the mariners, the men with a sea-training only, had been lacking; they had been men chosen for their known efficiency as commanders, and from them the seamen had learnt all they had to teach. With their passing of that generation (Sandwich was killed at Sole Bay), the day of the soldier-admiral passed also.

From that time the English admirals were seamen who had been trained in the sea-service, and in the

traditions which had been established in that service
when Blake and Monck were the chiefs, who implanted
their own military principles, so far as they applied to
naval warfare, in the colleagues and subordinates from
whom they in turn learnt their own seamanship.

## IV

We need not follow the ingenious shifts by means
of which Charles ultimately succeeded in marrying
his niece Mary to his nephew William the most stubborn
foe of King Louis, yet extracting the necessary funds
from Louis, checkmating Shaftesbury, reigning without
a Parliament for the last four years of his life, and
leaving the Crown to his brother in 1685 free from any
new limitations and with none to dispute the succession
except the illegitimate Duke of Monmouth. We must,
however, note a detail which aptly illustrates the
extent to which Charles, though with a lively consciousness of Imperial interests, was ready to set them
aside when they interfered with his monarchist programme. He had held on to Tangier at the beginning
of his reign, even when doing so involved parting with
Dunkirk. He had kept his hold on it for twenty years
—not perhaps uninfluenced by the fact that the garrison-
ing of it was an unanswerable warrant for keeping on
foot a standing regiment in addition to the household
troops which were otherwise all of the standing army
that he had been able to retain. Nevertheless in the
last year of his life Tangier was abandoned and dis-
mantled because, lacking the necessary funds to maintain its defences against the Moors, he did not choose
to call a parliament and face it with a demand for
money. Thus for the next twenty years, England was
again without a naval base on the Mediterranean;

where she was all the more in need of it owing to Colbert's development of the French navy which had now reached the highest point it was destined to attain. The last Anglo-Dutch war—not by its own actual achievements—had brought it within sight of effective maritime rivalry with the two specifically maritime Powers who were hammering each other's fleets to pieces. Charles was doubtless cynically satisfied—not without good reason—that his fleet would manage to make good against any adversaries; for though he knew its value, he was at no pains to increase its efficiency, while peculation and corruption were rife on the civil side of its administration; James, in his brief reign, could do little enough to remedy the disorganisation; and consequently for a moment while the crown of William III was still insecure the ascendency of the English fleet was unexpectedly hanging in the balance.

In 1660–1, when Charles returned to England and Louis at the age of twenty-two took into his own hands the reins of government which had hitherto been held by Mazarin, France was not a maritime power, even approximately in the same class with England and Holland. Charles had a royal navy of over 200 sail while the French Royal Navy had thirty. The Dutch mercantile marine had most of the world's carrying trade; only the English were beginning to encroach on that monopoly, and the goods even of French traders were borne largely in Dutch bottoms. In the Eastern and Western Oceans there were plenty of French as well as of English and Dutch privateers, as there had been in the previous century, but France was practically without oversea settlements except on the St. Lawrence. The idea of French rivalry had not presented itself seriously to the Dutch or the English. But in 1662, Louis was entrusting the very necessary reorganisation of the finances of France to Colbert, the bourgeois minister whose abilities had been commended to his notice by Mazarin.

Colbert developed a definite financial policy. Apart from the reorganisation which meant that the proceeds of taxation should actually reach the Treasury instead of being dissipated among its agents on the way, taxation was itself to aim at making the country entirely independent, so far at least as necessities were concerned, of supplies from potential enemies. It was therefore what we should now call an organised system of high Protection, securing to French agriculture and French industrialists the home market for everything France could produce for herself, while what she still required to obtain from abroad made a substantial contribution to the Treasury, though at the expense of the consumer. But there were still the goods needed which no amount of Protection would enable France to produce for herself in anything like adequate quantities. Such goods then ought to be obtained from countries which could not be regarded as potential enemies, and also to be available in time of war. The Dutch and the English were solving that problem by setting up colonies and a maritime commerce whose products might meet their requirements and were kept available by the strength of their fleets. To these they were largely indebted for their wealth and effective power, out of all proportion to their natural resources or their populations. France, taking example by them, must join in the race and surpass them both, in colonisation, in the expansion of maritime commerce, and in her fighting navy.

Private enterprise coupled with half a century of vigorous Government action had carried Holland to the leading place; private enterprise with no more than mildly paternal encouragement had taken England to the second place, which the vigorous Government action of the last decade had transformed into the first place. Private enterprise by itself had left France lagging far behind. It was necessary then that vigorous French Government action should cancel the handicap—and the more thoroughly the thing were done at the expense of the Dutch and English, the better. So Canada became a military Crown Colony; an East India, a West India, a Levant, an Africa Company, were set on foot, almost as departments of State; and a great navy was gradually built up which even in the Dutch war, only a dozen years after it began to emerge from embryonic conditions, was able to take the seas side by side with the two great fleets, though its independent activities were not displayed in first-class battles. In the following years it continued to be zealously nursed by Colbert till his retirement and death and after him by his son Seignelay, though Louis was absorbed in his armies, while the Dutch navy perforce and the English navy by neglect were losing their efficiency; so that in 1688 the French navy was not unprepared to challenge the English and Dutch together.

In the summer of that year, Whig and Tory leaders in concert invited the King's son-in-law, hitherto his heir presumptive in right of his wife, to intervene in England. The French fleet might have made William's landing impossible; a direct attack on Holland would certainly have done so. But Louis had offered James his help, James refused it, and Louis attacked the Palatinate instead of Holland. William landed at Torbay unmolested; the troops James sent west to oppose him went over to him instead; James made a midnight flitting to France; William and Mary became King and Queen of England in March, 1689 (o.s. 1688), and Louis promised to help James to recover his throne.

V

Louis had a powerful fleet and able admirals; but the military advisers to whom he gave ear had no more understanding than himself of the uses of the navy. At first, the French proved distinctly the stronger in the channel; early in 1690 a French squadron defeated an English squadron off Bantry Bay; French troops had already been carried over to Ireland; yet the French neglected to interfere with William's passage to that country, where he won at the Boyne Water a victory which was far from striking in itself but had the practical effect of breaking up the Jacobite resistance. Yet, only on the previous day the French had inflicted on the English one of the heaviest defeats in our naval annals, off Beachy Head. England had unmistakably lost command of the Channel. Still James, to his deep chagrin, found that the navy he loved was so fervently Protestant that it remained stubbornly loyal not to him but to his Protestant supplanter. The French navy made no further use of its victory; the English navy felt that it had suffered a disgrace not by its own fault but through mismanagement for which the landsmen had been responsible; and almost exactly two years after Beachy Head, Admiral de Tourville was forced by imperative orders from the King to join battle with half the French fleet against an immensely superior force. Even then the French losses were not much heavier than those of the English at Beachy Head— but the battle of La Hogue was decisive. There was no other fleet action in the war. England after a heavy defeat could recuperate and fight the harder. The French fleet could not. After La Hogue, it was not again able to take the sea in force, though a vigorous and damaging privateering war on the Anglo-Dutch commerce was carried on continuously.

The English and the Dutch were alike in this, that their naval development was instinctive. The Governments which built up their navies were pushed on by the natural inclination of their peoples. But, apart from the size of the populations, the problem of maintaining sea-power was a harder one for the Dutch than for the English because the Netherlands lay open to attack by land—that is to say, by land Powers rolling armies of invasion against them. England did not. She could be effectively attacked only by a sea Power; as long as she held command of the Channel and the North Sea, no invader could reach her shores. The invader could wreck Holland's prosperity but not hers. The French differed from both in that their instinct was not maritime but continental. Their fleet was not instinctively created and maintained; it was an artificial creation maintained only as subsidiary to the armies which were their natural instrument for the continental aggrandisement, to which maritime aggrandisement was only subsidiary. Defeat on the seas made them concentrate the more on victorious armies and the less on the defeated navy, except at moments when a Colbert or a Choiseul could make his influence felt; whereas for England a defeat or even a felt menace of defeat meant redoubled concentration on the navy. Therefore Beachy Head was followed by La Hogue, and therefore La Hogue—not because it was in itself an overwhelming victory—gave England the lasting supremacy of the seas; the supremacy which was to be the decisive factor in the approaching duel, to be fought out in the eighteenth century, with oversea empire as the stake.

Now it is worth while to observe that the policy of Louis XIV, indirectly and unconsciously but none the less decisively, fostered the further development of the English sea-power. It was not so at first. He did his best to keep English and Dutch fighting each other, to the detriment of both and the exhaustion of Holland. This strengthened England only in so far as it weakened her maritime rival; and that was fully compensated by the fact that it allowed France to develop her own sea-power without interruption. But it did not suffice to ruin Holland; and in the next phase, when France directly challenged England as well as Holland, the two sea Powers were united against her. The depression of Holland in the economic interest of France had the whole-hearted approval of Colbert. But Colbert's aims were crossed by his Master's continental ambitions, of which not the depression but the subjection to his own sway of all the Netherlands, Dutch as well as "Spanish," was an integral part. That would not of itself have brought England into the arena; but when Louis, in his character of *Grand Monarque*, deliberately posed as the magnanimous champion of the exiled James, he brought England into play, uniting her to Holland, and at the same time emphasising the fact that France intended to take Holland's vacated place as her naval rival—a tremendous incentive to her naval development. For England it meant that the naval issue must be fought out and her own predominance established—or lost. France began well, but she no sooner met with a heavy defeat than she fell back upon mere commerce raiding, because her continental ambitions demanded concentration on her armies, while England at war concentrated her martial energies on her navy.

That war ended with the Peace of Ryswick. But five years later France was again at grips with England and Holland, and half Europe as well, in the War of the

Spanish Succession, waged under the last reigning Stuart. The predominance of the English navy had been at best doubtful in 1690; in 1702 there was no doubt about it; the only question was whether England would make the best use of it. Again we may note that it was not English statecraft or statesmanship which brought England vigorously into that war, nearly so much as Louis' repetition of his old political blunder in posing as the champion of the Stuart exiles. In that war the military genius of Marlborough and Eugene saved Europe from a French domination. But for England it wrought far more; it made her supremacy on the seas indisputable, because it won her a permanent naval base in the Mediterranean. If Marlborough—whose military genius was such that he appreciated the military uses of sea-power as few soldiers have done—could have had his way, that base would have been at Toulon, as Ralegh would have had it at Cadiz. The co-operation necessary to the capture of Toulon was not forthcoming, but George Rooke, cruising with a different object in view, took the Rock of Gibraltar off its guard with an Anglo-Dutch squadron, a fortnight before Marlborough and Eugene broke the French Grand Army at Blenheim; four years later an expedition from Spain under Stanhope captured the still more valuable station Port Mahon with the island of Minorca; and both were retained as prize of war by England at the Treaty of Utrecht. If she could not have Toulon she could at least keep watch and ward over it. As long as she could guard it the French fleet could not concentrate to strike a decisive blow against her; so that it would be her own doing if she lost the maritime supremacy she had thus definitely achieved.

R

# CHAPTER XII

## THE EAST AND THE EAST INDIA COMPANY: 1660–1709

### I

THE East India Company was launched upon a new phase of its career under the Charter bestowed on it by Oliver Cromwell, as a Company trading upon a permanent joint-stock, instead of a series of joint-stocks, each individually wound up at the close of the particular venture. It had thus been enabled to raise a very much larger capital than had ever before been possible. The position was confirmed at the Restoration by a fresh Royal Charter, the Crown not regarding itself as bound by any acts of the Protectorate.

On the other hand the Company was faced by a new situation in India where the accession of Aurangzib, the result of successful rebellion, practically inaugurated a revolution in the Mogul Empire itself, which fundamentally affected the Company's immediate activities in India as well as its more remote future. It is also to be noted that, four years after the Restoration, Colbert started the French East India Company, which on Indian soil, was presently to prove itself a much more formidable rival to the English traders than either the Portuguese or the Dutch, both of whom the English had there already left far—and permanently—behind; but the presence of the French did not make itself felt as a menace till after the last Stuart sovereign was in her grave. Since the progress of the East India Company turned upon the political conditions in India produced by the half-century of Aurangzib's reign—which in effect corresponds with the era of English expansion now to be reviewed—this is the matter which demands our first consideration.

It was remarked in an earlier chapter that the Mogul Empire was at the zenith of its splendour in the reign of Shah Jehan. Roughly speaking, India north of the 20th parallel of latitude, extending up to Kabul, was under his dominion. South of that line lay the two sultanates of Bijapur and Golconda (Hyderabad), the representatives of Mohammedan overlordship in the Deccan except in so much of the northern part of it as had been already brought under the Mogul dominion. Bijapur retained its independence, but Golconda was tributary. East and west of the two sultanates respectively the coastal districts were held by Hindu princes in varying degrees of subjection to one or other of the sultans, while the southern triangle was under independent Hindu Rajas. Except in this southern triangle, all the Hindu dynasties and princes in India were the vassals of one or other of the three Mohammedan potentates, while the Mogul himself was lord of more than two-thirds of the whole, including about half the coast-line (the northern half in each case) both on the east and on the west.

Within the Empire, both Jehan Gir and Shah Jehan continued, or at least did not violently break away from, the policy Akbar had inaugurated and carried out, of giving complete toleration to Hinduism and, broadly speaking, not differentiating between their Mohammedan and Hindu subjects—a departure from the precedents set by all the previous Mohammedan dynasties, Afghan or Turk, that had ruled in Hindustan since Mahmud of Ghazni first led his zealots through the north-western passes to raze the temples of idolatry. Under Akbar Rajput princes, ruling their own domains, held high commands in his armies; his great finance minister was a Brahman, and Jehan Gir's mother was a Rajput. For Akbar, being a most unorthodox follower of Islam, was tolerant of all creeds, and being by blood a mixture of Turk Mongolian and Persian, with his mother's Persian strain predominating, was singularly free from racial prejudices, and dreamed of a unified empire. Under this régime the old animosities were at least pacified, and were not rudely revived under Akbar's son and grandson; though Moslem fanaticism might resent this toleration of the Infidel.

Shah Jehan was not too successful in the business of enlarging his empire. On the north-west, he lost Kashmir and his efforts to recover it were of no avail; and though he annexed territories in the northern Deccan, the rule of his officers there was by no means secure. In the latter part of his reign he distributed vice-royalties among his four sons; Shuja had Bengal, which included Behar and Orissa and was very nearly an independent sovereignty. The third son, Aurangzib, was in charge of the Deccan, the fourth had the western provinces of Gujerat and Sindh, and the eldest, whom he intended to be his successor, had the north-west. But each of the other three intended to secure the succession for himself. Shah Jehan fell ill, and the three younger sons revolted, having this in common, that they were bent on ejecting the eldest, Dara Shikoh. In 1658 Aurangzib, being much the most astute of them, captured his father who passed the remaining years of his life in captivity, hunted the other three brothers to death, and thus auspiciously opened the reign which ended in 1707 when he had passed his ninetieth year.

The two characteristic features of the reign, which in fact made the break up of the Mogul Empire inevitable, were provided by Aurangzib's determination to enlarge a dominion already too large for effective control and his reversion to Moslem bigotry in relation to the Hindus. While he made himself overlord of all India, so that it became a collection of Satrapies, he revived the hostility of the vast Hindu population to the crushing Mohammedan supremacy.

The Two Years' War of Succession postponed the decisive overthrow of Bijapur and Golconda, which Aurangzib had seemed to be on the eve of effecting when the expectation of Shah Jehan's death started the insurrection of his sons and the fight for the throne. The Mogul did not return to the Deccan till more than twenty years had passed, leaving it to lieutenants who found in the sudden rise of an entirely new power, that of the Hindu Marathas, a problem which none of them was capable of solving. The Marathas were to prove a particularly formidable factor in the coming disintegration of the Mogul Empire one reason thereof being the fervent hostility of Sivaji, the founder of their power, to the Mohammedan domination. And while Sivaji was doing his work, Aurangzib was unconsciously fostering it by his zeal in depressing the Hindus and Hindu principalities in the north and west. Sivaji's work was done before Aurangzib had sufficiently freed himself from his entanglements with his Rajput vassals and on the Afghan frontier to take in hand personally the overthrow of Bijapur and Golconda, which were themselves the strongholds of Mohammedan though not of Mogul power in the south. The rise of Sivaji himself, however, was at the expense of Bijapur rather than of the empire, because the Maratha country proper was mainly within the Bijapur sovereignty though bordering on Mogul territory. The Moslem sultanate was the primary object of the Hindu chief's hostility, though the Moslem empire was ultimately the enemy. The Mogul conquest of the sultanates was made easier by the rise of the Marathas, but the Marathas themselves were to prove enemies of the effective power of the Mogul dynasty much more dangerous than the sultanates, though the fact did not become fully apparent during the life of Aurangzib.

The Maratha development calls for some special attention; not only because in the next century the Maratha Confederacy threatened to become the paramount power in India but because the Maratha country lay on that side of Bijapur which brought it into contact with the Mogul dominion and the Imperial province of Gujerat in which the East India Company had its headquarters. The Marathas had never formed an organised State, though racially distinct from their neighbours, the western highlands where they abode being difficult of access, difficult to hold, not productive of booty for conquering settlers, but at the same time, like other highland districts, ill adapted for the development of political organisation. Their foreign rulers curbed them by planting garrisoned fortresses in their territory. But they had the hardiness of a highland folk; and when there arose among them a leader endowed with something at least nearly akin to genius, who, starting as a brigand chief, set himself to organising them as a brigand community, he did in effect transform them into a rebel robber-State. That is what Sivaji did, but commonly as the champion of Hinduism against its Moslem oppressors, while he levied tribute from the former as the price of his protection. When we recall the prolonged defiance that Wales was able to offer to the Kings of England, or the Highland clans to the Kings of Scots, it is not hard to understand how the Marathas under a great leader like Sivaji were able to defy the armies of Bijapur, or of the Mogul's viceroys. But that the thing should have been done by a bandit chief wholly without the prestige of high ancestry—no true Maratha was a Brahman though Brahmans among the Marathas had great influence—and that he should have organised his power to such a pitch that it did not melt away at his death, was an achievement of genius not easy to parallel.

## II

As long as Charles II and James II were on the throne, the London Company enjoyed the royal favour. It had accepted the Commonwealth without enthusiasm; it had been saved from dissolution and provided with a permanent basis by the Protector, not out of any tenderness towards it but because he regarded the Eastern trade as an Imperial asset; and it welcomed the Restoration on the full tide of the Monarchist reaction, with an eager loyalty. Its attitude to the other two East Indian oceanic powers, Holland and Portugal, had been for five and twenty years past and remained after the Restoration the attitude adopted openly or covertly by Charles II during the first fifteen years of his reign—it had aimed, that is, at friendly relations with the defeated Portuguese while cherishing its hostility to the Dutch who had ousted it from the Spice Islands. Created and even to some extent petted by the Crown in its early days, it had a naturally Royalist bias, though a considerable quasi-Puritan element had entered its composition. The astute and impecunious Charles II was quick to see its possible utility to himself if judiciously handled, apart from the general principle of encouraging trade and maritime expansion from which he only departed when it happened to clash with his personal convenience. It had just been launched on a rising tide of commercial prosperity, and was more than willing to pay a handsome price for the Royal favour in the shape of gifts and loans. The Duke of York's interests were engaged, because (or by reason of which) he became a very substantial shareholder; and on the one occasion when relations became somewhat strained, through the King's injudicious attempt to manipulate elections to the directorate, Charles was skilful enough to transform a possibly dangerous opponent, Josia Child, into an extremely valuable supporter. Crown and Company derived mutual advantage from the alliance.

We left the Indian activities of the Company at the point where, (its headquarters being still at Surat in the western Mogul province of Gujerat), having recently established a fortified factory at Madras under the Golconda sovereignty, it had still more recently been permitted to set up factories in Bengal—not fortified but under the protection of Mogul governors—first in Orissa, a sub-province of Bengal, then at Hugli in Bengal proper (under favour of the viceroy Prince Shuja, the second of the sons of Shah Jehan who were on the point of fighting each other for the succession), with a branch at Kasimbazar, higher up stream. The east coast factories were technically subordinate to Madras, while Surat exercised a general supremacy. The chiefs on the spot were constantly in the position of having to take decisive action on their own responsibility, in circumstances which could not be appreciated by persons not on the spot; action which on the one hand might involve exceeding their technical authority, or departure from the general rules of policy laid down by the Company sitting at the India House in London to whose severe censure they thus rendered themselves liable; while on the other hand they themselves judged such action to be essential in the Company's interest. To the judgement, the courage and sometimes the open insubordination of such men, who never hesitated to assume that dangerous responsibility—though doubtless their judgement was occasionally at fault—it was due that the Company was able to maintain and consolidate its position through the turmoil of Aurangzib's reign.

Four Presidents in succession ruled continuously at Surat from 1662 to 1690. The situation had been difficult enough during the actual progress of the War of Succession when the factions of Aurangzib and his younger brother were fighting each other, and to stand neutral was only a fraction less dangerous—or even for the moment more dangerous—than to accept protection from one party (which might in the end be defeated) as the lawful authority. That particular phase passed when Aurangzib had crushed the brother who had previously been Viceroy of Gujerat; but the war had made the restoration of an effective Government difficult. Sivaji had just struck a heavy blow at Bijapur, and was turning his attention to the Mogul province, when Sir George Oxenden arrived at Surat as President in 1662.

In 1664 Sivaji with a great army swooped upon Surat, the Mogul city in which the English traders had been permitted to set up their factory—that is to say their depot and offices; not a fortress—Mogul Governors tolerated no foreign fortresses within the Mogul jurisdiction. The Mogul Governor shut himself up in his castle; the Marathas ravaged the town; but the English President took a bold stand. Sivaji offered him terms, but he defied the bandit chief as a rebel, and succeeded in beating him off. The Mogul protection had failed ignominiously, but he had protected himself, brilliantly and in the sovereign's name, when no one else had dared to face the invader. He received a substantial reward from Aurangzib, but more important was the prestige and favour accruing to the English name. Oxenden was also in charge during the Dutch war of 1665–7 when Dutch squadrons threatened the coast. Surat itself was too far up the river for attack; moreover the Dutch, from motives of policy if nothing else, would hardly have assailed a Mogul city, so that there was not actually much to be feared from their presence, apart from their interference with the traffic by sea. Finally it was under his Presidency that the island and port of Bombay, acquired by the Crown in 1661, were transferred to the Company and attached to the Surat presidency.

The Portuguese had long ago taken possession of Bombay, as their own, not holding it from any overlord on the mainland. Its potential value had been recognised, but had never been turned to great account; and when it became the private property of the English Crown on the marriage of Charles II with Catherine of Braganza, as a portion, like Tangier, of the Infanta's dowry, it seemed at first as if the acquisition was likely to prove more troublesome than it was worth. As a beginning, the Portuguese Governor declined to hand it over to the Earl of Marlborough (James Ley, third and last of his line; he was killed three years later in the Dutch war) who was sent out with naval and military forces to take possession; and nearly all the troops died of scurvy and fever. There was not an open breach with Portugal; the English were actually allowed to take possession in 1666; but it was obvious that if effective use was to be made of Bombay, it would have to be put in the hands of the East India Company to take its place within the Company's organisation. After some bargaining, the Company accepted it (declaring it to be a most burdensome addition to their responsibilities) at the price of a quit-rent of £10 per annum, and set about planting it with settlers, English and Indian, mainly from Surat, supplemented by a score of women "of sober lives" from England to provide wives (for good Protestants only). Bombay was placed under a deputy-governor; it was not till some years later that the President's headquarters were removed thither from Surat.

In 1669, Gerald Aungier succeeded Oxenden as President of Surat. During the eight years of his presidency (terminated, as Oxenden's had been, by his death, in 1677), Aungier made Bombay; having realised its possibilities in the face of drawbacks and difficulties which might well have seemed insuperable to any man of a less dauntless resolution. But he realised also that the time had come when the failing control of the Imperial Government over the areas at a distance from the centre made it imperative for the English to rely upon their own powers of self-defence. There was no question about the soundness of the old principle of unarmed commerce under the old conditions, but the old conditions had passed—that had been made conspicuously clear when the Governor of Gujerat entirely failed to defend Surat against Sivaji while the President and servants of the English Company were left to uphold alone the banner of the Mogul. The emperor could no longer resent the claim of the English to take adequate measures for the security which his own Government could no longer guarantee. The fact that the old conditions had passed was confirmed in the second year of Aungier's Presidency; Sivaji again fell upon Surat, when Aungier himself and Streynsham Master (a nephew of Oxenden) shared the credit of rescuing the Company's property and defending the Company's quarters against the marauders. Mainly through Aungier's initiative the English in India took up the new attitude which the Company found itself inevitably compelled to endorse, involving its own gradual development as an actual military Power. It is worth while, however, to emphasise the point that but for the ravages of Sivaji the necessity for a change of front might not have become apparent till much later   They for the first time revealed inability on the part of the Mogul Government to protect its own subjects and foreign residents on its own soil.

The very lively account of the operations at Surat and the port at Swally Roads on Sivaji's second incursion, sent home by the Surat Council,* contains incidentally other points of interest. Not only the Dutch, but by this time the French also had factories in Surat. The French made their own terms with the marauders without fighting; it is inferred that the Dutch had already a secret understanding with them, as they were unmolested. When the Marathas attacked the English quarters they were received with so hot a fire that they withdrew to carry their depredations elsewhere. Later returning to the attack they were again repulsed, but Masters who was in charge did not decline a parley. (The little garrison had come up from Swally Roads whither the goods had already been removed for safety; it was only the unanimous pressure of the Council that induced the reluctant President to remain there while Masters "cheerfully

---

* This may be read in full in the *Diary of William Hedges*, ed. Sir H. Yule, Vol. II, pp. 226–9.

undertook the charge" of defending the factory itself with thirty sailors, in his place.) Masters told the Maratha captain that he had no wish to fight—but would fight to the last gasp if attacked. After which the Maratha captain became most polite; and Sivaji, having cleared out the rest of the town, withdrew his army, having satisfied himself that it was better policy to have the English as friends rather than enemies. Before departing, however, he informed the Mogul authorities of Surat that he expected an annual tribute of twelve lakhs of rupees (£120,000), failing which he would return at his leisure and burn down what was left of the city. They were his legitimate prey. Not so the English, who had made it clear that preying upon them was bad business; his main concern with them, at the conclusion of negotiations, was to persuade them to reinstate the factory at Rajapur (in the territory he had torn from Bijapur) which they had abandoned in consequence of his own depredations.

It is clear enough that it was his experiences with Sivaji that shaped Aungier's views on the new departure in methods which he urged upon the Company in a letter written not six months before his own death at his post in Surat. "The times now require you to manage your general commerce with your sword in your hand," since the native powers take no account of "paper protests and threatenings," though more particularly it was necessary to have a fleet competent to deal with that which Sivaji—with a perspicacity unusual among Oriental potentates—was now developing, and also with the pirates who infested the coast and in the intervals of their normal employment served the Mogul in lieu of a navy.

When Sivaji's departure left Surat in peace, Aungier devoted himself to the development of Bombay though

as yet the Company rejected his proposal that headquarters should be transferred thither from Surat—
their objection being not at all unintelligible, since,
during its brief career as a Crown Colony it had acquired
a very evil reputation as a death-trap for Europeans.
The Company, however, subject only to the English
Crown, was at this one spot, as Portugal had been
before it, unequivocally sovereign; no native power,
not the Mogul nor Bijapur nor the Marathas, could
lay claim to it. The native subjects of the Portuguese
had become the native subjects of the English who
could administer it as they chose.

The first essential business was to fortify it, though
the Company refused to sanction engineers for the
purpose, on the ground that their schemes were always
unprofitably costly. Aungier, however, went on with
the erection of Martello towers, already begun, armed
the existing fortress with guns, instituted a native
militia in which service or payment for exemption
was compulsory, with English officers, and enlisted a
miscellaneous troop of "regulars" consisting of such
Europeans as could be collected. With these materials,
when the last Dutch war broke out and a substantial
Dutch squadron appeared on the scene, he succeeded
in making such a deceptively imposing display that
the Hollanders, sighting three English and five French
ships lying in the harbour, took discretion to be the
better part of valour and retired. France as well as
England was at war with the Dutch at this time, the
new French East India Company was pushing its way,
and the new and growing French fleet was displaying
considerable activity in the Eastern seas against the
Dutch though with no marked devotion to the interests
of its English allies. The Dutch did not again threaten
Bombay. The real problem for Aungier was to get

the port in such a state of defence as to be secure against the pirates and to provide protection for the coastal traffic; and this he did, though by no means as effectively as he desired, his means being so limited by the economies of the India House.

But the great purpose in view was to develop Bombay into a better trading centre than Surat where the English could not be independent. Under Portuguese rule it had not been developed; Aungier gave it a sound government and a new trading population attracted to it from Surat, and he made it habitable by draining the marshes which had been the source of its evil reputation; carrying out his schemes under the same difficulties and limitations as his defence plans.

Aungier's vigorous policy was by no means in favour at the India House. His successor, Rolt, was appointed as agent of the extreme school of blind economy; and with the same intention John Child was then made Deputy Governor of Bombay, and was promoted to succeed Rolt at Surat in 1682; when his namesake Sir Josia Child had established himself as Governor and dictator of the Company in London. Next year, however, Sir Josia, hitherto a leader of the "economy" school, suddenly became the champion of reckless aggression—a *volte face* apparently due to the loss of Bantam owing to Dutch intrigues. In both policies, he knew that he could count upon his protégé John* as an instrument entirely at his service.

Meanwhile Madras had had its own troubles: for on the Coromandel coast there had never existed such a controlling authority as that of the Mogul's viceroys in Gujerat and Bengal. Fort St. George had to take

---

* Until recently, the established fiction that Josia and John were brothers was never called in question. In actual fact however, they were quite certainly not brothers; nor is there any shadow of evidence that they were even remotely related. See *Keigwin's Rebellion* (p. 625), by R. and O. Strachey, p. 162.

care of itself, while the Directors in England remained firmly convinced that expenditure on defence was a prodigal extravagance. When a vigorous Governor, Sir Edward Winter (1662–5), proposed to take vigorous (and expensive) action, the Directors promptly superseded but did not recall him. But the new Governor was a Puritan with a taste for republican doctrines; so Winter, with the support of the more Royalist party took the government back into his own hands, imprisoned the Governor for his treasonable proceedings, declaring that he himself was only doing his duty as a loyal subject of the Crown, and for some years defied the Company's emissaries, finally retiring on his own terms; but the defensive policy was not advanced. A few years later, Sivaji was carrying his victorious arms through the southern Deccan, England and Holland were at war (1672–4), and the Madras Government, threatened by sea and land, seriously contemplated abandonment of the position as untenable. The Dutch war, however, was soon ended; Sivaji met with reverses and shortly afterwards died; and Streynsham Master who had distinguished himself at Surat was sent out as Governor. Madras recovered prestige, though the Company as usual was very ill-pleased with his methods; and the advance of the Mogul's armies in the south gave at least comparative security—provided that the English kept on good terms with the Mogul's officers.

In Bengal, as at Gujerat, the English were present by grace of the Mogul and the Nawab, Shaista Khan, Aurangzib's uncle; their only means of defence when he chose to deal with them tyrannically or extortionately was to threaten withdrawal; active resistance would have been madness, and appeal to Aurangzib himself futile. Such was the general position of the English in India when John Child, who for some years had, with doubtful credit, served the Company at Rajapur and elsewhere, was appointed Governor at Surat, in 1682.

About this time there occurred, within the Company's jurisdiction, two episodes which illustrate the anomalous character of its authority. We have already seen Sir Edward Winter, himself in the Company's service, defying it at Madras and seizing the Governorship on the plea that the official President was disloyal to the Crown and that the Company in London was evading its obligations and misusing its powers; similar action on the like plea was now taken at Bombay and in St. Helena (which, though in the mid-Atlantic, was one of the Company's Governorships). That island had formerly been held by the Dutch as a port of call on the way to the East, but was seized by the English when their rivals occupied Table Bay to take its place, initiating the Dutch colony in South Africa, in 1652. In both of the later Dutch wars it was again captured and then recaptured. The Company planted it with English settlers under its own Government, which became so harsh that in 1684 there was a serious revolt, though it was crushed with a savagery not unworthy of Judge Jeffreys himself.

The revolt of Bombay in 1683 was more surprising. It was headed by a fighting and popular member of the Bombay Council, Richard Keigwin, who had previously done good service at St. Helena. The ruinous economies and autocratic methods of John Child and his brother-in-law Charles Ward as Deputy Governor at Bombay, had become intolerable. Keigwin, being in command of the troops, arrested the Deputy-Governor in the King's name, ruled as elected Governor —always in the King's name—for eighteen months to the satisfaction of the settlement, wrote home denouncing Child at Surat (who found himself powerless), and

s

only resigned at the end of 1684 in obedience to direct
orders from the King who knew perfectly well that the
new Child domination in the affairs of the Company
would be entirely in his own interest.

### III

The rebels were not penalised. But Sir John Child,
with a knighthood, was now officially made "Governor
and General" of the whole Indian establishment. He
was merely the instrument, not the deviser, of Sir
Josia's new policy. The actual fact had been obvious
to Aungier that the Company's position in India could
no longer be allowed to be dependent on the capricious
goodwill and very uncertain protection of Mogul
viceroys. It must compel respect for its own power to
defend itself. Bombay was, or could be made, secure;
Surat could not, Madras was threatened alternately by
Moguls and Marathas, the settlements in Bengal were
at the mercy of the ruling Nawab, the Mogul himself
was nearing his seventieth year. What would happen
in case of a quarrel with Aurangzib it was hard to guess,
but it was imperative that the potentates who, from the
Mogul down, held us in contempt, should be made
"sensible of our power." In Bengal particularly it came
to this, that either the trade must be abandoned or
the rights granted in return for heavy payments must
be enforced with arms in our hands. In the past, the
Mogul could be relied on to see that his officers carried
out his promises; that was so no longer. Protests had
been vain.

Aungier however had not contemplated anything like
the fantastically grandiose scheme which was now set
in operation by the despotic Governor of the Company
in London. In 1686, with the Royal Assent—James II,

now on the throne, was a large shareholder—it declared war on the Mogul empire with an armament of ten ships and six companies of infantry in addition to the ships in Indian waters and the miscellaneous "soldiers" of sorts already on Indian soil. Regarded as a war, the thing was no doubt a fiasco; it ended in 1690 with peace upon terms which Sir John Child represented as highly honourable to the English, while hostile critics with better reason treated it as an ignominious admission of complete defeat. Aurangzib was probably quite unconscious that his might was being challenged; he condescended to make some concessions which cost him nothing, mainly because hostile English ships on the sea-route to Mecca would make the pilgrim voyages of the Faithful extremely dangerous. But incidentally the war had the effect of inaugurating that fortification of the English settlements upon Mogul soil, under shelter of the Imperial authority, which had hitherto been rigorously forbidden, but without which the British power in India could never have developed. Specifi-cally, however, its main interest lies in the fact that it brought about the establishment of the English in the new station on the Hugli which was destined to become the British Capital, as Calcutta. At the time, and for long afterwards, the supreme position was held by Bombay; the transfer thither from Surat, which Aungier had not been allowed to carry out, having been at last sanctioned when Sir John Child bcame in effect though not by actual title the first Governor-General of the English in India, Scotland and Ireland not being as yet participants.

The foundation of Calcutta was the work of Job Charnock, who after nearly thirty years' service in the Bengal factories was appointed Chief Agent and head of the Hugli settlement at the critical moment when

the Court of Directors in England was resolving to
declare war in India. He had joined the service as a
young man, was junior "member of Council" at the
Kasimbazar factory in 1658, and was made head of
Patna from 1664 to 1681, during which period he was
several times disappointed by the Madras Government
—Bengal being under its presidency—of promotion
which he thought, and the Board in England thought,
was his due. The latter habitually referred to him as
"our old and tried servant" until he was at last allowed
to succeed to the Hugli Agency. From 1681 to 1685,
a period during which Bengal was made temporarily
independent of Madras, Charnock was head of Kasimbazar, the general Agency being given to William
Hedges; but in 1685, when it was again subordinated
to Madras, Charnock received the long-deferred promotion, though he was detained for another year at
Kasimbazar by the action of the Nawab.

Charnock is a strange figure; evidently the kind of
person who habitually outraged the conventions of his
fellow Europeans—he married a Hindu wife, and laid
himself open to charges of apostasy from the Christian
Faith—and was obviously disliked by most of the
authorities with whom he came in contact, while his
merits were more readily appreciated by those at a
distance; not a tactful or a brilliant person, but one
of indomitable courage, endurance and determination;
the last person to be bullied. At Hugli he found the
native authorities bullying the English settlement.
Hugli was a hundred miles up the river, practically
out of reach of big ships. The position there was
intolerable, especially after a violent *fracas* between
the English—who had not four hundred fighting men
in the place—and some native troops. But there were
armed light craft available; on these he embarked

the English, and, dropping down the river to Chitanati, the point where Calcutta now stands, where there was practicable harbourage for big ships, occupied the shore, hoping to be permitted to substitute it for Hugli as a permanent station; its two apparent merits being that the surrounding land was practically impenetrable for an army during a part of the year, while by water it could be reached by the larger English ships from the sea.

Thence he opened negotiations and actually obtained a fresh agreement guaranteeing the trading rights which had been guaranteed so often, but over-ridden. The agreement was waste-paper. For in the early months of the year, the guardian swamps were not so impenetrable as they had seemed; an attack in force was threatened, and Charnock was constrained to re-embark and move down to Hijili near the river mouth, which was itself little better than a swamp. Here he succeeded in making a stand for three months with his four hundred men, cut off from supplies and supports, and occasionally fiercely attacked by swarms of the Nawab's troops, till between fever and fighting he had scarcely a hundred men left fit even to pretend to bear arms. But the arrival of an English ship enabled him to bluff the Nawab's commander into the belief that he had received a powerful reinforcement. Negotiations were re-opened, the old agreement was renewed, and Charnock with his remnant evacuated Hijili with all the honours of war. (June, 1687.)

Presently he returned to Chitanati and tried to make the place habitable; but next year arrived Captain Heath to take over the command of the forces and seize Chittagong—an enterprise which testifies the Company's ignorance of the geography of Bengal. Chitanati was abandoned. Heath went off on the fatuous Chittagong expedition, and the fugitives—for such, in effect, were Charnock and his party—were deposited at Madras.

Meanwhile on the other side of the peninsula Sir John Child's ships were harassing the pilgrim-route and the Mogul's ships by sea, while the Mogul's officers (Aurangzib himself being more seriously occupied with the suppression of Golconda) were harrying the Company's factories ashore; the process was destructive to the interests of both; and in 1690, as previously noted, Aurangzib granted the peace which from his point of view was a magnanimous concession. In consideration of their humble prayer for pardon, their payment of substantial compensation for damage done, promise of good behaviour in future, and the expulsion of " Mr. Child " (who perhaps rather conveniently died three weeks before), a new licence to trade was granted.

The practical outcome was more advantageous than the terms of the Mogul's ordinance would suggest. On one side, Indian governments had learnt, from the stoppage of trade, that to strangle trade was in their own interests a mistake. The English on the other hand knew that their command of the sea was the weapon which had made Aurangzib prefer magnanimity to vindictiveness; but they had also learned that to challenge the Mogul Empire on land was futile, while the military conditions only emphasised the necessity for making their main factories strongly fortified garrisons with open communications on the sea side where they were masters. Bombay and Madras could be made into such fortresses, and Job Charnock, whether by chance or prescience, had fixed upon the site for a third in Bengal at Chitanati.

Moreover, when Aurangzib issued his ordinance a more enlightened Nawab, Ibrahim Khan, was taking

Shaista Khan's place in Bengal. When Charnock returned in 1690, it was under new guarantees which gave promise of being honestly observed, and with a fixed resolve to establish the English headquarters not at Hugli but at the new site. Before his death in 1693 Calcutta was definitely born, though as yet its cradle was a very uneasy one. In 1700 it became Fort William, so christened in compliment to William III.

## IV

We have followed the doings of the Company's servants in India during the thirty years succeeding the Restoration of Charles II; that is, to the point when the "Glorious Revolution" of the Whigs was an accomplished fact and William of Orange was seated, not yet securely, on the English throne. When Sir John Child died and Aurangzib issued his pardon to the English, the battle of the Boyne had not yet been fought, or the decisive issue of La Hogue between the French and English fleets; but the European interests of Dutch and English had become so closely identified that Dutch hostility or even Dutch rivalry never again required to be seriously reckoned with in Indian waters or on Indian soil. On the other hand the Company had definitely entered upon its departure from its old purely commercial policy but had at the same time arrived at a critical epoch in its own constitutional history, partly generated by the crisis in the constitutional history of England.

The Company, as has already been noted, welcomed the Restoration with a warmth which was generally shared by the country at large till the awkward business of reconciling conflicting claims created by the Civil War and the Interregnum damped the first enthusiasm.

The entire business community hailed it with joy because the aggressive attitude of the Commonwealth and especially the development of the Navy had entailed heavy expenditure and unprecedented taxation, to the immediate detriment of England's own trade though much more so to that of her rivals; and the Company was a Company of traders. As such, moreover, its prosperity was largely dependent upon alliance with the Government and the privileges derived therefrom. Charles, on the other hand, was no less alive to the advantages to himself derivable from such an alliance, and, unlike his father, far too shrewd to throw them away. Consequently the Company received from him freely whatever they could reasonably ask, and he received from them freely whatever his own astuteness suggested that he might judiciously hint. Each of the parties got a very substantial *quid pro quo*.

For the profits of the re-constituted Company proved to be immense. Whatever doubts there may have been in the first years were dissipated by the statement of results at the end of seven years; so that in spite of the first Dutch war the shares in 1669 were at a premium of thirty per cent, which in the next ten years rose to 150 per cent, and continued to rise, till in 1683 shares that had been purchased on the reconstruction were worth between three and four times as much as had originally been paid for them.*

Trade prospered, then; but within the Company there were discordant elements, and outside it there were always the free-traders denouncing and invading the monopoly. The Company itself had been re-formed by the absorption of a rival Company and the admission of many members who were actually advocates of the free-trade doctrine or of the old Regulated system

---

* Hunter, vol. II, p. 278; Macaulay's *History*, ch. 18.

instead of joint-stock; and not a few of the old Parliamentarians or Cromwellians, who, though they accepted and even welcomed the Restoration, did so without any intention of allowing the restored monarchy to become absolutist; men of the type who presently under the leadership of Shaftesbury became the Whig Opposition. They were never dominant in the Company, but there was a constant risk that they might become so, though that risk was averted partly by the fact that its rivalry with the Dutch kept it in line with the King's anti-Dutch policy (as it was understood) when the popularity of that policy in the country was fading, partly by the diplomatic tact wherewith Charles attached to himself the ablest and wealthiest of those whose antagonism threatened to become inconvenient, Josia Child.

That remarkable man, the son of a London merchant, was already in possession of enormous wealth and varied administrative experience when he joined the Company's Board in 1674. He had been brought into the directorate by Thomas Papillon, the leader of the party within the organisation who desired reconstruction on a broader basis which would meet the economic argument of the free-traders (which was, broadly, that while monopoly was all to the advantage of the monopolists, trading in general for the country was not advanced but retarded by the suppression of competition). Papillon, moreover, was of Shaftesbury's political school, the Opposition (not yet known as Whigs) was beginning to take shape, Popish Plots and Exclusion Bills were in the air, and the reforming party in the Company, with Child as yet among them, were regarded as being associated with the rising political Opposition in the country and in Parliament. In 1676 Charles tried to prevent the election of Papillon and Child to the directorate, but two years later Child was made a baronet. Sir Josia became the most ardent champion of the Company's monopoly, the Company became a pillar of Toryism, and Papillon and his friends were finally ejected from the Board in which Sir Josia became Governor in 1681. The last Parliament of the reign had met only to be dissolved instead of being opened; in that hour Charles had routed the Opposition, and Child was his ally.

It was not, however, until Papillon's party was decisively defeated at the moment of the King's triumph over the Opposition that the Company was generally recognised as unequivocally Tory, though in actual fact it was always, as a corporate body, on excellent terms with Charles. It was between two fires—those who emphasised its dependence on and subserviency to the Crown, and those—of the High Cavalier tradition—who persuaded themselves that its governing body was disloyal; though the latter were to be found in its distant possessions rather than in England. Hence Winter at Madras and Keigwin at Bombay, rebelling against the Company's authority, regarded themselves as the stout champions of loyalists against disloyalists, though their actual grievances had nothing whatever to do with political parties and the political situation in England. Charles himself on the other hand thoroughly understood the position, and gave the Company his backing when necessary—but the rebels were not penalised. Now, from 1682 on, not only the Crown but popular opinion in general recognised the Company as a Tory organisation from which the Whig element was weeded out, the opposition to it identified itself with the Whig party, and the political Revolution of 1688 entirely changed its relations with the Government of the new King and Queen, while it became a target for Parliamentary attack.

SIR JOSIA CHILD          [Rischgitz
The Autocrat of the East India Company

[Face page 274

The change in 1682 was the work of Child, who from that time forward was virtually the despotic ruler of the Company, crushing all opposition to his will. Coupled with his remarkable ability and a dominating character, Child's immense wealth gave him great influence and made him a more than formidable antagonist. In England the battle was definitely joined between Sir Josia as Governor and Papillon as Deputy-Governor on the direct proposal for a reconstruction which would open the corporation to the public; Sir Josia won, with the result described. The appointment of Sir John to Surat ensured harmony between the dictator in London and the virtual dictator on the spot in India itself.

Sir Josia, we may say, captured the Company when he defeated Papillon in 1681. The other side were vindictively attacked when possible as "Exclusionists"; in 1684 Papillon's principal ally Barnardistone and Papillon himself were made victims in succession; both were subjected to huge fines—Jeffreys was Chief Justice—and Papillon had to take flight to Holland. But the opposition continued to be strenuous. They challenged the legal validity of the powers granted to the Company by the Crown in curtailment of the liberties of other traders, the Company having taken proceedings against an Interloper, Thomas Sandys—thus making the question one of Royal Prerogative in respect of regulation of trade, a definitely political issue. There was a long battle in the law courts, but judgement—delivered by Jeffreys—could hardly have gone against the Crown. For there was no Parliament, and Charles by the revocation of borough charters had just ensured that in the next House of Commons at least the Whigs would be a powerless minority, and judges were still removable at the King's pleasure.

As a matter of fact, however, the legal precedents were heavily on the side of the Prerogative.

The natural result was that the Company fell upon the Interlopers; the Interlopers waxed the more defiant of the law which trampled on what they regarded as their rights and also of the law about which there could be no question at all, some of them taking to sheer piracy. The development of buccaneering, already rife in the West Indies, proceeded apace in the East Indies also during the last twenty years of the century. These buccaneers, however, were after all no more than a small portion of the determined interlopers, most of whom continued to regard themselves as honest traders victimised by an unconstitutional and arbitrary law. Moreover, the number of these was continually swelled by some-time servants of the Company itself, who left the service for one reason or another and made use of their experience to trade on their own account—with no disposition to active interference on the part either of native potentates who had no antipathy to bribery or of officers of the Company who sympathised with them and could be conveniently blind.

## V

The Company, under Sir Josia Child's guidance, was doing an immensely profitable trade, which was increasing the wealth of England; that fact could only be disputed by those who clung fast to the belief that it took more treasure out of the country than it brought in. But however it might enjoy the Royal favour, it stood out amongst the whole mercantile community as not only a close corporation entirely controlled by a small oligarchy, but as enjoying special privileges from which the rest of the community were unjustly excluded, and as bringing into the country goods which competed disastrously with her industries, all without Parliamentary sanction and in virtue of Royal prerogative. While Charles II and James II reigned, attacks on it were vain; but the position changed with the accession of William and Mary. The practical supremacy of Parliament was guaranteed by the terms on which they had been called to the throne; William had no reason to feel goodwill towards the oligarchy; its opponents had identified themselves with the Whigs on whose support he was himself mainly dependent; and the powerful commercial interests in Parliament were antagonistic to it. Child had won the battle in 1681, but now he had to fight it all over again. Then the King and the Judges were all on his side, and there was in effect no Parliament; now the King was cold, and Parliament was always there on the other side.

Again the opposition was organised by Papillon who returned to England and to Parliament in 1689. A great Association of merchants was formed outside the Company; a hostile resolution urging the formation of a new Company was passed by the House of Commons; in 1791 the Mogul war ended, and the terms of Aurangzib's peace-ordinance became known. The Company had reason to feel uneasy. Apart from the unqualified free-traders, there was general agreement on two fundamental points—that the trade with the East was of benefit to the country, and that it could best be carried on on a Joint Stock basis by a Company enjoying exclusive privileges. But the old Company was bent on keeping its preserves to itself intact; the Association demanded, as in 1681, a reconstruction which should place it on a much wider and more inclusive basis. The House passed resolutions in this sense, but a Bill to give them effect could get no farther than the second reading, since Child would not give way. Thereupon the House petitioned the King to withdraw the Charter and issue a new charter to a new Company. William, acting always on the constitutional principle of not taking sides if it was possible to avoid it, replied that he could not legally withdraw the Charter without three years' notice; at the same time making it clear that he favoured the principle of the scheme which the Commons had failed to pass. The House petitioned him to give the three years' notice, but his presence was needed with the armies in the Netherlands, and he departed to the front, leaving the question in abeyance.

There ensued a period of intense intriguing and lavish bribery—incorruptible ministers were rare, Child's purse was deep, and the King was more concerned with battles and sieges than with the commercial dispute. Child succeeded in getting the charter renewed, with only some modifications in the direction that Parliament had proposed. Thus strengthened, the Company seized an Interloper's vessel, in the Thames. The House, which felt that it had been tricked, took the matter up; and the result was a Resolution that no English subjects could be prohibited from trading in the East, except by Act of Parliament. Neither King nor Parliament was disposed for a battle on the question of Prerogative, and the King cancelled the provisions in the charter prohibiting unlicensed trading (1694).

The result was chaotic. In effect the Interlopers were let loose, and that was what neither the Company nor the Association wanted. A throat-cutting competition was to the interest of no one except the very few who understood how to make their own individual profit of the welter; there was a popular panic over the cry that Indian goods were flooding out English manufactures, which produced dangerous riots. The Company and the Association openly pitted themselves against each other in endeavours to purchase from the Government the confirmation or the acquisition of an exclusive charter. In 1698 the Association's offer of a loan of £2,000,000 seemed to have carried the day; an Act was passed—opposition in the House of Lords being over-ridden by claiming that it was a supply Bill which the Lords could not amend—"creating * a corporation to whom the King was to grant charters," a Company called the "General Society" for floating a loan of £2,000,000 to the State, subscribers to which should have the exclusive right of trading to the Indies, saving the rights of the old Company till its expiry in three years' time, and of the owners of ships which had already sailed. Any one might be a subscriber. Subscriptions poured in—but about one-sixth of the entire amount was taken up by the East India Company itself, which thus became very much the largest shareholder.

Still the fight was not over. The General Society was not constituted as a Joint Stock Company, but as a Regulated Company in which each member was free to trade on his own account. But its members were also free to combine as Joint Stock Companies. In effect the old Company could carry on, though not—after the three years—with any special privileges. It was, however, in possession of immense advantages over its competitors; it had a great organisation, a great staff of experienced servants, an established trade, established settlements, and a great capital of its own to work on; its competitors within the General Society, though most of them formed themselves into a Joint Stock "New Company", had none of these things.

* Hunter, Vol. II, p. 317.

While they struggled to push their way in, the old Company used every possible artifice to keep them out. It was a sort of civil war, ruinously costly to both sides. Both found themselves faced practically with the alternatives of compromise or disaster. The great champion of the old monopoly. Sir Josia, died in 1699; the other side was still led by Child's old adversary Papillon, whose attitude was always consistent with Joint-Stock amalgamation. The old Company, however, saw a chance of winning if, when it perished as a Company in 1701, it could still hold its shares as a corporate body in the General Society; but that could only be secured by an Act of Parliament, and the Company's Bill was defeated in 1700.

Meanwhile, in India the old Company held its own against the officers of the New Company— claiming with entire justification that the sovereign rights bestowed on it by charter were valid until the expiry of the charter in 1701, Beard in Bengal and Thomas Pitt at Madras particularly distinguishing themselves. The latter, William Pitt's grandfather, made his fortune as an Interloper, but had reconciled himself with the Company in 1694 and was by it made Governor of Madras when the New Company was launched.

The crisis came when the defeat of the Company's Bill in 1700 forced it to revive the negotiations it had hitherto rejected. Compromise was hastened by the rapidly growing menace of the outbreak of the great European War of the Spanish Succession, and the rivals came to a definite agreement which was ratified at a General Court of the two Companies on April 27th, 1702. They were to be merged in the "English" company, so named in contradistinction to the "London" or Old Company; their several properties

would become its sole property; the government and
direction of all would be in the hands of a single body
in which both would be represented equally; though
the complicated process of amalgamation took six
years to complete, the unification of the British power
in India dates from 1702, the first year of Queen Anne.
The consolidated Company was to be known as the
"United Company of Merchants of England Trading
to the East Indies." The surviving difficulties as
between the two Companies were finally settled by
the award of the Treasurer, Lord Godolphin, embodied
in the Act of 1709. From that date the business of
actual as well as technical consolidation went forward
without violent disturbance, till the Company suddenly
found itself, a generation later, involved in a duel
with the European Power which, avoiding collision
with the English, had been making good its footing as
a rival for empire.

T

# CHAPTER XIII

## BIRTH OF THE OLD COLONIAL SYSTEM, AND THE NEW EXPANSION UNDER CHARLES II

### I

THE Commonwealth, we have said, marks the Imperialist turning point in our history, because it was during the Interregnum that the Government of England consciously took upon itself the functions of rulership over an expanding oceanic dominion, an Empire comprising diverse elements with possibly divergent interests in diverse regions of the globe having taken the place of an insular State. It fore-shadowed the incorporating union of England and Scotland; it created for the first time, an Oceanic Navy; it made a beginning, though no more, of regulating relations between the parent State and its off-shoots across the Atlantic; it was Cromwell's charter that provided the basis on which the Indian Empire was to rise; it was Cromwell's West Indian adventure that emphasised expansion as an object of State policy; and it was the Commonwealth Navigation Act, along with the development of the Navy, that stressed the development of sea-power as the means to empire, though "empire" and "imperialism" were not yet terms adopted into the political vocabulary.

We have seen how in the next half century, growing from these beginnings, the Navy established its Oceanic supremacy, and the East India Company its position as a potential Power in India. We have now to see a Colonial system evolving itself under Government control; on the one hand, a multiplication of Colonies, on the other a continuous effort on the part of the Government to direct and control the expansion upon the lines most beneficial to the State as a whole. The wisdom, the justice, and the honesty of its methods, its measures, and its intentions, may of course be called in question, but neglect is emphatically not the fault which can fairly be laid to its charge during the period of the Restoration.

During the previous half-century, colonisation had been experimental. The Home Governments, which before the Civil War meant the Kings, had contented themselves with sanctioning the occupation of hitherto unoccupied territories by particular groups of their subjects who were to enjoy exclusive rights and privileges therein upon terms, without forfeiting their normal rights as Englishmen; provided always that their operations should not contravene the laws of the realm, or be injurious to other English interests, a point on which not they but the Crown would be the judge should any question arise. Subject to observation of the conditions laid down in their respective charters, each group was left free to go its own way. Even the Commonwealth Navigation Act had not differentiated between Colonial and English shipping and seamen, and such restrictions as had been previously placed upon their commerce had been counterbalanced by the privileges they enjoyed. The modern idea of a Colony as an independent State in the making had had no part in the creation of any colony, English or otherwise, except so far as it may have been latent in the minds of New Englanders.

But the regulation of trade by the State in the interests of the whole State was an integral part of the mercantile doctrine. The colonies were outlying portions of the State, which as a matter of course was entitled to regulate their trade accordingly, and the State for obvious reasons meant primarily England herself, the portion of it which bore the burden of protective armaments in a competitive world where protective armaments were a necessity among armed rivals. The essential aim of the regulation of trade was to make England powerful, and to no one was it more essential than to the colonists who, without the protection of English fleets would find themselves open to the attacks and their commerce at the mercy of the maritime Powers. The advantages derived by England from the colonies must be such as made it worth while for her to bear the burden of protecting them. Negatively, the trade of the colonies must not either damage her by competition, or strengthen her potential enemies by supplying them with the material of power; positively, it should pay toll by way of compensating her for her expenditure on defence. The more definitely financial control in England passed from the Crown to Parliament, the more definitely passed with it the regulation of trade—and the more definitely was the regulation of trade controlled by the mercantile interests in Parliament. The elimination of outside competition was the constant aim of the mercantile interests. This aim was applied destructively to Ireland and was perhaps the most persistent obstacle to the Union with Scotland; and it was presently to become the vital source of the constant friction between England and the Colonies, which was the most real though not the ostensible cause of the final rupture. But it must not be forgotten that for a full century after the Restoration the colonies depended for their existence upon the protection afforded by the English navy to which they contributed nothing; the regulation of their trade in the interest of England, short-sighted though it was on the part of the English and irritating to the Colonists, was by no means a tyrannous or excessive *quid pro quo* to demand in return for the benefits conferred.

Now we can in fact see that theoretically Imperial statesmanship had to make choice between three alternative lines of economic policy. It could treat the whole empire, mother-country and colonies, as a single fiscal unit just as England itself was a single fiscal unit with absolute freedom of internal trade and identical tariffs on foreign imports and exports—the ideal of "Empire Free Trade." That would have been to carry mercantilism to its logical conclusion, to make the whole empire independent of all foreign supplies except such as it was incapable of producing for itself, the competition of the foreigner being excluded by tariffs. Secondly, it could adopt the system uniquely developed in the modern British Commonwealth of Nations, of treating each of the several communities as an independent fiscal unit controlling its own tariffs, which would have been to discard mercantilism altogether as applied to the Empire. It rejected both those courses, and adopted a third. It assumed that the Colonies were dependencies to be fostered and protected so far as by fostering and protecting them the power of England would, in the judgement of those responsible for the welfare of England, be increased; the power of England being the necessary condition of the welfare of the Colonies themselves. In so doing, the characteristic which distinguishes England's treatment of her colonies from that of other colonising States is not her arbitrary subjection of their interests to her own but the very much greater latitude of action which she allowed her colonists to enjoy; and, during the Restoration period, the pains taken at home by those who were in general charge of colonial affairs to promote their welfare.

## II

The purpose of the Commonwealth Navigation Act had been quite simply to "protect" English shipping (inclusively) against the competition of the maritime rival—the Dutch—who actually held the supremacy. The desired result followed, though not immediately; but there were many contributory causes, so that it remains an open question whether the said result, the increase of shipping so that it gradually overtook and passed that of the Dutch, would not have been attained if there had been no Navigation Act at all. The general consensus, however, of opinion in its favour was so strong that it was the one measure of the Commonwealth Government which was forthwith re-enacted on the Restoration.

But the Restoration Navigation Act (1660) went farther, supplementing the former Act by applying new regulations to the Colonies. It laid down that certain "enumerated" articles—sugar, tobacco, cotton-wool, indigo, ginger, and woods used for dyeing—should be shipped only to English (or Colonial English) ports. A second Act in 1663 required that European goods should not go direct to colonial ports but be landed in England to be exported thence to the colonies; and a third in 1673, the Plantation Duties Act, required the same customs duties to be paid on goods carried from one colonial port to another as if they had been brought to an English port. The three collectively are included as The Navigation Acts.

It will be observed that goods which, if sent to England, would compete in England with goods produced in England were not on the enumerated list —they were free to go abroad; but the non-competitive goods must come to England first and pay the duties. It may also be observed in the same connection that with the exception of tobacco, which was the principal export of Virginia and Maryland, all the enumerated articles were West Indian products. With the trivial exception of furs, all the products of New England were of the competitive order, and therefore from the home-producer's point of view undesirable imports.

The second or Staple Act of 1663 requires some further explanation. The Navigation Act permitted European goods to be carried direct to the colonial ports in English or colonial but not in foreign bottoms. This tended to throw the colonial port to port trade into the hands of the colonial shippers, and at the same time to multiply the trading routes from Europe thereby making it more difficult to protect them. The Staple Act made England the central mart or staple for imports to the colonies, which would all follow the regular Anglo-colonial trade routes, while tending to attract it to home rather than colonial bottoms, to increase the trade between England and the colonies, and—directly —adding to the English revenue by the customs duties which would have to be paid at the English ports. But another motive is suggested in the wording * of the Act; the closer commercial relations involved in the centralisation will maintain "a greater correspondence and kindness," a stronger sense of interdependence, to the mutual benefit of the colonies and the mother-country.

* Beer, *The Old Colonial System*, Vol. I, p. 76; Egerton, *British Colonial Policy*, p. 71, *N*.

Now Massachusetts, having no enumerated products of her own, succeeded in doing a substantial direct export trade of her own—evading the Navigation Act —with enumerated goods from other colonies. The Act allowed Virginia goods to be carried to other colonial ports as well as to ports in England; it allowed Massachusetts to export her own products (which were not "enumerated") to foreign ports; consequently she was able to carry on, in circumstances which made detection very difficult, what was in effect an extensive smuggling trade with foreign ports, in enumerated goods. The purpose of the enumeration was so far frustrated; the smuggled goods went to the foreign ports without having paid the English customs, and undersold the goods which the English merchants had bought for re-export; to the detriment on the one hand of the revenue from customs and on the other of the English exporters. To counteract this, a third Plantation Duties Act was passed in March, 1673. (It is sometimes referred to as the Act of 1672, as the official year 1673 still began not on January 1, but at Lady Day. But as a matter of fact it passed in the House of Lords on March 29, after the official as well as the popular New Year's Day.)

This third Act was intended to stop the gap which the Navigation and Staple Acts had left open for the evasion of the principle on which they were based— that England should derive revenue and English merchants should derive profits from the export of the specialised products of the colonies; it was the rounding off of the system which claimed that the State which gave the colonists their privileges and their security was entitled to its *quid pro quo*. It enacted that a duty equivalent to the English customs duty should be paid on the embarkation of enumerated goods, unless

bond were first given that the goods would be taken
to ports in England but not elsewhere. Even this,
however, did not stop the gap completely, because the
machinery for enforcing the Act was defective.

There is, however, another point in the Navigation
Act of 1660 which differentiates it from that of 1651.
Under the earlier Act, Scottish shipping and seamen
were on the same footing as English. In the Restoration
Act, the question was again regarded from a specifically
English point of view, and Scotland was treated as a
foreign country which had no right to privileges though
it might be admitted to them as a matter of convenience.
For the temporary incorporation effected under the
Commonwealth was dissolved by the Restoration;
England and Scotland were again, as they had been
before, two separate kingdoms, though they had the
same King; so that Scottish shipping and seamen
were no longer included in the term English. Scotland
passed her own retaliatory Navigation Act, copying
England's, *mutatis mutandis;* but retaliation is merely
futile, or worse, unless the retaliator is definitely better
equipped for conflict than the aggressor. If England
lost something by being shut out of the trade with
Scotland, she gained or believed that she gained much
more by shutting Scotland out of the trade with the
Plantations; though there was a doubt whether, under
the Common Law, Scotsmen, being in the allegiance of
Charles II, were not technically Englishmen when
aboard an English ship as they were when on English
soil.

It must not be overlooked, however, that while the
laws were restrictions upon colonial trade in the
interests of England, the system also "protected"
colonial trade in the economic as well as in the military
sense. In respect of their own special products, they

had the English market secured to themselves, the foreign competitor being in general entirely excluded. They enjoyed in short that preferential treatment which is to-day the nearest approach to Empire Free Trade that meets Dominion acceptance—an interesting reversal of the seventeenth century attitude.

### III

"Commerce brings wealth to the State; the right kind of wealth means the power which it is the supreme object of the State to attain; colonies therefore which provide either a power-producing commerce or the power derived from strategic vantage points are to be fostered and developed by the direct action of the State, but always, primarily at least, with an eye to the power of the State itself—on which the prosperity of every colony must ultimately depend. The time has come when the State in its own interest must organise a colonial system, directed to increasing the power of the State; which is as much as to say, of England." Thus we may summarise the attitude of the Restoration statesmen towards the colonies.

So far, we have seen the application of the doctrine to legislation concerning the commerce of the colonies. The colonies must be a preferential market for English goods; therefore there should be obstacles in the way of their procuring competing foreign goods. England must be a preferential market for colonial goods; therefore there must be obstacles in the way of their seeking foreign markets till England's needs are satisfied. From these two propositions it followed that exports from and imports to the colonies must pass to, from, or through England or between colonial ports, incidentally paying toll in the shape of duties to the revenue of England in return for English expenditure on their military or naval defence against the foreigner.

But colonial organisation demanded much more than the formulating of commercial regulations. It meant active expansion on the lines most advantageous to the nation; and that appeared to mean in the tropical and subtropical area, because the products of those regions were of the kind which the Empire wanted but which England could not produce for herself. All the "enumerated" goods, the goods which England and Europe wanted but could not produce for themselves, came, as we noted above, from those regions. These were the nationally profitable colonies, and so it was to the West Indies and the development of Plantation colonies of the Virginia and Maryland type that politically-minded colonisers like Ashley and Arlington turned their thoughts. New England might itself flourish but it brought little enough profit to the nation. England and New England did not to any appreciable extent want each other's products; England and Virginia, England and the West Indies, did. It was the same motive that had led Pym and other Puritan leaders a generation earlier to make the West Indies the objective of their own scheme when those other Puritans whose primary object was to escape from England were sailing for Massachusetts. In the Restoration era, we shall find Massachusetts presenting itself rather as an embarrassing problem than as a source of power and profit to England. On the other hand, in the northern area Newfoundland held a unique position. The island itself was unproductive but its occupation carried with it control of the fisheries. They in effect were its product, and the most useful kind of product according to the criteria of mercantilism. The fishing industry in any case helped to develop shipping, seamanship, and sea-power; the Newfoundland fisheries supplemented the English fish-supplies from the North Sea fisheries, but their main market was southern Europe; in other words, the fishing trade was a great exporting trade, exporting goods which England did not want for her own consumption in exchange for money or goods which she wanted but could not herself produce.

Colonisation as an outlet for surplus home population had ceased to be an objective; that is to say, it was no longer considered advisable to encourage emigration from England. At the beginning of the century, it was generally held that the population of England was greater than the soil could support; the view now was that England herself wanted all the man-power she could keep at home. Every emigrant was a potential fighting man lost, and France had twice as many fighting men as England. Colonial expansion was desirable as increasing the national wealth, but the expanding colonies should preferably be populated as far as possible from the expanding population of the existing colonies, and from elsewhere. (Cromwell had already endeavoured, though unsuccessfully, to plant Jamaica from New England; though it is at least probable that he had another motive thereto in the suspicion that the concentration in New England might give it a dangerous independence.)

But there was still another objective for colonisation besides the direct production of wealth which was indirectly power; what we may call the strategic colony; the occupation of territory which in other hands might be put to hostile uses or in English hands might serve the contrary purpose. In this lay the essential importance of the Dutch territory on the Hudson. Its products did not meet England's commercial requirements any more than did those of New England. To the Dutch themselves it was of little commercial value, and in the North American Continent they had no chance of developing into serious competitors. But if the French from Canada could have established themselves in the basin of the Hudson, they might have succeeded in doing there what in the next century they sought—and failed—to do on the Ohio and the Mississippi. Here again we can see that the idea was one which had planted itself in the minds of the Puritan statesmen. Pym's Company selected Providence Island with an eye more to a naval base than to the ostensible commercial value of the island itself, and strategic values were always a dominant consideration in the mind of Cromwell.

During the experimental stage, the Crown left the Adventurers—Companies or Proprietors—to shape and apply their own administrative systems and methods. Questions arising in the Colonies which were referred to the Crown were dealt with by a Committee of the Privy Council; though in theory it reserved to itself over-riding powers which it only sought to enforce when Charles I instituted Laud's Commission of Plantations with the specific purpose of imposing a regulation of religion more in accordance with the ideas he shared with the Archbishop. Otherwise the only exception was in the withdrawal of the Virginia Charter, transferring the powers of the former governing body to the Crown itself. Except in the cases of Virginia and the proprietary settlements, the governing body was resident in the colony itself. No over-ruling Parliamentary powers were recognised till, with the fall of Strafford, the Long Parliament assumed the sovereign powers and substituted its own Commission of Plantations for Laud's. The colonies found themselves under the necessity of recognising the sovereignty

of Parliament, even before the fall of the monarchy—
we have seen that afterwards, under the Commonwealth,
it intervened forcibly to depose Royalist Governments,
and recognised Rhode Island as a community not dependent on Massachusetts. That the powers of Parliament covered the financial relations between England
and the Colonies was taken for granted at the Restoration
and assumed in the Navigation, Staple, and Plantation
Duties Acts—the King's claims to arbitrary powers
of taxation having been abandoned at the Restoration.
But once more the Government was the King's Government and the Ministers were the King's Ministers,
not yet responsible to Parliament. Only both Government and Parliament had learnt to look upon the
Colonies as something with which they had more than
a formal concern.

We may put the point in another way by saying that
in one sense the Crown became much more active in
its relation with the colonies, but, in that relation as
in others, with a tacit recognition that powers which
Charles I and his father had assumed as Royal Prerogative
were in fact shared by Parliament. The fact was most
conspicuous in matters of finance, as exemplified in the
Acts of Parliament enumerated in the second section
of this chapter, all of them carrying the implication
that the authority regulating trade was not the Royal
Prerogative but the King in Parliament. But the time
had not yet arrived when the King exercised prerogative
only on the advice of ministers who were responsible
to Parliament for the advice they gave. That stage
arrived not with the Restoration but with the Revolution.

At the moment of the Restoration, however, the
King's course was marked out with some definiteness
—Clarendon must be the head of his Government;
and in Clarendon's eyes the Expansion which James I

and Charles I had been content merely to patronise had become a matter of first-rate political importance as a source of national power—as it had been to Cromwell, whom Clarendon admired almost as fervently as he detested him, as having been the most powerful if also the most unscrupulous ruler of his times. The Chancellor took a special pride in what he regarded as his own success in imbuing Charles II with his own zeal for colonial development, though it may very well be that the King's own astuteness had as much to do with it as his Chancellor's advocacy.

## IV

The King's Government was carried on by the Privy Council—the King's Councillors chosen by himself without reference to Parliament, necessarily including the chief officers of State and other persons of eminence in whom the King chose to repose confidence or whom he thought fit to consult on matters of importance. Its business was not legislative—that belonged to Parliament—but executive. Matters which were not appropriated to specific Ministerial departments came before the Council as a whole or were referred to committees of its members for consideration and advice upon which the King would presumably but not necessarily act. The Colonies had not hitherto been a State department; questions concerning them which touched the Crown had been referred, if necessary, to committees of the Council. Charles II was hardly seated on the throne when it became clear that a mass of questions, arising out of the dislocation produced by the Civil War and the Interregnum, were in urgent need of settlement, and a small General Committee for Plantations was promptly appointed to meet twice a week to examine such questions and report upon them to the Privy Council; it included the Lord Treasurer, the Lord Chamberlain, and the two Secretaries of State. This was soon found insufficient and special committees were appointed for special questions.

A larger scheme, however, was already in preparation. Before the year 1660 was out the place of the General Committee was taken by a Council for Foreign Plantations, among whom were the members of the first committee, with Clarendon and Ashley (Shaftesbury) added from the Privy Council, a number of persons who had already an active interest in Colonial administration, and others who were personally experienced in Colonial problems. This new Council, moreover, was supplemented by a parallel Council of Trade specially concerned with that particular aspect of the colonial problem, as a part of the general problem of the advancement of national trade. The two Councils were to work in conjunction; a large proportion of the members of each were common to both; the one dealt wholly with the commercial side, the other primarily with the political; but the two were co-ordinated by the substantial element of joint membership, and when both met on the same day they did so at different hours so that it was practicable for the same members to attend both meetings; while on each there was a body of advisory experts not directly concerned with the operation of the other council. But whereas the Council for Plantations had to deal exclusively with Colonial affairs, the Council of Trade was occupied with the regulation of trade generally, including that of the colonies—"to enquire into and certify all things tending to the Advancement of Trade and Commerce"*; so that all the great incorporated Companies individually and a

* Beer, pp. 913-915.

number of unincorporated Companies collectively were officially represented upon it. Both Councils, it may be said, consisted of a number of persons politically eminent who were members of the Privy Council, and a number selected as experts in some branch or branches commercial or political of colonial affairs, while the Council of Trade included a number of experts in other branches of commerce.

The Councils were merely advisory bodies, clearing the ground for the Privy Council. The Dutch War broke in upon their activities, and in effect, though they had done valuable spade-work, they ceased to function. Clarendon fell; Ashley, Arlington and Clifford became the leading members of the "Cabal"; and in the reorganisation which followed (1668), the Privy Council set up four Standing Committees, one being a Committee for Trade and Plantations (of which the five Cabal ministers were all members). Incidentally this Committee, reinforced by the law-officers of the Crown, was made a judicial Court for hearing Appeals in the first instance from the Channel Islands, and from this developed into that Judicial Committee of the Privy Council which is now the Empire's final Court of Appeal. In connection with it were reconstituted in a modified form a Council of Trade in the same year, and a Council of Plantations in 1670. The old difficulty, however, the fact, that is, that the Councils, however efficient, were still only advisory bodies without executive powers,—remained, and in 1675 their functions were transferred to a reconstituted Committee of the Privy Council known as the Lords of Trade; which practically controlled the colonies for the next twenty years, because, though it was not itself formally endowed with the authority, the Privy Council learnt in effect to adopt its recommendations as a matter of course;

U

mainly perhaps owing to the confidence inspired by the skill and judgement of the Committee's permanent secretary, William Blathwayt.

In certain of its aspects, however, control or direction of colonial administration was within the spheres of two of the departments of State, the Treasury and the Admiralty. It was the business of the Admiralty to enforce sea-laws and of the Treasury to collect Customs dues, while theoretically it was the duty of the Government of each colony to enforce the Acts in the area of its own jurisdiction. Comparatively speaking this was a simple matter in those colonies, originally chartered or proprietary, which for one reason or another had reverted to the Crown, as in Virginia; because there the Governor was appointed by the Crown. It was not at all simple where the appointment of the Governor was vested in the Colony itself or in a proprietor under its charter, as in Massachusetts and other New England Colonies which looked upon the Navigation Acts as grievances, laws imposed upon them, not to be actively resisted but to be legitimately evaded. Even in the Royal colonies the Governors were for some time apt to be not over-zealous in enforcing unpopular regulations emanating from England, and there was at times considerable friction between Colonial Governments and Treasury authorities; a fact which was in some degree due to the Crown's sound practice, generally maintained throughout the Restoration period, of choosing as Governors the best men available for the post. For such men were apt to find themselves viewing disputable questions at the colonial angle, and to protest against the English point of view with outspoken frankness. After the Revolution there was marked deterioration in the quality of the Governors chosen.

The Central Government, then, claimed to intervene

—to impose for fiscal purposes common regulations upon the wider England overseas which had grown up in such haphazard fashion outside the normal English governmental system, forming a number of units, without co-ordination, having separate interests diverse and it might be mutually antagonistic, diverse religious standards, varying forms of government; to which others were to be added by settlement or by conquest in the next decade, and still others later; none of the existing colonies having been created by the English Government except Jamaica, though all were dependent for their existence as English communities upon the protective power of the English Government. Neither in the past nor in the present did the world provide any parallel for such a position. The Spanish colonies were the private estates of his Catholic Majesty the King of Spain. The Dutch Colonies had been developed, and remained, under the direct control of the Dutch Republic. Canada was on the point of being made a highly organised military colony under the French Crown. Only the English colonies were still without more co-ordination or common authority than the minimum involved by the group of Navigation Acts and the need of their enforcement which was still mainly in the hands of the several governments.

What we ought to find surprising, then, is not a despotic assertion of unreasonable Authority by the English Government but its abstention from exercising the despotic control which every other colonising power adopted as a matter of course. It did indeed by degrees draw the appointment of the Governors into its own hands; not however with the object of curtailing legitimate local liberties but on the generally accepted principle that local liberties must not be made a cover for virtual independence—against which the only other safeguard was the consciousness in the colony that actual independence would leave it unprotected. As yet the Home Government was in the full flush of zeal for the development of the colonies themselves as members of the Empire; and Governors were appointed on their merits as administrators.

### V

From the English point of view at the Restoration, the existing colonies would have been classified in two groups according to what was regarded as their commercial value to England; those which produced goods which England wanted but could not herself produce, and those whose products were mainly the same as England's own. The former would have included Virginia, Maryland and the West Indies, with the Newfoundland fisheries; the latter the whole New England group; though Newfoundland was actually unique, being in the nature not of a land settlement but of a maritime station which gave lucrative employment to English ships and men and increased the maritime strength of England. Apart from Newfoundland the commercially valuable colonies were those which produced "enumerated" articles. The modern point of view is obviously a different one; it is that of political development; we group together the colonies from which one day a new nation was to be evolved. That was a conception not present to the minds of seventeenth century statesmen, or if present, only as something no less inadmissible than that of Secession to the Northern statesmen two hundred years later. But in this modern point of view, Virginia and Maryland are associated with the northern instead of the southern group: and to this group is added the expansion (in the sense of planting new colonies), on the north American continent which took place in the period under review.

Of this expansion to which we have now to turn, there were three main centres, besides a fourth in the Arctic or sub-Arctic region of the continent on the north of the French colony, which was in the nature of a commercial venture in the wilderness rather than of serious colonisation; the Carolinas on the south of Virginia, New York on the west of New England, and Pennsylvania north of Maryland; the first by settlement of the Virginian type, the second almost simultaneously by conquest from the Dutch, while the third, subsequent to the other two, was a proprietary experiment by the Quaker William Penn actuated by motives *mutatis mutandis* similar to those of the first Lord Baltimore.

New Amsterdam and the New Netherland were converted into an English colony or colonies under abnormal conditions, by force of arms, in the first Dutch War of the Restoration, and were retained by England at the end of the War, under the Treaty of Breda. We may conveniently give their story precedence, though the Carolina proprietary group had already begun its operations in 1663.

Henry Hudson, a great English navigator in the Dutch service, discovered the River Hudson—as well as the Arctic Hudson Bay—in 1609. It lay within the unoccupied territory granted by James I to the Virginia Company; but as it remained unoccupied the Dutch planted a trading station at the river mouth in 1613. The Dutch West India Company took possession, established New Amsterdam in 1622, and proceeded by degrees to plant more stations some distance up the river, and also eastward of the river mouth towards

New Plymouth and southward on Delaware Bay; which was clearly legitimate till they should encroach upon territory claimed as in actual occupation by the English. A fairly miscellaneous infiltration of foreigners was admitted, including some English who had failed to accommodate themselves to the narrow church-systems of New England. Nevertheless quarrels over questions of territorial rights did in course of time arise on one side with Maryland and on the other with Connecticut, and there would probably have been a resort to arms but for the disinclination of Massachusetts to take joint military action with her fellow-members of the New England Confederacy either during or after the Dutch War of 1652-4.

But we have seen that from the moment when Charles II returned to England he was drifting if not consciously steering towards a Dutch war; and the purpose of annexing New Netherland (on the very flimsy pretext that it was on territory already under English sovereignty when it had been filched by Dutch trespassers) was not only a motive to the war but was actually made the occasion for bringing it on.

The Dutch Government and the Governor Stuyvesant—as much perhaps on account of his merits as of his defects—were unpopular, the population of the colony was mixed, and so conquest would probably be easy; the Dutch wedge between the northern and southern English groups was extremely inconvenient and might become more so; and in particular a Dutch trading centre at that point materially complicated the business of enforcing the Navigation Acts which had just been initiated as a weapon against Dutch trade-rivalry. It does not appear that there was as yet any consciousness on the English side of the importance of the Hudson river in relation to the rival French expansion on and from the St. Lawrence and the Great Lakes.

From a modern point of view, the scheme of asserting a *de jure* English sovereignty over territory which had been for forty years *de facto* in Dutch occupation was obviously inexcusable, as Cromwell's seizure of Jamaica from Spain had been. But there was in the seventeenth century no single power concerned with colonisation which was not prepared to assert—where it had any prospect of making good—its own right of sovereignty in occupied territory in virtue of prior discovery, or its own right to hold by occupation territory not already in effective occupation, as might be most to its own advantage. Where all alike were in the habit of acting upon "the good old rule, the simple plan" and appealing alternately to mutually incompatible legal maxims by way of providing a technical justification, recriminations were little more than a matter of form.

So, the peace being then unbroken, Charles in 1664 granted his brother James Duke of York the lands north of New England from the St. Croix to the Kennebec, the islands off the New England south coast, and the coast and mainland between the Delaware and Connecticut rivers—in other words, New Netherland. James sent out as Deputy Governor Colonel Nicolls—no better man could have been chosen—with three ships of war and a small military force to take possession. They reached Boston at the end of July; a small co-operating force was set in motion from Connecticut; and on August 29th Stuyvesant was compelled by his own people to surrender New Amsterdam without firing a shot. He and they took the oath of allegiance to the English King and their new proprietor, accepting the change of sovereignty with equanimity. The Dutch and other colonists remained undisturbed in their possessions, though there was some unnecessary violence (for which Nicolls was not responsible) displayed in bringing in the coastal settlements between the Hudson and the Delaware, presently to be known as New Jersey, and south of the Delaware estuary (bordering on Maryland) which became the province of Delaware.

This last portion was not included in, but was now attached to, the grant made to the Duke, who in his turn, while Nicolls was on his way out, conveyed the New Jersey area to his friends Lord Berkeley (brother of Sir William Berkeley of Virginia) and Sir George Carteret, another of the Carolina proprietors,* who had distinguished himself in the Civil War by holding the island of Jersey for the King against the Parliament; hence the name of the new colony; and hence also it did not fall within the jurisdiction of Nicolls—much to his disappointment, as he considered that the Duke had parted with the most profitable part of his new possessions wherein he was sovereign—subject to the Crown.

Nicolls, who was also associated with a simultaneous commission sent out to enquire into and settle the affairs of New England to which we shall return later, remained in charge till 1668 after the annexation of New Netherland had been ratified by the Treaty of Breda. He re-christened the province and its capital by the same name—New York—in honour of the Duke. His policy of conciliation was evidently successful; for throughout the war, though Dutch squadrons appeared, there was no symptom of revolt. The Dutch institutions were not rudely suppressed, and on the other hand the representative system, which in one form or another had developed in all the other colonies, was not yet

* *Infra*, p. 308

set up; he ruled by a code known as the Duke's laws which accorded with English custom and gave the fullest religious liberty—in favourable contrast to New England rigidity. The Government continued on the same lines; but in 1673 during the third Dutch war, a strong Dutch squadron raided the American coast, and without difficulty recaptured New York, which was quite unprepared, together with New Jersey and Delaware. For the moment the Dutch domination was revived, but only till the Treaty of Westminster at the close of 1674 ended the war, the Dutch surrendering their conquests.

The desire of Charles and Clarendon to close the gap on the coast line and hinterland between the northern and southern colonies by ejecting or absorbing the Dutch intruder needs no very subtle explanation. There might be no great value in the territory itself, but the presence of an alien wedge was an immediate inconvenience and a barrier to ultimate unification. That the States General of the United Provinces should not be greatly disturbed over the question is not surprising; the Province was not lucrative, while in case of war with England it provided rather an objective for enemy attack than a stronghold from which the enemy could be seriously threatened. The one person who really appreciated the fundamental importance of the Hudson River basin would seem to have been Jean Talon, the Intendant of New France or Canada; who urged Louis to make a point of insisting on the restitution of New Netherland in the negotiation of peace-terms and of following that up by purchasing it from the Dutch for France, which would then be in possession of a line of immense strategic value from Lake Champlain to Delaware Bay, completely closing in New England—as she subsequently sought to do by occupying the Ohio basin. But Louis missed his opportunity. In the later Dutch war it did not recur, since he was then not in alliance with Holland but at war with her.

Meanwhile Berkeley in West and Carteret in East Jersey had been occupied more with their own interests than with those of the colonists they at first succeeded in attracting thither, with whom dissensions soon arose. With the war, confusion became worse confounded, and another phase for the whole group appeared when a fresh grant of the entire territory was made to James after the peace and he sent Sir Edmund Andros as Deputy Governor in charge of the whole; Andros being honestly but tactlessly bent on asserting what he conceived to be the Duke's rights, without regard to what the other proprietors conceived to be theirs. In 1682 however—when the King had won the fight over the Whig Exclusion Bills and the Crown had become to all intents absolute—a very able Governor was sent out to take the place of Andros, in the person of Thomas Dongan; Charles having just issued to William Penn, the Quaker son of the Admiral, himself in high favour, oddly enough, with both Charles and James, the patent for the new proprietary colony of Pennsylvania, on the north of Maryland and Delaware; the last of the group known as the Middle Colonies.

## VI

The New York group differs from the rest of the seventeenth century colonies on the American continent as having been acquired by conquest from Europeans, not through settlement by private enterprise. The same singularity applies to the last colony already inaugurated before the Restoration, the Island of

Jamaica, which was conquered or taken by force of arms from Spain which was undeniably in occupation, by direct Government action—and was moreover planted by Government action without the interposition either of a company or a proprietary. There was, however, this difference between the two, that New Netherland was not in theory conquered territory but *de jure* Crown property resumed by the Crown and conveyed by the Crown to a proprietor who happened also to be heir-presumptive to the throne (though with reasonable probability of being displaced by the birth of an heir-apparent), so that, though virtually a Crown colony, technically it was not so. The rest of the West Indian plantations, on the other hand, had been seized as actually unoccupied territories by private adventurers and held under proprietary patents issued to them by the Government, whether of James I, Charles I, or the Commonwealth and Protectorate. Jamaica, however, will be more conveniently treated in relation to the rest of the West India islands, since its progress as a Plantation was retarded by its position as the headquarters of the buccaneering which was a pervading feature of West Indian history through the greater part of the reign of Charles II.

After the Restoration, but before the seizure of New Netherland was organised, what may be called the speculative desire of expansion again took shape in the projection of a new colony on the south of Virginia. It was in fact the revival of the scheme which had failed to materialise in the first years of Charles I, when Sir Robert Heath, the Attorney-General, had been granted a patent for the purpose. Nothing had come of the plan then—"Carolana" had been dropped; but in 1663 the "Carolina" patent was granted to eight joint Proprietors, the list being headed by the names of

Clarendon, Albemarle, and Ashley (who afterwards became the most active of the promoters). The other five were Sir William Berkeley (reinstated as Governor of Virginia), his brother, Lord Berkeley, and Sir George Carteret, who almost immediately transferred their interest to New Jersey, Sir John Colleton already a leading planter in Barbados, and Lord Craven. Clarendon and Monck were the two men of greatest mark in England; Ashley, soon to be made Earl of Shaftesbury, was the keenest witted and most ambitious of the Restoration politicians or statesmen; Colleton was and Berkeley ought to have been typically representative of experienced planters. The proprietors in short formed a remarkably distinguished and influential group.

Little enough was known of the region that was to be exploited beyond the historical fact that Ralegh's ill-starred settlement had lain within it. The intention was to draw settlers to it not from England but from the multiplying population of Virginia, Barbados and New England; and it was expected or hoped that it would be productive of the wines, fruits and silks for which England was dependent upon Mediterranean countries, without interfering with the sugar and tobacco industries of the existing colonies. In actual fact, however, the progress of the colony was slow and desultory; the only one of the proprietors who appears as taking more than a perfunctory interest in it was Ashley; it disappointed the expectations of its productive capacity until at the end of the century it discovered its own peculiar staple product, rice; and it played little part in the general colonial history of the period, except so far as its coastline became a resort for buccaneers and provided cover for illicit trading.

Carolina, however, has a unique though hardly

practical interest of its own, inasmuch as a wonderful constitution was elaborated for it by Shaftesbury's secretary, John Locke, the philosopher, whose *Essay on Civil Government* subsequently became the textbook of the Whig political theory. Locke was in fact a practical man of affairs as well as an academic theorist, but ideal systems of governments are apt to overlook the human factor, and, if born at all, not to outlive infancy. It was hardly attempted to carry out in practice any part of Locke's "Fundamental Constitutions" and those which were attempted had no root and withered away. The Carolina settlers evolved their own constitution by what may be called the normal methods of conflict and agreement between representative Assemblies and the governor appointed by the Proprietors. For the Charter itself, unlike earlier charters, expressly provided for the institution of Assemblies of freeholders, and limited the legislative powers of the Proprietors, while giving the latter powers of imposing taxation.

The history of the Carolinas then is somewhat meagre and lacking in interest. It began from two points of settlement in 1663, one near Cape Fear and the other on the river re-named Albemarle after the duke; the southern broke up or was absorbed into the northern which was the nucleus of North Carolina. The settlers, mainly emigrants from Virginia, were supplied by Berkeley with a governor from that colony; the extreme laxity of the laws the settlement compiled for itself made it a somewhat disreputable asylum for disreputable characters and a centre of illicit trading, the Proprietors only concerning themselves with it when the scandal became flagrant. Its annals are scanty till its tardy emergence into respectability in the next century.

In 1670 a fresh southward settlement was made, of which Charleston presently became the headquarters, and capital of South Carolina, as the two did not coalesce though it was not at first intended that they should remain separate Governments. Here progress was steadier, and the society in general was less irregular than that on the Albemarle. Primarily at least the population was drawn mainly from Barbados and Bermuda. Later Huguenot refugees from the persecution under Louis XIV and Scottish refugees from the persecution of the Covenanters came into the colony. The former failed to develop the silk industry as it had been hoped that they would do; the latter dwindled in numbers and were finally wiped out in a Spanish raid. As with all the southern plantations, Carolina was largely dependent on coloured slave labour; and it brought trouble on itself in the shape of Indian wars by enslaving Indians in defiance of reiterated instructions from the proprietors in England.

One more experiment in expansion remains to be recorded—the establishment of the Hudson's Bay Company and the occupation of Rupert's Land. Explorers, Englishmen for the most part, had investigated the more northern latitudes in search of the North-West Passage; but no attempt at settlement had been made; while the French had found enough to do in working up the St. Lawrence to the Great Lakes. It was a Frenchman, however, who conceived in 1659 the idea which he endeavoured to persuade the French Government to take up, of pushing north to the Hudson Bay region for the sake of the fur trade. He failed with the French Government, but saw Arlington who was at the Paris Embassy in 1665; Arlington sent him over to England; there he interested Prince Rupert; and Rupert, after sending out a preliminary exploring expedition, succeeded in forming a Company (including Ashley and Arlington) with a small capital, of "Merchant Adventurers trading into Hudson's Bay," and obtained a Royal Charter for it in 1670, giving the colony his own name. Its business was the fur trade, its employés were fur-traders and hunters, and its stations more or less fortified trading posts. Between 1682 and 1686, the French from Canada, claiming the territory in right of discovery, attacked and captured most of the English posts, but were ordered by the then friendly French Government to restore them; an agreement of mutual colonial non-interference having been made between Louis and James, who had just succeeded Charles on the English throne.

# CHAPTER XIV

## THE SOUTHERN PLANTATIONS, UNDER RESTORATION AND REVOLUTION, 1660–1702

### I

VIRGINIA, Maryland, and the West India Islands, had submitted to the Commonwealth and Protectorate sovereignty with varying degrees of reluctance, but on the whole with general acquiescence after the first shock of royalist resistance; and this was in fact all that these Governments had demanded of them. Intransigent Royalists had been removed from office or from the colony and replaced by officers pledged to loyalty to the Commonwealth, but there had been little disturbance, no fresh burdens had been imposed, and the Navigation Act in no way differentiated between the colonies and the Mother-country in respect of trade or shipping. But the sympathies of the southern colonies were always, in the nature of things, with Church and King, and they welcomed the Restoration with rejoicings.

In Virginia the popular feeling immediately reinstated Berkeley in the governorship. No ostensible changes in the system of government were instituted; as a matter of form, all Acts of Assembly passed during the Interregnum were invalidated, for the most part merely to be re-enacted under the legitimate authority of the Crown instead of the usurped authority of the Commonwealth. Yet it was soon apparent that the Crown, through the Privy Council, intended to interest itself more actively in the affairs of the Colony than it had done in the past.

Moreover there was no colony, except perhaps Barbados, more directly affected by the new Navigation Act, for the simple reason that Virginia was wholly absorbed in the cultivation of tobacco for export, and tobacco was one of the enumerated articles for which the market, so far as the producers were concerned, was restricted to the colonies themselves or to England. For Virginia as for the rest, the Staple Act permitted the import of foreign goods only through England, and the Plantation Duties Act imposed upon the inter-colonial trade the same duties as those imposed at English ports, the revenue from all alike being appropriated to England herself. Virginia like every other colony felt very consciously that she was being taxed and her export and import markets restricted for the benefit of English traders, but only very subconsciously that this was the way in which she paid her share of the burden of Imperial defence borne by the Mother-country.

Moreover, there was a secondary grievance. Loyal Virginia grumbled but did not attempt to evade the Acts, while it was notorious, if difficult to prove, that her less scrupulous neighbours profited by the comparative ease with which they could evade them, and that Virginian tobacco found its way to foreign ports from Massachusetts without paying the English duties; it seemed, so to put it, that loyalty was bad business; which did not encourage the spirit of loyalty.

The actual duty on the tobacco, however, was by no means crushing; it was no more than twopence on a pound of tobacco, and only a half-penny if it was for re-export.*

* Williamson, *Short History of British Expansion* (First Ed., p. 292 *n* .

x

On the other hand, it was no fault of the English Government that Virginia was wholly dependent on her production of a single article of commerce. She was so for the single reason that in spite of restrictions nothing else was equally attractive as a paying proposition. Berkeley received instructions, which he did his best to carry out, to develop the production of iron, flax, hemp, silk and pitch, all of which were reasonably available, and the English Government backed him up by remitting duties on some of those articles; but little came of it. Tobacco was not as paying as it would have been had the tobacco trade been free, but it still paid better than anything else the colony could or would produce even with unrestricted entry into England. Still the fact remained that tobacco itself was not so profitable under the Navigation Act as it had been before. There were, however, co-operating causes of the smaller profits accruing. There was in fact over-production, since although Virginia led the way it was not the only tobacco-growing country. Maryland was a competitor; and while Virginia sought to restrict output beneficially by planting-regulations tending to eliminate the inferior kinds by limiting periods of exportation, they were regulations which did not appeal to the Marylanders who declined to adopt them as definitely injurious to their own trade. To effect the object in view the co-operation of Maryland was necessary, and so the attempted cure was abandoned.

It may also be remarked that while the colony was paying for defence by England, that defence was not always sufficiently adequate to convince the colonial mind of its value. Almost at that humiliating moment in the Dutch War of 1664–7 when a Dutch squadron was amusing itself in the Thames estuary while the King of England was moth-hunting, a small Dutch squadron sailed into the Chesapeake Bay, captured or destroyed a score of merchantmen, and burnt the English man-of-war which ought to have been but was not on guard; a performance which was repeated with some variations of detail in 1674. The Virginians were the more annoyed when they found themselves called upon to set up a quite useless fort which was intended to command the river entry; but they were admittedly responsible for defence on land.

It is certainly difficult to accept what has until recent times been the popular view that the Virginians suffered from a crushing burden of taxation—very much as it used to be a popular belief that Charles I heaped taxes upon the people of England. Charles demanded from England and England demanded from the colonies a revenue not at all out of proportion to the needs of State. The grievance in both cases was not that the burden was excessive but that in levying it the assent of the taxed was not asked and their protests were ignored. A grinding oppression can scarcely have been the condition of a colony of which the population rose from some 12,000 in 1640 to 40,000 in 1670, ten years after the Navigation Act, and again was nearly doubled a dozen years later—though about one-sixth of the total population were indentured servants who at the end of five years' service became free men, and five per cent were negro slaves. Material prosperity can hardly have been wanting. But the Navigation Act made it less than it would otherwise have been, while increasing the prosperity of English merchants—and the Colonists themselves were allowed no voice in the matter; that, not the weight of the burden, was the real grievance.

Disturbing, too, was a curiously arbitrary act on the part of Charles II himself. In 1673 he granted what might be called certain proprietary rights to Arlington and Culpeper in the province of Virginia; rights which, had they been exercised, would practically have destroyed security of land tenure besides conveying other powers which would have been intolerable. It was, however, nothing but a trick to provide them with money out of Virginian pockets; they cheerfully agreed to resign all the rights except quit-rents in face of the unanimous protest of the colonists—and the whole affair lapsed after ten years. But it had not advanced the loyalty of the colony.

Berkeley, a born reactionary, was already past fifty when he was reinstated as governor. He was always zealous in upholding the colony against encroachments upon its freedom, and in maintaining an ultra-conciliatory native policy; but there his merits seem to have ended. Personally he became autocratic and vindictive. The Assembly of Burgesses elected at the Restoration was naturally something of a counterpart of the "Cavalier" Parliament elected in England at the same time on the flood-tide of the reaction; and like that Parliament it remained undissolved for sixteen years. The government of the colony became government by a corrupt clique of Berkeley's friends, and mainly to that fact, not to hostility to the Crown, was due the explosion of 1676 known as Bacon's rebellion, of which the immediate occasion was an Indian War.

For the war itself neither Berkeley nor the Indians were really responsible. In the course of a local quarrel arising from a theft, some Indian Chiefs were treacherously trapped and put to death by the settlers; reprisals resulted in a rising and the massacre of some three hundred English; Berkeley did not choose to take the action necessary to restore order; and a recently arrived colonist, Nathaniel Bacon, took the law into his own hands, raised a troop in defiance of Berkeley, and attacked the natives. Berkeley declared Bacon a traitor, dissolved the Assembly, and summoned a fresh one —which was on Bacon's side and proceeded to pass legislation directed against the misrule of the Governor's clique. Berkeley again declared Bacon a traitor, and it seems probable that Bacon would have overthrown the Government and possibly have proclaimed Virginian independence, had he not died of a fever.

With the loss of its leader, however, the rebellion collapsed; and Berkeley took savage vengeance on the ringleaders. Before the tale of executions was completed, commissioners to enquire into the matter arrived—with a regiment—from England. Berkeley, who was much disposed to defy their authority, was removed and sent to England, where he died soon afterwards; the colony quieted down. The activities of the commissioners show that there had been no slackness or indifference on the part of the authorities at home who appointed them; they tackled their task with vigour, tact, and understanding, and an evident determination to be fair and just to all parties; and not the least successful of their efforts was the conclusion of a peace with the Indians which was never afterwards broken. But the appointment of Lord Culpeper to the Governorship—which he discharged mainly by deputy—in 1679 marked the new departure which was to characterise relations between the Mothercountry and the colonies: the Governors sent out ceased to be men whose homes and personal interests centred in the colony itself.

Of Maryland during these years there is little to be said. Baltimore's main object was to preserve his proprietary rights, with a minimum of friction with the Crown on one side and with settlers on the other. The

actual Governorship he put in the hands of the son
who succeeded him as third Lord Baltimore in 1675.
The Colony had lost its originally Roman Catholic
character, because its basic principle of toleration had
brought into it numbers of the Puritan independents
who were not at home either in New England or in
more emphatically Anglican colonies; but Maryland
was free from serious disturbance.

II

Of all the English colonies existing when Charles II
landed in England, the one which almost any Englishman at that time would have named as the most valuable
was assuredly Barbados. It offered indeed no opportunity of expansion except by way of overflow into
other islands; but it very precisely met the requirements of what a colony ought to be in the view of
mercantilist imperialism. In proportion to its area it
was immensely productive of goods for which there
was a great world-demand and world-market, goods
which England needed but could not herself produce;
it produced nothing which competed with England's
own products, while providing an unfailing market for
English goods; it was defensible, as it proved by the
fact that no enemy force ever made footing on it; for
lack of space it did not attract the type of emigrant
which England was now convinced she could ill spare,
while it could still welcome indentured servants drawn
from the classes which England herself reckoned as
undesirables, in default of the negro slave-labour of
which she employed an immense quantity, the number
of black slaves being about double that of the entire
white population. Its actual relative prosperity in this
period may be judged by the fact that although its

ANTHONY ASHLEY COOPER, BARON ASHLEY AND
EARL OF SHAFTESBURY
One of the founders of Carolina, and the most bitter enemy of Holland

[*Face page* 318

area is only ten per cent above that of the smallest English county, the value of its exports to England at the end of the century was thirty-five per cent greater than that of all the other colonies put together.*

Barbados complained bitterly of the burden of the Navigation Act, but it is clear that there was no colony which could so easily afford to pay it. For twenty years after the first introduction of the sugar industry she had developed by leaps and bounds; she was aggrieved not because her trade fell off but because many causes combined to diminish the rate of its increase as she neared the limit of her own productive capacity while other competing sugar areas of later date were still developing; and she naturally selected the English restrictive laws, by which England benefited, to denounce as the cause of her rather imaginary woes, though those laws were probably far from being the most important of the adverse factors. But they were undeniably an adverse factor, and governor after governor did not hesitate to say so in very plain terms, as long as there appeared to be any shadow of a chance that their remonstrances would produce any mitigation. There never was in fact any such chance, because the English Government had adopted them as an integral part of a considered Imperial policy which it had at no time any disposition whatever to change.

The story of Barbados, the most easterly of the West India islands except Trinidad, is intimately bound up with that of the immediately neighbouring group, the Windward Islands, and also of the chain stretching westward, the Leeward Islands (the Lesser Antilles), beyond which lay the three much larger Spanish islands (the Greater Antilles), Porto Rico, Hispaniola, and Cuba, north of which were the Bahamas,

* Williamson, *op. cit.*, p. 288.

and south the fourth large island, Jamaica, which Cromwell had torn from Spain. The Dutch share was represented by Tobago, Curaçoa, and St. Eustatins.

At the moment of the Restoration, the English in the Leeward Islands were in occupation of Nevis, Antigua, and Montserrat, and of half St. Kitt's, of which the other half was occupied by the French, who also held Guadeloupe and (in the Windwards) Martinique, St. Lucia, and Grenada. Barbados and Nevis excepted, all these islands were at least once captured and recaptured in the course of each war with France, and generally, when peace was made, reverted (if not already recovered) to the first owner; but the one English possession on the mainland—Surinam—passed permanently to the Dutch at the Treaty of Breda, and bears to-day the alternative title of Dutch Guiana. Such exchanges took place during this second Dutch war, the French being then in alliance with the Dutch; very greatly to the detriment of the English in the Leeward Islands.

Francis Lord Willoughby, the exiled Royalist Governor and principal proprietor in Barbados, was recalled after the Restoration, and the Leeward Islands were made part of the Barbados Governorship, in view of the confusion of proprietary claims and counter-claims resulting from the civil broils. Both he and his brother William, who succeeded to the title and the Governorship in 1666, proved able governors and stout advocates of free trade for the colonies. In 1671 the Leeward Islands were separated from Barbados and placed under the Governorship of Colonel Stapleton, an administrator of the best type, under whom—with little enough support from England—the islands made up much of the lost ground; each island having local self-government, with its own Assembly and Deputy-

Governor. Besides sugar, their main industry, the islands produced other enumerated articles, indigo and ginger as well as tobacco. But it is to be remarked that while all the Governors openly protested against the Navigation Acts and shared the popular objection to them, all did loyally if reluctantly endeavour to enforce the law, without advantage or hope of advantage to themselves.

### III

The West Indian waters and islands had provided a continual cockpit for rival adventurers of all nations who refused to acknowledge the Spanish sovereignty without effective occupation, whether the adventurers were acting with Government authority, or on their own responsibility as independent traders. For the Spaniards claimed that foreign traders were prohibited, and when they appeared might be treated by them as pirates—while all other nations denied the Spanish right of prohibition. Dutch, French, and English, equally defiant of Spanish claims, and generally not unwilling to co-operate with each other against the Spaniard—or on occasion to cloak sheer piracy under the profession of legitimate trading—were all alike active "beyond the line," where what would have been palpable acts of war anywhere else were perpetually committed by all the parties, whether their respective Governments were at war or not. The last and most flagrant act of aggression had been the Protectorate seizure of Jamaica as a *pis aller* when its attack—without declaration of war—on Hispaniola failed. The affair had been a bitter disappointment to Cromwell, who was nevertheless resolved to make the island the base for what he regarded as England's right to conquer the Spanish dominions in America; while he was also zealous to develop the productive resources of the island itself, though time for organising such development was not left to him, and all organisation was at a standstill in the twenty months between his death and the return of King Charles.

When the expedition which captured Jamaica returned to England in disgrace, it left in the island, under command of Colonel Doyley, a garrison which was meant to be the nucleus of settlement and development. Doyley held it successfully against Spanish attempts to recover it; but his men were not good settlers, the Spaniards had done practically nothing in the way of development, recruits for settlement did not pour in, and those who did come in were of inferior type. Doyley did his best with his materials, started the usual representative form of government, held his own, and was at first continued in office after the Restoration. In 1662 he was succeeded by Lord Windsor whose stay was brief, and in 1664 Sir Thomas Modyford of Barbados was appointed Governor.

Throughout Modyford's Governorship, and indeed from an earlier time, the task of ruling was complicated by the ambiguous position of the adventurers who had become known as Buccaneers—originally the French name for a particular class of adventurer; while the French themselves invented the title *fléboutier* from which we in turn derived "filibuster," but which was itself the French adaptation of the entirely English term "free-booter." The *boucaniers* proper were the hunters who visited the uninhabited north-west of Hispaniola which was full of wild cattle—originally imported from Spain. They slew the beasts, dried the meat by a process which the Indians called *boucan*, and traded with it. This was the strict sense of buccaneering. But it was apt to be merely a minor part of the

operations which brought them in conflict with the
Spanish authorities, and the term soon came to be
applied to all those who to the Spaniards were inclusively
Pirates, whatever they might call themselves.

The buccaneers, in short, were all sorts of unauthorised
free-traders who, generally claiming that their "trading"
was entirely legitimate, were in perpetual conflict with
the Spanish authorities; we have met them already, in
the account of the attempted settlement of Providence
Island. They resorted principally to the creeks and
harbours of the Bahamas; the French had headquarters
at Tortuga, off the north end of Hispaniola. Their
ships frequently acted in concert, and they evolved
among themselves a sort of common international
pirate law of their own. When England was desirous
of being on friendly terms with Spain, it was obviously
necessary to profess anxiety to suppress the dubious
traffic, but when England was in conflict with Spain
it was no less convenient to issue privateering com-
missions to buccaneer captains, or at least for the
Government to adopt Elizabeth's characteristic method
of coupling public disavowal with private encouragement.

England and Spain were at open war when Cromwell
died and peace between the two countries had not
found its way "across the line" when the King was
recalled. England was in possession of Dunkirk and
Jamaica. Spain had been on friendly terms with Charles
in exile, and hoped for restitution; but Charles declined
to give up Jamaica, sold Dunkirk to France, married
the Portuguese Infanta, and renewed the demand for
Free Trade in the West and religious liberty for English
subjects; and the desultory war went on with intervals
of negotiation. Correctly interpreting the situation,
Modyford called in the buccaneer chiefs, commissioned

them to act against the Spaniards by sea, and carefully gave the commission in a form which would enable the home Government to denounce them and himself in true Elizabethan style, if policy should make that course necessary. Previous Governors had done the like on occasion.

The most redoubtable of the men employed by Modyford was Henry Morgan whose exploits recall, so far as concerns audacity of design and desperate valour in execution, some of those of Francis Drake, though the buccaneer lacked the chivalry of his great prototype. He does not appear to have been exceptionally barbarous, but barbarity was the order of the day on both sides, and he did little if anything to restrain the revolting barbarity of his fellows. The most remarkable of his feats were the sack of Porto Bello and of Panama. But these came at a stage—in 1670— when Charles had made up his mind to patch up the Spanish quarrel. Both Modyford and Morgan were summoned to England to answer for their misdoings; the former was sent to the Tower for a time, but Morgan, who had Modyford's commission for his warrant, became a popular hero, was knighted, returned to Jamaica as Lieutenant-Governor, and was active in what had now become the serious and quite necessary task of suppressing the buccaneers themselves, who had become uncontrollable. Some of them came in to the King's peace and many of these betook themselves to the illicit business of cutting logwood in unpopulated Spanish territory in which for long they were not discouraged; while some, the buccaneer organisation having been broken up, betook themselves to unequivocal piracy. For a full decade during the reign of Charles II, they had appeared definitely as an instrument of which English Governors could make active use;

their successors, though the old name still clung to them, became the enemies of all Governments, and indeed of civilisation. It was a curious episode, but one not to be overlooked.

With the elimination of the buccaneer organisation which during the troubles necessarily centred on Jamaica, with demoralising effect, the progress of the island became more rapid; especially aided thereto by the judicious rule of Sir Thomas Lynch, who having long served there in various capacities, was Governor from 1672 to 1676 and again in 1682. Its products were particularly various, though as in the West Indies generally, sugar before long took the leading place; but it was not till the end of the century that Jamaica showed signs of rivalling Barbados in value.

## IV

The logwood traffic remained a continual source of friction with the Spanish authorities, and the Navigation Acts continued to be a grievance to which the island colonists at last submitted though without ceasing to protest. The suppression of the buccaneers at least made it less difficult to exercise some control over West Indian piracy and the illicit traffic which was not always clearly distinguishable from piracy. In the decade preceding the Revolution, however, it was becoming clear that there was more reason for anxiety in French rivalry than in the secular antagonism of Spain. After the Revolution, and especially in the War of the Spanish Succession, the progress of the islanders was retarded by the eternal but futile process of capture and recapture and the constant menace of attack, even when it did not materialise, which had been initiated in the war of 1666-7: since, although after

La Hogue the French fleet was out-classed, French privateering and commerce-raiding increased and multiplied. Nevertheless the West Indies did indubitably prosper. By the end of the Stuart period, Jamaica was rivalling Barbados or at least Virginia in her commercial value, from the English point of view.

For a short time after 1678 an attempt was made to organise her government on the analogy of that of Ireland under Poyning's Law; but the normal method was soon reverted to. Generally speaking no change in the islands accompanied or followed the Revolution —other than the universal tendency to slackness in the appointment of Governors. The Revolution itself was accepted as a matter of course; but it did not occur to anyone in England to apply to colonial assemblies the principles which had been laid down in the Declaration of Right and Bill of Rights as governing the relations between the Crown and the English Parliament.

With the exception of Jamaica, the islands had practically reached the limit of their productive capacity by the end of the century, a fate which had not yet overtaken the great territories on the mainland. The progress of the Carolinas under the proprietors was desultory—until rice-production became the centre of the Carolina economy, with a large European market— and South Carolina, bordering upon the Spanish Florida, had Spanish as well as Indian conflicts on her hands. The valiant defence of Charleston in 1706 against the attack of a combined Franco-Spanish squadron was a notable event in the annals of the colony.

In Maryland, the controlling powers of the third Lord Baltimore were suspended, owing to his being a Roman Catholic, soon after the Revolution, and remained in suspense till the close of the period. Virtually, Maryland was for the time a crown colony.

The government of Virginia after Bacon's rebellion presents points of interest. After the settlement effected by the Commissioners, an inefficient Deputy acted for Culpeper till his own arrival on the scene in 1682, with instructions to curtail the powers of the Assembly by limiting the franchise and depriving it of all powers of initiating legislation except in the case of money-bills, and by other measures in the enforcement of which he displayed a judicious laxity—more perhaps with personal interests in view than out of regard for the colonists. Also, for a consideration, he resigned most of the proprietary rights which he had not already abandoned. In 1684 he was succeeded by Lord Howard of Effingham who was in no respect fitted for the post, but fortunately left the discharge of his duties for the most part—after the Revolution—in the hands of a very competent Lieutenant-Governor, Francis Nicholson. Howard's instructions very definitely confirmed the Assembly's powers of taxation, but said nothing of the English Parliament's concurrent powers in that respect.

Nicholson had already been Lieutenant-Governor of New York under the régime of James; subsequently he was transferred for a short time to Maryland, where he did valuable service. In both colonies he was zealous in promoting education and in endeavouring to remedy the haphazard disorder into which religious institutions had fallen, though his motive therein was no doubt mainly political. It is to be noted that in opposition to the economic policy previously current he held the view that the artificial stimulation of other industries than tobacco was useless, and in the long run unsound; instead of trying to make Virginia self-contained and self-supporting, she should concentrate on the wealth-producing tobacco, and supply her own needs by purchase from England. It may be suspected, however, that the main motive was to discourage the production of goods which would compete with English products. We see in him also a far sighted perception of the fundamental weakness of the colonial system—its incoherence for defensive purposes in relation to the menace of French expansion. Nothing came of his plans for a general military confederation of the colonies under Virginian hegemony—the tentative New England confederation under Massachusetts hegemony having long ago lapsed—and it was largely this very lack of cohesion which in the eighteenth century kept the colonies dependent on English defence until the Seven Years' War.

# CHAPTER XV

## THE NORTHERN COLONIES; UNDER RESTORATION AND REVOLUTION, 1660–1702

### I

THE problem of the relations between the Restoration Government and New England differed from that of the colonies south of the Delaware area, new or old, and from that immediately presented by the acquisition of New Netherland, though before the reign of Charles II ended the story of the new colonies in the north becomes intimately associated with that of the rest of the northern group. We have therefore still to follow out first the course of affairs in New England during the period to the end of which we have already carried the sketch of the Middle colonies.

In New England, Massachusetts was the immensely dominating factor. She had attained a degree of *de facto* independence which Cromwell himself had found disturbing. She had established a system of rule by Church membership so intolerant and narrow that the Connecticut and Rhode Island settlers had withdrawn outside her boundaries; and the government itself had, after Winthrop's death passed into the hands of an oligarchy representative of the worse side of Puritanism, as Winthrop and his colleagues had at least to a great extent represented its better side: and while she was ready enough to ride rough-shod over her smaller neighbours, going so far as the practical annexation

of Maine and New Hampshire—a fate from which
Roger Williams saved Rhode Island only by appealing
to the English Government—she had no intention of
yielding to encroachments on her practical independence
by the authorities at home. Whereas the home authorities
were naturally bent on reducing it.

The new Council of Plantations was soon ready with
an indictment against the colony which, although it
officially hailed the Restoration with a somewhat
unctuous enthusiasm, was nevertheless in the habit of
referring to itself as a "commonwealth" and of, in effect,
prohibiting the forms of worship established by law
in England. Clarendon, however, refrained from drastic
measures; but Connecticut, which was itself tolerant
and always jealous of its big neighbour, was given a
new charter which enabled it to absorb its rigidly
Puritan but small neighbour New Haven. Rhode
Island received a charter also. New Plymouth was
offered one but declined it since it would have imposed
on her a governor appointed by the Crown. The
Massachusetts charter was confirmed, but with a
condition that involved the withdrawal of the limitation
of the electoral franchise by church-membership which
was ostensibly accepted but surreptitiously evaded.
These measures, while they certainly acted as checks
on the unauthorised power of Massachusetts, provided
no plausible ground for complaint.

The next step was the appointment of that Royal
Commission of enquiry into New England affairs in
1664, of which Colonel Nicolls was head at the same
time that he had on his hands the business of annexing
and settling New Netherland, as previously related.
Massachusetts, ever skilful in devising legal expedients,
refused to recognise the authority of the commission,
as infringing her charter: but could not prevent Nicolls

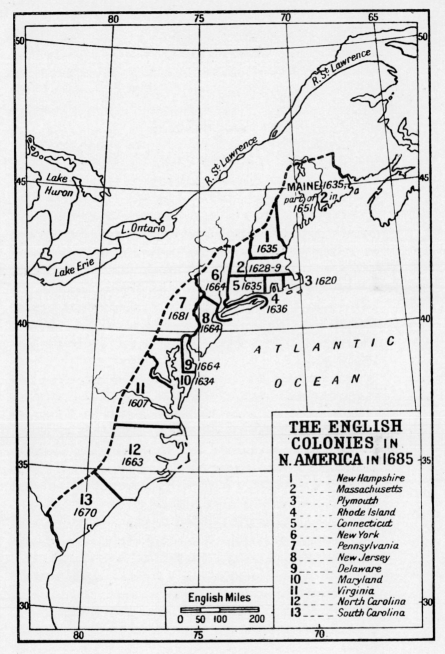

THE ENGLISH
COLONIES IN
N. AMERICA IN 1685

1 ..... New Hampshire
2 ..... Massachusetts
3 ..... Plymouth
4 ..... Rhode Island
5 ..... Connecticut
6 ..... New York
7 ..... Pennsylvania
8 ..... New Jersey
9 ..... Delaware
10 ..... Maryland
11 ..... Virginia
12 ..... North Carolina
13 ..... South Carolina

English Miles

0   50  100       200

[Face page 330

from resuming Maine where no charter had conveyed authority to her. Otherwise, his preoccupation with New Netherland prevented Nicolls from actively pushing the work of the commission. A few years later Maine, with her own consent and without reference to the home Government, was again attached to Massachusetts, which succeeded in buying out the claims of the proprietors, though New Hampshire was finally constituted as a separate Crown Colony.

Practically in the matter of the Commission Massachusetts scored a diplomatic victory. At the same time, since she produced no enumerated goods herself, she profited by the Navigation Act since her shipping and her ports were free and were largely employed in contraband traffic, while she studiously abstained from active enforcement of the regulations, as the penalties on Governors who neglected their duties in this respect applied only to those who were appointed by the Crown. This evasion became the more scandalous when the Navigation Acts were rounded off by the Plantation Duties Act of 1673. The Lords of Trade sent commissioners on behalf of the Treasury to collect the duties. The activities of Edward Randolph who was thus sent to Boston in 1676 were regarded with extreme hostility by the Bostonians, and on the other hand his report of the conditions there established a conviction in England that the whole system of the Navigation Acts was vitiated by the wilful recalcitrance of the Massachusetts authorities, and could never be properly enforced until the Government was brought under direct home control. Coupled with the sense that the military organisation of the colonies as separate units was inadequate for defence against an aggressor, this developed the idea—in England—of organising New England as a single Crown Colony.

Here it may be well to emphasise a point on which popular impressions require revision. Cromwell, Charles II, and James II, were all three tolerationists. Their motives were different, but all three desired to concede the widest latitude of private religious opinion compatible with social and political order. For Cromwell, however, there was one exception; he was uncompromisingly hostile to Rome and the Roman hierarchy. For him the prelatical Church of England was also a partial exception; partly because when dominant it had been a persecuting organisation, partly because, when no longer dominant, it continued to be a Royalist organisation; but provided that it was politically powerless he and his officers winked at the private practice of its rites and ceremonies. So far as the Puritan Government in England intervened in the colonies, it was for the protection of minorities.

Charles II and James II were both tolerationist, because both wanted something more than toleration for the Roman Church, and toleration for Rome involved toleration for the large body of Protestant dissenters. It is the hostility of the Cavalier Parliament to both Rome and Dissent that gives to the reign of Charles II in England the character of an era of persecution. With the Parliament against him, Charles experimented with tolerationist measures on his own responsibility, but found his own security so seriously endangered thereby that he dropped them. But in the colonies, where the constitutional powers of the Crown so far as the English Parliament was concerned were not in question, the intervention of the Crown was habitually in favour of toleration.

It may appear paradoxical to say in one breath that James II was a tolerationist and that he lost his crown because he was a bigot. But the "bigotry" which lost him his crown was not the bigotry of intolerance; it meant merely that where what he regarded as the true Faith was concerned he was blind to all other considerations. It does not appear that he had any hostility to other forms of religion as such. He was, however, blindly determined to advance at all costs the Church his own adherence to which had all but lost him the succession to the throne in a country which, when excited was apt to become rabidly Protestant. Seeing no other means of advancing that Church otherwise than by arbitrarily over-riding the law—actually the most fatal course he could possibly adopt—he proceeded to over-ride the law in the most flagrant manner, and in consequence ended his days as an exile. Louis XIV had just given example in the *dragonnades* of the savage intolerance of which Roman Catholicism was capable and the English people were probably right in their conviction that a Romanist monarchy would be incompatible with a Protestant England. But in actual fact, James never did show any inclination to persecute any form of religion; and his type of bigotry was perfectly consistent with the fact that whether as Duke of York or as King he used his powers on behalf of toleration for all forms of Protestant Dissent. Surprise is not seldom expressed that the Quaker William Penn should have held a high place in the favour of both Charles and James; but Quakers had learnt tolerance in the school of adversity, and poles apart as were the Quaker and Romanist creeds, in the state of England at that time Quaker and Romanist had many grounds of sympathy.

Now over against this attitude the Stuarts—troubled in England by an intolerant Parliament—found in New England a Puritan intolerance very fully established in Massachusetts and not altogether absent

in the other colonies. Only Church-members enjoyed full political freedom, admission to church-
membership was in effect rigidly controlled by a
Puritan oligarchy in whose eyes "heresy" was a grave
offence, and heresy included much that was definitely
taught in the English Church as by law established on
the one side or by divers independent sects on the
other. The Massachusetts Church was a State Church,
and one which persecuted Dissent as markedly as the
Cavalier Parliament persecuted Dissenters in England.
The Anglican there was among the Dissenters, and the
Quakers in particular were treated with extravagant
severity; not perhaps so much because of their unorthodox mysticism as of their "presumptuous and incorrig-
ible contempt for authority" in refusing to adopt the
conventional forms of expressing respect for it. In
the other colonies, too, the authorities looked askance
upon the Quakers who were endeavouring unsuccessfully
to provide themselves an asylum in New Jersey; when
William Penn devised the scheme which took shape in
his proprietary colony of Pennsylvania.

From all these considerations, it will be clear that
the ambitions of Massachusetts presented a difficult
task to the rulers who governed her under the Charter.
She of all the colonies was most conscious of a menace
from the French in Canada. Menace from the Dutch,
never very serious, was negligible after New Netherland
had been annexed; but she was nearest to the French,
most open to attack either by sea or by land, and most
likely—excepting Newfoundland—to come into collision
with them over fishery disputes. There was therefore
no colony which could less afford such a break with
England as would leave her exposed, unaided, to the
active hostility of Canada supported by the power of
France. On the other hand much of her wealth was

derived from her success in evading the Navigation
Acts which the English Government was bent on
enforcing, but could not enforce without encroaching
not necessarily on her chartered rights but on that
complete control of the administrative machinery
which she had enjoyed so long that she had come to
regard it as her inherent right: a control moreover
which she knew she was in fact exercising, in respect
of religion, in contravention of her chartered powers.
In short, to preserve her "rights," she had little to
rely upon besides the argument that any encroachments were breaches of her charter, while she had to
meet the counter-argument that it was her own
infringements of her charter that not only warranted
but necessitated encroachment.

## II

In the settlement of the Middle colonies, it is evident
that the Duke of York's intention was to keep the
sovereignty in the Proprietor's own hands, though with
no tyrannical purpose. Neither Nicolls nor his successor,
Francis Lovelace, was authorised to concede even a
Representative Assembly such as every previous
English colony had acquired. Lovelace was Governor
when the whole of New Netherland was recaptured
by the Dutch and the Dutch system was for the time
restored. The loss cancelled all the proprietary grants,
but with the restitution of the colony under the Treaty
of Westminster James was again constituted proprietor
of the whole, and again granted East Jersey to Carteret,
an arrangement fruitful of jurisdictional controversies.
Then came the Duke's unfortunate selection of Sir
Edmund Andros as the new Governor; unfortunate
because he was the well-meaning but stupid agent of

a well-meaning but stupid Proprietor. Even when Andros went so far as to submit to James for consideration the clamant demand in the New York colony for a representative Assembly, he was quite incapable of explaining to the Duke, who was quite incapable of seeing for himself, why the demand was reasonable. Neither James nor Andros wished to play the tyrant, but both did so without a suspicion that they were guilty of anything of the kind, under the mistaken impression that they were only being resolute. Unfortunately Andros was later sent to Massachusetts, again with disastrous effect and always for the same reason. James was one of those unfortunates who cannot learn—who if they make a blunder only continue to repeat it under the obstinate conviction that it must be the right thing to do.

In 1680 Andros sailed for England; the Deputy he left behind him was incapable of governing at all; the demand for an elected Assembly became more active than ever, and this time the Duke gave way, probably persuaded by the counsels of William Penn who was in high favour. In place of Andros, Thomas Dongan in 1683 came out to New York as Governor with authority to summon an Assembly elected by the freeholders of the colony.

Meanwhile New England had undergone the unwonted and costly experience of a great Indian war, and the question of cancelling the Massachusetts charter and reorganising her Government under direct control of the Crown had become acute.

Apart from the episode of the Pequod war, the relations between the white settlers whether English or Dutch and the Indians had always been creditably amicable. The intercourse was limited; there had been no violent expulsion of the Indians: their territories had been acquired from them by purchase; but they had been pushed back by the inevitable pressure of civilised communities upon barbaric and still semi-nomadic tribes. Those with whom the English came in contact were outside the great confederacy of the "Five Nations" otherwise known as the Iroquois, west of the Hudson, who were presently to take active part in the Anglo-French struggle. But the Iroquois themselves blocked the way for further retirement before the encroaching English, so that the up-country Indian tribes were between the upper and nether millstones. The spirit of hostility awoke, while the English had forgotten the need of being prepared for it; and the leader of the outbreak was Metacom, better known by his English name Philip, the younger son of that Massasoit with whom the Pilgrim Fathers established such friendly—and lasting—relations on their first arrival.

The tribes concerned were quartered roughly speaking in the districts between the Naragansett and Connecticut rivers. The immediate occasion of the war was the execution of some Indians who had been found guilty of murdering a Christian Indian who had given information to the Plymouth government. It began with a raid into outlying Plymouth territory in June 1675; it was decided by a crushing blow at the Naragansett tribe which prevented any further combination, at the end of the year; it was ended by the hunting down and slaying of Philip himself in the following autumn. And it was said to have cost Massachusetts the lives of ten per cent of her men of military age and an expenditure of £100,000—the equivalent certainly of more than half a million now—besides the destruction of property, before it was over. The New Englanders appear to have begun by regarding it as a 'judgement' for laxity in enforcing religious discipline, and ended—some of them—by searching the Scriptures to find precedents warranting merciless punishment of the conquered foe, very much as two or three years later England herself went crazy over the Popish Plot panic. But the governments were sane enough to mitigate the full fury of the popular vindictiveness, the not unusual offspring of popular panic. The whole episode is known in the colonial annals as King Philip's war.

In the same year Randolph was sent out—to return to England with the report which was to prepare the way for the cancellation of the Massachusetts charter. In 1684 the charter was annulled and Massachusetts became a Crown Colony.

Randolph's report was that of a man who suffered from an extreme form of the diseased mentality which we are apt to attribute to officialdom at large. He looked with a distorted vision upon everything which ran counter to his own ideas, as an official, of what ought to be; and he succeeded in convincing himself that the people of Massachusetts were almost as ill-pleased with the existing Government as he was. He was honest, zealous, industrious, interfering, and tactless. On the other hand Massachusetts was perfectly conscious that it habitually evaded the law, and its leaders were divided between those who were bent on standing out for the maintenance of the existing system and those who favoured judicious compromise. Randolph in England urged extreme measures; but the Privy Council committee was clearly in no haste to adopt his recommendations. On the other hand the political movement in England was turning in favour of the power of the Crown, while Randolph's return to Boston as Inspector of customs increased the friction. Early in 1681, Charles dissolved the last Parliament of his reign; the Whigs had been routed;

the succession of his brother was secured; before the year ended he was issuing the first writs of *Quo Warranto* for enquiring into transgressions of their charters by the English boroughs with a view to revocation. The like process was adopted with regard to the Massachusetts charter. There was a more than sufficient technical case; and so in 1684, the Massachusetts Bay Company ceased to exist and its powers reverted to the Crown. The legality of the forfeiture was quite indisputable, whatever opinions might be held as to its justice or expediency. What use the Crown would make of its power was another question.

Massachusetts, by her dominating attitude towards the smaller New England Colonies, had isolated herself, and received no support from them in her effort to preserve her own liberties, legitimate or otherwise.

### III

In 1681 Penn obtained the Charter for and started the Proprietary Colony of Pennsylvania: in 1683 Dongan arrived at New York as Governor, on behalf of the proprietor James Duke of York; in 1684, the Massachusetts Charter was revoked; early in 1685, Charles II died, and James Duke of York became King of England. At the end of 1688, William of Orange landed in England and James II fled to France. These eight years, then, form the closing chapter of the Restoration colonial system as inaugurated by Clarendon; the period in which the Crown was asserting its supremacy both in England and the colonies.

For New York, owing to the happy choice of Thomas Dongan as governor—the first but not the last Irishman who had the chance of distinguishing himself as an Empire-builder—it was a period of marked success.

James, as we have seen, had at last been persuaded to concede the repeated demands of the colony for a representative Assembly, and Dongan's first act was to give that concession practical effect. Although numerically the Dutch were preponderant in that most heterogeneously settled colony, the ideas prevailing in the Assembly when it met were essentially English. It promptly passed a series of resolutions (which had no legal validity till sanctioned by the Proprietor, a sanction that the Duke in his conciliatory mood did not refuse, at least if silence gives consent) implying its own control of taxation and affirming freedom of conscience for all professing Christians; resolutions which were known as the "charter of liberties." Three years afterwards King James enacted a new constitution which deprived the Assembly of its powers, which were vested in the Governor and council nominated by the crown; but so long as Dongan remained Governor the colony offered no protest.

The fundamental importance, however, of Dongan's rule lay in his conduct of relations with the great Iroquois confederacy and with the French in Canada. The Iroquois power extended from the Great Lakes on the north to the Virginian border on the south; that is to say, over most of the interior west of the Upper Hudson and the extended range of the Alleghanies and east or south of the upper St. Lawrence and the chain of lakes. Thus they presented a formidable barrier to French expansion southward and to English expansion westward, the two inevitably clashing movements of the future. With a view to the coming clash, it was of vital importance to each of the European rivals that the Iroquois territory should ultimately be absorbed into its own dominion and should certainly not be effectively dominated by the other. The Five

WILLIAM PENN
The founder of Pennsylvania

[*Rischgitz*

[*Face page* 340

Nations (the three most familiar names among them are those of the Mohawks, the Oneidas, and the Senecas) were a very much more powerful combination than was possible among the other greater tribes of the north such as the Hurons and the Algonquins, their natural enemies, with whom the French had thoroughly established friendly relations, and the Mohicans eastward—to say nothing of the numerous minor tribes in what modern terminology would describe as the English sphere of influence.

So far as Dutch or English had hitherto come in touch with the Iroquois, the relations had been friendly. But during the last ten years, the great Governor of New France, Frontenac, had cultivated the friendship of the Iroquois and planted the fort which afterwards bore his name at the north-east corner of Lake Ontario; which should have been the centre for extending French influence, though the missionary efforts of the Jesuits among them tended rather to irritate and alarm the Mohawks and the Senecas. Unluckily for the French Frontenac was superseded in 1682, the same year in which La Salle had carried exploration south to the mouth of the Mississippi, creating, so far as discovery could do so, a French claim to that river basin from the Great Lakes to the Mexican Gulf. Next year Dongan arrived at New York, and was prompt to grasp the menace of the situation which had thus arisen.

Charles was the pensioner of Louis. The new and inefficient French Governor, La Barre, had made up his mind to an aggressive policy, directed to the splitting up of the Five Nations, and expected the English to stand neutral. Dongan saw that the confederacy must be preserved as a buffer between French aggression and the English, and that it must be done without bringing on a dangerous quarrel between the Governments on the other side of the Atlantic. La Barre, demanding English neutrality, warned him that the Iroquois were subjects of France. Dongan replied that they were under English protection, and that if territorial questions were in dispute, they should be dealt with by the home Governments. The Iroquois declined to admit that they were in any way the subjects of either; the French were their " fathers "—a title which Frontenac had gratified them by assuming—the English their " brothers "; all they desired was to live in amity with both. La Barre made a display, but only a display, of force which came to nothing; whereupon he in turn was displaced by Denonville. The Iroquois sought closer relations of alliance—not subjection—with the English. Lively but still polite communications passed between Denonville and Dongan, to the Irishman's evident enjoyment, but neither would recede from the position that the Iroquois territory belonged to his own Government. Then at the end of 1686 James II made a treaty of colonial neutrality with Louis. In the improbable event of war between the two countries, the colonies of both were to remain at peace with each other, and if one went to war with Indian tribes the other should render no assistance to the enemy. Denonville went to war with the Iroquois. Dongan could not send them armed assistance—but he did not prevent arms and ammunition from reaching them, and Denonville's ill conducted expeditions into the Iroquois country were attended with more failures than successes. The Iroquois were confirmed in their resolve to resist French aggression and to look upon the English as their friends; while Dongan also succeeded in persuading James to stand by his claim that Iroquois territory was English territory. Dongan would have proceeded to a more active policy of fortifying the frontier; but at this moment—1688—James had resolved to unify the whole group of the northern colonies—New England and New York together—of course as a Crown colony, under a single Government; a project for which there was indeed much to be said. But with characteristic blindness, he chose for Governor not Dongan but Andros. Dongan's career was ended.

Pennsylvania, it need hardly be said, occupied a quite peculiar position. The Quaker son of a fighting Admiral, a man who had suffered persecution for his religious convictions while entirely tolerant of the religious convictions of others, whose own moral standards were the highest, who was yet a friend of publicans and sinners, a "Friend" who was suspected of being a Jesuit, William Penn himself was, to say the least, an unusual person. The project of his colony presented itself to him when he was endeavouring to find for his persecuted sect an asylum in New Jersey. It was to be in the nature of a social experiment carried out according to the projector's own ideas and under his own direction. Charles was the more ready to assent, because the granting of the proposed charter was to be purchased by the cancellation of debts owing from the Crown to William Penn's estate. James was favourably disposed because he held Penn in high regard. The projector should have at his disposal for colonisation the territory which lay unoccupied on the north of Maryland and west of the New York territory of which the Duke was himself Proprietor. The boundaries were occasion of dispute with the Proprietor of Maryland but the Proprietor of New York was generously disposed and conceded the land necessary to give the new colony a port of its own.

The charter itself made no stipulations as to religion, while it required the assent of the Proprietor, the acting Governor, or the Assembly, to any taxation except by Act of Parliament. Penn himself promulgated a "frame of Government" or Constitution somewhat experimental in structure and based on a wide electoral franchise, and affirming the principle of religious freedom of conscience. Perhaps the most striking feature of the actual Government which Penn inaugurated in person in 1682 was the liberality of its attitude towards the Indians, in consonance with Quaker doctrines of human brotherhood. Quakers of course provided the kernel of the population, but with many other elements added. Penn's own idea would seem rather that of exercising an intelligent and benevolent despotism by assent of the community. The numbers of the colony swelled rapidly, as did its general prosperity; and it belonged to the northern not the southern type, with small rather than large estates, the soil not lending itself to such products as were most "economically" worked on large estates run by slave-labour. When King James on his accession planned his northern unification, Pennsylvania did not fall within the compass of his scheme. The association between James and Penn was too genuinely friendly to permit the King to think of interference with Penn's colony.

When Charles II procured the cancellation of the Massachusetts charter, so that the colony, like Virginia in 1624, reverted to the Crown, he clearly felt no goodwill towards it; since the Governor he appointed was the notorious Colonel Kirke, back from Tangier which the King had just chosen to abandon on the plea of expense. It was doubtless well for Massachusetts that the appointment did not materialise, since Charles died, James succeeded him, Monmouth raised his abortive rebellion, and Kirke was congenially employed in hunting down rebels. It is worth noting that Randolph, whatever his faults were, did all he could to prevent the appointment. Actually, a New Englander, Joseph Dudley—an ally of Randolph—was provisionally made "President," with a Council of Seven members and Randolph, still collector of customs, as secretary: and then at the end of 1686 arrived Edmund Andros, some-time Governor of New York, now chosen by King James as the fittest man to be Governor of New England—including New Hampshire, Maine, and part of Rhode Island. Connecticut and Rhode Island very soon learnt that their own charters were in question and would certainly have to be surrendered—the sooner the better; and in 1688 James added his own proprietary provinces, New York and New Jersey, to the jurisdiction of the Governor of New England whose commission made him the arbitrary ruler of all the provinces north of Maryland, Pennsylvania alone excepted. On the next New Year's Day, James himself was a fugitive, a discrowned guest at the court of Louis XIV, and the Emergency Government in England was considering how best the crown might be offered to William and Mary.

## IV

The flight of James did not cancel the position of Andros. The English theory was that the King *de jure* having abdicated a new King *de jure* took his place in due course; though the *jus* might be disputable he would anyhow be King *de facto* and those who came in to his allegiance would be undisturbed, unless they were Roman Catholics appointed by James in defiance of the law which debarred them from office. Very few people had qualms about coming in—they

z

could always change sides if convenient. There was trouble in Scotland till Dundee fell at Killiecrankie and in Ireland till Sarsfield capitulated at Limerick, but in England, though there were non-juring clergy, there was no revolt—only, William's loyal subjects maintained a secret correspondence with St. Germain, in case of accidents.

Andros did not conceive himself to be, and in fact he was not, what we commonly mean by a tyrant, but his methods were outrageously arbitrary and constantly transgressed the terms of his commission as Governor. Both he and Randolph were intensely unpopular, and below the surface the idea of armed rebellion was being secretly fostered, coupled with hints that Andros in addition to his other crimes was a Papist. In New York, Francis Nicholson, who was afterwards to do good service in Virginia and Maryland, was Lieutenant-Governor for Andros, and he too had made himself unpopular. Dongan who was an avowed Roman Catholic was still in the colony. The news of the Revolution and the flight of James to France created something of a panic in New York as well as in Massachusetts; James and Louis were in league! James's papist confederates in New England would play into the hands of the French in Canada! Boston and New York each consequently carried out a bloodless revolution on its own account; Andros and Randolph were shipped off to England, whither Nicholson also retired, and the revolutionists sent dispatches to the home Government to declare their loyalty to the new monarchy in England, in whose interest they had ejected the agents of the former King. The revolutionary Governments were in effect left to carry on as best they could—they had at any rate declared for the Revolution at home, with no attempt anywhere at a

Jacobite counter-revolution—until William could spare time from home and European affairs to give some attention to those of the colonies.

Now the scheme of James, constituting a single Dominion of New England, the whole to be under the direct administration of the Crown—to which he gave effect in the last year of his reign—had in it a very sound basis of statesmanship; carried out by able hands it might well have had far-reaching results. With a common military organisation and a common system of fiscal control at the ports, the menace of French aggression would have been minimised, jealousies between the provinces would have faded, the Government would have been permeated with those principles of religious toleration of which James imagined himself to be an advocate. The substitution of despotic control for virtual self-government was not involved in the ideas. Under other auspices it might have shaped out as a Dominion with a Parliament of its own bearing the same relation to the Vice-regal Governor that the Parliament in England bore to the King.

But that, unfortunately, was not the shape it took in the mind of King James, who was zealously striving to over-ride the English Parliament itself. By choosing as Governor a man so like-minded to himself as Andros he had at once produced—through Andros's actions— the impression that his aim was to establish a tyranny over a people accustomed by tradition and practice to self-government. What would have happened if he had ruled England for another ten years it is impossible to say. But he was not given, or did not give himself, the chance of carrying the scheme farther, and his successor on the throne did not take the chance of giving it a statesmanlike shape.

William was a European statesman whose interest centred not in England but in Holland. It was essential from his point of view that England should be on his side in his life-long struggle with Louis; he knew that, whether she saw it or not, it was in her interest to be so. With that end in view, he accepted the English crown to which his wife had been heiress-presumptive until the birth of her half-brother in 1688. Having accepted the crown, it was his business in England to keep it secure and to rule with justice and what the prayer-book calls "indifference"; but he took no personal interest in England's empire. His hostility to France might have suggested that to strengthen English against French colonists in America was a commendable policy, but whatever New England might feel, Old England herself was hardly alive to the coming importance of the Anglo-French rivalry on the other side of the Atlantic.

So William—and his English advisers—dropped what had in fact been the revolutionary Dominion scheme of his father-in-law and reverted to the separate-colonies system; but retained so much of the former as gave to the English Crown an increased control through the appointment of Governors; accompanied by the more active insistence of the "King in Parliament" on their sovereign rights.

Maine, Nova Scotia and Plymouth were incorporated by charter with Massachusetts as one Province; the Governor, Deputy-Governor, and Secretary were to be appointed (and removable) by the crown; the Assembly was to meet, as of old, but was to be elected on a property, not on a Church-membership, franchise. New Hampshire was not included in the new Massachusetts charter. The Connecticut and Rhode Island charters were restored. The New Jersey proprietors were recognised—later they surrendered their title

and the Jerseys became a single Crown Colony. New
York had been always in fact, and in form also since
its proprietor succeeded to the throne, a Crown Colony.
Baltimore's political rights as proprietor in Maryland
were forfeited because he was a Roman Catholic;
Penn's rights in Pennsylvania were temporarily forfeited
because of his personal relations with James, but were
restored after two years. The southern colonies were
of course unaffected.

While the Revolution was being carried through
and completed in England, all the New England
colonies were carrying on under provisional Governments of their own making—more or less, one might
say, the pre-Andros Governments. Also, Frontenac
was back in Canada, France and England were at war,
and of course the 1686 treaty of colonial neutrality
between James and Louis had lost any validity it ever
possessed. Frontenac at once developed an attack,
having as his instrument for the purpose the eastern
Indian tribes who were for the most part completely
under French influence. With the fall of Andros, his
scheme of English defence went to pieces. Massacres
were perpetrated at Schenectady on the New York
frontier, at Salmonfalls, and at Falmouth in Maine.
But by sea a volunteer force, organised by Massachusetts
and commanded by Captain Phipps, dealt a counter-
stroke by seizing the Acadian capital of Port Royal—
always a thorn in the side of the English. A few months
later, Phipps with a much larger armament was in
the St. Lawrence, threatening Quebec, while a composite
force of New Englanders was marching on Montreal.
But the land expedition was ill-managed and was soon
retreating instead of advancing; Quebec was reinforced
by the return of the troops which had been sent to
meet it, and after an abortive attack, Phipps, too, had

to abandon his attempt. There was a temporary truce. Frontenac on one side and Phipps on the other were each anxious for an aggressive policy; but for the latter an organised frontier policy was out of reach because the colonies would not act in concert, while the designs of Frontenac were paralysed by the blow to French sea-power dealt by the battle of La Hogue in 1692, and the peace of Ryswick in 1697 suspended hostilities and restored Port Royal to the French.

By that time Phipps himself had held a brief tenure of office as Governor of Massachusetts, the first appointed under the new charter; doubtless with the idea that a New Englander would be more acceptable than a governor from England; but as an administrator he was a failure, and was succeeded in 1697 by Richard Coote, Earl of Bellamont, an Irishman like Dongan; honest, courageous, and generally tactful, but imbued with the ideas of a Whig aristocracy—in other words, of a class which regarded itself as born to govern. Throughout the period, the Assembly kept in its hands the traditional weapon of Parliament by making the governor's allowance the matter of an annual vote. That fact was typical of the New England attitude towards the central Government—it was fundamentally the attitude of the English Parliaments to James I and Charles I; whatsoever the Crown desired was *ipso facto* suspect. There could be no confident co-operation, of which one unhappy result was manifested in the failure to organise the defences of the north-east against the French and their Indian allies, which only missed being absolutely disastrous in the next reign through the crippling effect on the French of their failure in sea-power.

Bellamont, who held simultaneously the governorships of New York and New Hampshire with that of

Massachusetts, died in 1701. But his holding of the
joint governorships did not remedy the fundamental
defect of disunion and conflicting interests or what
we might call provincialism; nor did it reconcile the
antagonism between the collectively provincial and
the metropolitan points of view, the colliding interests
of the colonists as a group and the mother-country on
whom they were so largely dependent for defence.

The time in fact had arrived when there was a
permanent undercurrent of distrust if not of actual
hostility between the colonists on one side who were
desperately jealous on behalf of their individual local
liberties which they assumed to be their rights as
Englishmen, and on the other the governors who were
sent out by the English government primarily to
represent the principle—unquestioned in any other
colonising state—that the supremacy of the central
government was not to be disputed. And that mistrust
was intensified by the failure of the home government,
after Bellamont's death, to provide governors who
were, whether in character or in ability, in any sense
equal to a task which demanded high qualities of
statesmanship.

# CHAPTER XVI

## THE CLOSE: 1702-1714

### I

UNTIL 1707, except during the brief period of compulsory union under the Commonwealth, England and Scotland were separate kingdoms with separate legislatures, separate administrations, and separate fiscal systems, though in both countries the same monarch was King. James I and VI would have made the union much closer if he could have taken his own way, but Scotland dreaded practical subjection or at best the constant subordination of her own interests to those of her wealthier and larger neighbour, while England, secured from active hostility by the union of crowns, had no disposition to admit the smaller kingdom into her own commercial ring-fence. Therefore throughout the seventeenth century Scotland had no share whatever in the English expansion. On the soil of England or aboard an English ship, the Scot was an English citizen: elsewhere he was a foreigner. The arrangement was reciprocal.

Scotland thus had no part or lot in the English chartered companies or in the proprietary rights granted to Englishmen through which the English expansion was effected. James I bestowed what was in effect a parallel charter for a Scottish East India Company on Sir James Cunningham in 1617, but the London Company procured the cancellation of the grant on terms which satisfied the granter. The Scottish settlement of Nova Scotia under grants from James I and Charles I never got beyond the embryonic stage. The colonising rights in Newfoundland were conveyed to a Scottish proprietary in 1637, but this came practically to an end under the Commonwealth. After the Restoration the Scots were again excluded from the English plantations, as from all other English trade privileges, because in the English Mercantile view the Scot was a competitor—though there was a limited supply of Scottish "indentured servants" who on emancipation passed into the ranks of free colonists. The "rebels" deported by Cromwell after Preston, Dunbar and Worcester to Barbados and New England supplied an appreciable and efficient element of the population in both; but this could scarcely be counted as Scottish participation in the benefits of English colonisation. The wars almost eliminated the traditional Scottish trade with France and the Low Countries. The London merchants complained that the Navigation Acts which were made for their own profit were evaded by illicit traffic with Scotland—which did not tend to make the English mercantile community any readier to make concessions to the Scots.

Scotland was poor but energetic and ambitious. The result was the launching, in 1695, of the Darien scheme; primarily intended to be English as well as Scottish. But to the London Merchants it appeared to be a menace to their monopolies. The whole scheme was, financially speaking, wrecked by the English boycott—which was more than countenanced by the language of William III and of the English Parliament. In reply, Scotland staked every penny she could raise on the venture; but in such circumstances it was doomed to disaster from the outset, and in Scotland it was an article of faith that the failure and attendant ruin were wrought by the deliberate malignity of England.

England's trade might prosper as a result of England's wars with French or Dutch; but those wars, (in which Scotland was not directly concerned, and on her own account would have been—as in the past—much more inclined herself to join England's enemies than England), merely wrecked the Scottish trade with France and Holland without bringing to Scotland any benefit at all. Commercially speaking, Scotland would be better off as an independent State with a separate king of her own than tied to England by the union of crowns while her commerce was deliberately depressed in the interests of English Merchants. With the death of William III, however, England awoke to a new menace. England had fixed the course of the succession to the English throne, deflecting it from the legitimate line. She had chosen a cousin of the reigning Queen, Anne, whose children had all died; but she had no power of imposing that choice upon Scotland. The Scots proceeded to make it abundantly clear that on Anne's death the legitimate line would be recalled to a Scotland which in those circumstances would certainly renew the ancient alliance with France, unless England would make a treaty of union giving her all the securities she demanded, including complete participation in all English commercial rights. At last mercantilist hostility in England and Nationalist sentiment in Scotland yielded to political exigencies assisted by profuse bribery, the incorporating Treaty of Union was passed by both Parliaments, and the first united Parliament of Great Britain assembled in 1707; thenceforth the Expansion of England was superseded by the Expansion of the British Empire, though more than another generation passed before Scotland was really reconciled to the amalgamation.

## II

For half a century England had planted colonies on the west of the Atlantic without following any system, and without definitely relating the successive settlements either to each other or to the home Government. For another half century she was endeavouring, on the basis of mercantilism, to organise the relations between the colonies and the mother-country on the assumption that the former existed and were sanctioned and protected primarily to increase the wealth and power of the latter. Thus in the years which followed the Revolution, the old Colonial Systems attained completion.

That system, then, was born with the Restoration Navigation Acts. At the close of the reign of Charles II and in that of his brother it was following a line of development which in the hands of a powerful ruler with able subordinates might have unified the whole continental group of colonies into a consolidated dominion, a Province not of England but of a British monarchy. James being what he was, the Revolution came and stopped that development. Unification went by the board; while the colonies did not share in the constitutional gains that the Revolution brought to England herself. They were still a congeries of dependencies of "the Crown" which exercised its authority not less but more actively than before. Like England they retained their representative institutions, but, unlike England, with diminished rather than increased powers. For in England the actual effect of the Revolution was to make the executive Government in England responsible to the English Parliament instead of to the monarch, and to establish the principle that the only taxing authority was that body; the limitations imposed on the power of the Crown in the Bill of Rights were all professedly declarations of immemorial Parliamentary rights which the Crown had never admitted but were now established by statute; but they were rights which neither statute nor custom had ever acknowledged to be vested in provincial Assemblies. Precisely to the extent to which the Crown lost powers, the English Parliament's powers were increased for all purposes; but without any corresponding extension of the powers of the provincial Assemblies, so that in effect the legal powers of these were only those which the Crown lawyers would have recognised under the first Stuarts. In the previous New England with its elected governors, the executive had actually been responsible to the electorate, but under the new system it was so no longer. The Assemblies had over their Governors no other hold than their power of restricting supply. And over the imposition by the home Government of taxation or legislation they had no hold at all.

The advantages of unification for administrative purposes are too obvious to need setting forth; yet, although after the break-down of James II's experiment, as well as of the very tentative and half-hearted earlier movement of the New England Confederation, various other schemes were suggested, none materialised. The failure then calls for some explanation. To the home Government, its own supremacy over the administration would have been an essential condition of unification, but this would have involved the burden of providing a military force as well as of naval defence; whereas to the colonists it would have implied—as James II's experiment implied—the final abrogation of their liberties. On the other hand the home Government could not view with equanimity the idea of a consolidated dominion not under military control, which would have a far greater power of combined resistance to civil control than a number of communities with no common organisation. This objection would no doubt have been, in itself, an inducement to the colonists to aim at a consolidation on those lines; it had probably been, in reality, the main motive of the New England Confederation. But it ran counter to the individualist prejudices of the colonists themselves, prejudices which were only temporarily set aside in the War of Independence and continued to permeate their history until the Secession or Civil War of the middle nineteenth century.

Thus on the Roman principle *Divide et impera* consolidation was not desired in England, while the sentiment of particularism held the several colonies apart from each other, so that it required a tremendous common emergency to impose upon them willing acceptance of a common supreme authority.

The governors chosen by Charles II and James II were, more often than not, men of ability, and, almost though not quite without exception, men whose heart was in their work. But colonising zeal had waned before the Revolution arrived; the right men were not easy to find and pains were no longer taken to find them. Governorships were obtained by interest as easy and profitable jobs for placemen, who were generally inclined to follow the line of least resistance, varied by occasional displays of arbitrariness sufficient to keep alive the tradition that the system was "tyrannical." General laxity with interludes of spasmodic activity in the administration of laws which were generally resented and habitually evaded, caused more irritation than would have resulted from their rigid but scrupulous enforcement.

Nor can it be denied that those laws—made in England—were unjust. The three Navigation Acts from 1661 to 1673 could be justified on the ground that the duties were no more than an equivalent for the contribution to Imperial defence which England was reasonably entitled to claim; since the colonies would certainly not have voluntarily taxed themselves to provide it. Moreover, they fell only on the export of goods which in the English market were protected from foreign competition. It seems now tolerably clear that the long established impression that they constituted a crushing burden of taxation was derived partly from rhetorical exaggerations familiar to students of fiscal controversies, and partly from demonstrable misinterpretations of actual figures. But the manner of the imposition made it a double grievance. It was imposed by an external authority without the assent of the taxed; England was therefore debarred from defending it as a tax for revenue—its real moral justification. From the official English and American point of view, these were duties imposed not for revenue but for the regulation of trade, so that their actual legality was difficult to contest. But they were imposed by England for the regulation of trade, avowedly in order that English trade might benefit at the expense of the colonies; which from the colonial point of view was, whether legal or not, palpably unjust to the colonies. When people feel that a law is unjust they do not usually feel much serious moral compunction about evading it; and if they are too law-abiding to break it themselves, the grievance still rankles, and their sympathies are apt to be with the law-breakers. That was inevitably the attitude of the great majority of the colonists to the Navigation Acts. There was not merely a tax upon goods; there was a positive restriction to England and the colonies of the market open to colonial exporters, imposed by England for the profit of English traders.

We may sum up the position by saying that a tax for revenue would have been in itself just, but would have broken the constitutional principle adumbrated by the Petition of Right in 1628 and definitely laid down by the Declaraton of Right in 1689 that revenue taxes may not be imposed except by consent of the taxed through their representatives. On the other hand the regulation of trade by the Sovereign was legal, but regulation on the avowed principle that the interests of the colonies must be subordinated to those of the English mercantile community was unjust in its incidence and galling in its expression. And it became the more unjustifiable when the English Government set about its extension by endeavouring to check the production, through prohibition of the export, of colonial goods which competed with those of English producers. In the English view, the Colonists' business was to produce, for themselves and for the English market, but for no one else, the goods which England wanted but could not produce, while supplying themselves from England and from nowhere else with all the goods that England was able to sell to them. In exchange they got the naval protection without which they could hardly have escaped subjection to a foreign power which would have exploited them mercilessly and would have left them no "liberties" at all; they actually got value in return for the injustice. But that did not prevent the injustice from rankling. And the injustice, or the memory of it, rankled for two centuries, while the value received was forgotten.

For half a century the colonies grumbled but submitted, because of the ever-present consciousness of the menace of French aggression and their own need of protection against it by the British Fleet. The need passed when Canada was incorporated in the British

Empire; and its passing was the doom of the Old Colonial system.

III

The first decade of the eighteenth century saw the definite establishment of "The United Company of Merchants of England trading to the East Indies." After a century, the old "London" Company had finally absorbed its last rival, and under its new title held the Eastern trade exclusively in its own hands. During the later years, the Great Mogul Aurangzib had compelled every prince in India to acknowledge his supremacy but died in his ninetieth year just as the New Company's arrangements were being completed—and from that hour no Mogul was ever again master of the great dominion; in which, fifty years later, the Company which had so vainly challenged him under Sir John Child was already the leading territorial Power. In 1709, however, it owned only a few square miles of Indian soil about Bombay, Madras, and Fort William or Calcutta acquired by purchase in 1698, the total area in which it could claim to exercise sovereignty being less than that of the Isle of Man.

The powers and jurisdiction of the Company derived on one side from the 1698 charter of the New or English Company into which the Old or London Company was technically absorbed under the Act of 1702 and the final arrangements of 1708–9 when the Old Company surrendered its separate Charter; though practically it was the Old Company which absorbed the New, and the rights and powers conveyed were in effect the rights and powers accumulated under the series of charters from 1661 onwards. On the other side they derived from agreements or Imperial decrees under direct authority of the Mogul, his viceroys, or potentates who before Aurangzib's completion of his conquests had been independent rulers. The country powers inevitably held the Company responsible for the doings of English subjects, whether members of the Company or not; and it followed that the Charters gave it at least a limited jurisdiction over all such within the area to which their powers applied.

The early charters gave the Company powers to make and enforce regulations upon their own servants. In the first charter granted by Charles II the Governor and Council in each of the major factories were empowered to judge "all persons under them" in all causes according to the English law; in the minor factories where there was not a governor, the chief factor might send offenders to a major factory or to England for trial and punishment. The Company had "power of command" over its fortresses, power to send ships of war—its own ships—and military supplies where they were needed, and to make peace or war with any non-Christian peoples. The special Charter of 1669 relating to Bombay in effect delegated the sovereign powers of the Crown to the Company, the island and port being Crown property, actual territorial sovereignty then coming into play for the first time. Bombay had hitherto been occupied by the King's officers and troops—not the Company's; and on the transfer, the Company was authorised to take into its service such of the officers and troops as were willing to remain: the troop then formed at Bombay became the nucleus of the Company's army. A charter in 1683 gave power to raise such troops as might be necessary, though it was not till after the foundation of Calcutta that the Bengal Nawab sanctioned a garrison within the imperial territory. The Company's own fleet

AA

had already been the strongest in the actual Indian waters ever since it proved its superiority to that of the Portuguese.

The position of the Company in the first decade of the century remained unchanged; what did change in the course of the next forty years was the position of the French and the organisation of the Mogul Empire. An immensely wealthy trading corporation had acquired from the Indian powers trading privileges—to the advantage of both parties—and three fortress-stations at points far remote from each other on the enormous coastline of India: with a military garrison for its fortresses numbering only hundreds, and an armed trading fleet; with authority over its own nationals and over Indians within its own estates. As concerned Britons its trading rights were exclusive. Theoretically it traded only as a corporate body: practically its servants, whose salaries were palpably inadequate, could grow rich by participating in the internal and coastwise trade, provided that they kept clear of the trade to England and Europe. The Company's rights were conveyed in a charter granted for a term of years, with a moral claim but not actual title to renewal; it was self-governing, but wholly dependent on its own resources.

The Company then had at last attained the Constitution which remained unchanged until the French challenge inaugurated the era of expanding Dominion. Though Sir Josia Child in England very definitely contemplated the "foundation of a large, well-grounded, sure English dominion in India for all time to come," and his own and his namesake's ill-judged and ill-managed war with Aurangzib was intended as a move in that direction, there was no farther attempt at expansion in the first half of the eighteenth century.

Aungier's doctrine that we must "trade sword in hand" did not mean that trade was to be pushed at point of sword after the Elizabethan manner of dealing with the West Indies, but that the English must make it abundantly clear that where they were legally established they could not be attacked or their legal rights assailed with impunity. The aggressively ambitious policy that Sir Josia had in view was clearly impracticable as yet; nor was it one that ever commended itself to the commercial magnates at home until it was forced upon them as the only alternative to expulsion at the hands of a European rival.

As yet, however, there was no sign of the presence of a dangerous rival. Portugal had faded out; the Dutch, with their hands full elsewhere, had never established more than a precarious footing in India and would never be able to recover their lost maritime ascendency; and the French had as yet had only the first far from conspicuous foundations of future power laid for them by François Martin. It certainly did not appear to the English in India that French rivalry was a serious menace to their trade; and though the armies of the respective countries were battling with each other in Europe all through the reign of Queen Anne, there were no hostilities between the two Companies in India till another generation had come and gone.

## IV

On the last day of the sixteenth century, two years and three months before the accession of the first Stuart sovereign, the first charter of the London East India Company launched the English Expansion, in the wake of the Dutch Expansion. In the first decade of the eighteenth century, when the last Stuart sovereign was on the throne, England had advanced to the position of the premier colonising and premier maritime power in the world, with no rival to fear in either hemisphere except France, which had been long behind her in entering as a competitor for oversea Empire. Her colonial system was established; her position in India was established; her commercial supremacy was established; her naval supremacy had at last been won decisively, and that decision had been confirmed by the War of the Spanish Succession. Six years after she took Scotland into partnership, the seal was set upon her achievement in 1713 by the Peace of Utrecht. The accession of the new dynasty in the following year brought no new development; it only guaranteed the continuity of the system which the last century had gradually brought into being.

The Utrecht Treaty reconstructed the map of Europe and the relative positions of all the European powers, but with that we are not here concerned. Its significance for us lies in the fact that its terms were practically dictated by the British maritime supremacy which was to be the decisive factor when the antagonism between France and England developed into a duel for oversea dominion, in the wars of the eighteenth century. That supremacy was the more thoroughly secured under the treaty by England's retention of Minorca and Gibraltar, the naval bases in the Mediterranean which she had captured from Spain. France's military ambitions on the Continent had proved incompatible with the continuous maintenance of a Navy which could meet that of England upon equal terms; when she concentrated upon a great naval effort, as she had done under Colbert's influence, she was capable of becoming extremely dangerous if at the same time English naval administration fell into incompetent hands. Holland was still a maritime Power but her supremacy had passed for ever, through no fault of her own but simply because she had reached the limit of her capacity for development, like Portugal before her. Great Britain had now left her far behind not only as a naval Power but as the world's maritime carrier.

The possessions confirmed to Great Britain by the Treaty of Utrecht were the Mediterranean naval stations captured by her during the war which gave her fleets a permanent ascendency in Mediterranean waters, the Hudson Bay Territory which had been over-run during the war by the French from Canada, and the perennial bone of contention Acadie or Nova Scotia, which the Massachusetts men had succeeded in recapturing a year before the treaty was signed, though attempts to seize Quebec had failed; while French claims in Newfoundland were withdrawn except in regard to fishing rights, which were compromised. The cession of Acadie did not include the island of Cape Breton where the French established the invaluable fortress of Louisbourg. In the West Indies the French ceded their share of the island St. Kitt's. All these provisions were simply recognition of the *fait accompli;* the ceded areas had become untenable by the French by reason of the British naval ascendency.

Nevertheless France remained with a footing in India where the ambitions of her representatives— unlike those of the English—were much more political than commercial, and securely entrenched in Canada under a centralised military Government with aspirations for conquest, most unlike the very decentralised civilian communities of English traders planters and agriculturists who were practically without military organisation. And she was not only entrenched in

Canada; on the south of the English colonies she was in possession of the Mississippi Delta and from north to south on the west of the English colonies, from the Great Lakes to the Gulf of Mexico her explorers had traced and laid claim to the great river basins.

For the English in 1713 an era of expansion had been brought to completion. That chapter had reached its conclusion. But that conclusion was in actual fact the starting point for the new era of conflict in every field which was to develop thirty years later.

# INDEX

367